THE EVOLVING PROTECTION OF PRISONERS' RIGHTS IN EUROPE

The Evolving Protection of Prisoners' Rights in Europe explores the development of the framing of penal and prison policies by the European Court of Human Rights (ECHR), clarifying the European expectations of national authorities, and describing the various models existing in Europe, with a view to analysing their mechanisms and highlighting those that seem the most suitable.

A new frame of penal and prison policies in Europe has been progressively established by the ECHR and the Council of Europe (CoE) to protect the rights of detainees in Europe. European countries have reacted very diversely to these policies. This book has several key benefits for readers:

- A global and detailed overview of the ECHR jurisprudence on penal and prison policies through an analysis of its development over time.
- An analysis of the interactions between the Strasbourg Court and the CoE bodies (Committee of Ministers, Committee for the Prevention of Torture ...) and their reinforced framing of domestic penal and prison policies.
- A detailed examination of the impacts of the European case law on penal and prison policies within ten nation states in Europe (including Romania which is currently very underresearched).
- A robust engagement with the diverse national reactions to this European case law as a policy strategy.

This book will be of great interest to scholars and students of Law, Criminal Justice, Criminology and Sociology. It will also appeal to civil servants (judges, lawyers, etc.), professionals and policymakers working for the CoE, the European Union, and the United Nations; Ministries of Justice; prison departments; and human rights institutions, as well as activists working for INGOs and NGOs.

Gaëtan Cliquennois holds dual PhD in Sociology of Law from the Ecole des Hautes Etudes en Sciences Sociales, France, and the University of Saint-Louis, Belgium. From 2010 to 2013, Gaëtan was a Postdoctoral Researcher at the FNRS, Belgium, and worked on human rights in penal and prison matters. He was also Visiting Scholar at the University of Cambridge and at the London School of Economics, UK. Since 2013, he has been a permanent Research Fellow for the French National Centre for Scientific Research (CNRS) at the University of Strasbourg, France (SAGE: Societies, Actors and Governments in Europe) and since 2018 at the University of Nantes, France. From February 2021 he has been the Director of Law and Social Change and works in the field of Law and Sociology of Law. As a Visiting Scholar at the European University Institute, he worked on the relationships between human rights and austerity policies. He has also worked on the creeping privatization of human rights and the European justice system. He has expertise in European human rights justice, the potential privatization of this system, litigation, penal and prison policies and management in Europe, and prison monitoring and strategic litigation by prisoners, NGOs and private foundations. In 2014, he was awarded an IDEX by the University of Strasbourg to work on 'the impact of funding and auditing mechanisms on the protection of Human Rights in Europe in times of crises'. In 2017, he was awarded a grant to work on human rights and pretrial detention for two years by the European Commission.

Routledge Frontiers of Criminal Justice

Life Without Parole
Worse than Death?
Ross Kleinstuber, Jeremiah Coldsmith, Margaret E. Leigey and Sandra Joy

Penal Responses to Serious Offending by Children
Principles, Practice and Global Perspectives
Nessa Lynch, Yannick van den Brink and Louise Forde

A Restorative Approach to Family Violence
Feminist Kin-Making
Joan Pennell

Interviewing of Suspects with Mental Health Conditions and Disorders in England and Wales
A Paradigm Shift
Laura Farrugia

Convictions Without Truth
The Incompatibility of Science and Law
Robert Schehr

The Evolving Protection of Prisoners' Rights in Europe
Gaëtan Cliquennois

Protest Policing and Human Rights
A Dialogical Approach
Michael Smith

The Politics of Prison Crowding
A Critical Analysis of the Italian Prison System
Simone Santorso

For more information about this series, please visit: www.routledge.com/Routledge-Frontiers-of-Criminal-Justice/book-series/RFCJ

THE EVOLVING PROTECTION OF PRISONERS' RIGHTS IN EUROPE

Edited by Gaëtan Cliquennois

Routledge
Taylor & Francis Group
LONDON AND NEW YORK

Cover image: gettyimages.co.uk

First published 2023
by Routledge
4 Park Square, Milton Park, Abingdon, Oxon OX14 4RN

and by Routledge
605 Third Avenue, New York, NY 10158

Routledge is an imprint of the Taylor & Francis Group, an informa business

British Library Cataloguing-in-Publication Data
A catalogue record for this book is available from the British Library

ISBN: 978-0-367-32153-6 (hbk)
ISBN: 978-1-032-04798-0 (pbk)
ISBN: 978-0-429-31703-3 (ebk)

DOI: 10.4324/9780429317033

Typeset in Bembo
by KnowledgeWorks Global Ltd.

CONTENTS

TABLES

INTRODUCTION

Gaëtan Cliquennois

During the first decade of the new millennium, the European Court of human rights (ECtHR) along with bodies of the Council of Europe (the Committee of Ministers of the Council of Europe and the European Committee for the Prevention of Torture) and more recently the Court of Justice of the European Union (CJEU) worked on highlighting substantive human rights law. Using procedural[1] and substantial obligations and expanding its power and control over national countries over time, the Strasbourg Court is now following a judicial policy that is resolutely aimed at driving national jurisdictions to take stock of and remedy the failures of their penitentiary systems, most specifically in terms of prison overcrowding, poor and degrading conditions of detention, the lack of medical care, absence of effective and efficient domestic remedies etc. In particular, using pilot and quasi-pilot judgements[2] and other judgements requiring a monitoring of their execution (through submission of condemned member states of action plans detailing their remedial actions to the Committee of Ministers), the ECtHR hopes to answer the structural/systemic issues encountered in certain States by ordering them to implement effective redress mechanisms. In this perspective, the book analyses this process by studying more generally the decisions rendered by the European human rights bodies relating to obligations applicable to prisons on national level on the basis of international and European standards such as the European Convention on Human Rights (ECHR), the updated 2020 European Prison Rules, the 2015 UN Nelson Mandela Rules for the treatment of prisons and the 1985 UN Beijing Rules for the administration of juvenile justice.

Therefore, prisons and other penal institutions are under the ECHR and CoE's (Council of Europe) scrutiny as the Strasbourg Court indeed requires Member States to:

1. Limit prison overcrowding and poor conditions of detention, situations which, according to the Strasbourg Court, limit to a certain measure the

DOI: 10.4324/9780429317033-1

degree of discretion that States enjoy in developing their criminal policies[3]. The Court has imposed in this sense procedural obligations on certain states which are constrained to develop judicial remedies and compensate prisoners victims of bad and inhumane treatment[4].

2. Reduce long sentences (in the sense that life sentence prisoners must have the right to request parole, but not the right to be granted parole), solitary confinement, disciplinary sanctions and repeated transfers[5].
3. Implement and develop prisoner suicide and homicide prevention programmes based on risk management[6].
4. Introduce procedural guarantees before imposing disciplinary sanctions[7].
5. Introduce regular evaluations of the risk of recidivism using risk management techniques[8].
6. Regularly assess the mental health of prisoners subject to long sentences or indeterminate preventive measures[9].
7. Establish independent parole boards and judicial processes for deciding on conditional release and recalls to prison[10].
8. Empower courts to release detainees whose state of health and illness are exceptionally serious[11].
9. Develop healthcare structures, particularly the provision of appropriate psychiatric treatment for mentally ill prisoners[12].
10. Create effective and efficient domestic remedies in order to give access to justice and the opportunity to complaint about conditions of detention for prisoners. According to the ECtHR, this last objective can be achieved by equipping the courts with appropriate legal tools allowing them to consider the problem underlying an individual complaint and effectively deal with situations of massive and concurrent violations of prisoners' rights resulting from inadequate detention conditions in a given facility[13].

While the European judicial review and monitoring of penal policies are growing, scant attention has been paid to the impacts of the case law of the ECtHR on national penal and prison policies. In this regard, the lack of intersection among human rights, European law and the criminological literature is striking. The socio-legal analysis of the Council of Europe's Recommendations and CPT (Committee on the Prevention of Torture) Reports, Prison Rules, prisoners' litigation and rulings of the ECtHR and the CJEU and of their impact on national penal and prison policies is still rare (Snacken, 2014). This is clearly an unexplored perspective by both criminologists and lawyers. On the one hand, criminologists tend to underestimate the impacts of law and human rights law in particular on penal and prison policies adopted by national states. On the other hand, lawyers tend to propose a narrow reconstruction of this or that ruling of the ECtHR and the CJEU, or an analysis of the techniques and methods of interpretation of the court without analysing the inputs (litigation) and outputs (execution and politicisation of judgements), and compliance, non-compliance and use (including its instrumentalisation) of law by national governments and administrations.

In particular, when addressing human rights, the sociological analysis of prisons pays exclusive attention to institutional practices and the implementation of prison law, with little attention to the oversight and judicial review exerted by international and European bodies, their regulations and their impact on national prison law and jurisprudence (Cliquennois and Snacken, 2018; Daems and Robert, 2017; O'Connell and Rogan, 2022; Snacken, 2011; van Zyl Smit and Snacken, 2009). In this respect, we have to remind that a bulk of the sociological literature casts doubts with some convincing arguments about the integration of human rights and their efficacy and efficiency in prisons and psychiatric institutions. It also questions the ability of human rights institutions and law to make penal and prison institutions accountable and transparent, to limit and soften harsh penal policies and the state's right to punish, to improve access to justice and legal aid for prisoners in this specific context and to fight persistence of human rights violations in the face of reform. The literature in sociology and criminology mainly convincingly argues that the authoritarian nature of the prison administration is in contradiction and even clashes with human rights law (Chauvenet et al. 2005) and undermines its efficacy. In this way, prison litigation could make no significant changes to prisoners and could even rigidify interactions between prisoners and prison staff, and lead to a backlash in the form of so-called disciplinary governance from the prison authorities that oppose and fight this trend (Herzog-Evans 2012). Sociological studies also underline the distance of prisoners and prison officers' culture and habitus from human rights law (Piacentini and Katz 2016). The negative effects of the human rights framework and litigation efforts on the prison complex constitute an additional argument which is twofold: human rights legitimatise prison institutions by improving superficially its conditions (Cartuyvels 2002; Kaminski and de Schutter 2002; Mary 2013) and prison conditions litigation even increases the prison population as litigators (such as NGOs) as it requires indirectly the building of new prisons to put an end to bad and poor prison conditions characterising old prison facilities (Boyland and Mocan, 2014; Gottschalk 2006; Guetzkow and Schoon, 2015; Schoenfeld 2010). Nevertheless, this argument related to the increase in prison population seems perhaps to be a little bit exaggerated as the institutional context, the adoption of harsh penal policies such as the war on drugs and on terrorism and the privatisation play a significant role (Feeley 2018). Finally and according to this sociological and criminological literature, prison litigation is also counterproductive as it usually reinforces the bureaucratisation of the prison services to the detrimental of prisoners (Feeley and Swearingen 2004).

While most of these arguments are very convincing, a more optimistic socio-legal literature exists and points out the progressive integration of human rights into the prison world (Cliquennois and Snacken 2018; Cliquennois, Snacken and van Zyl Smit 2021; Daems and Robert 2017; Simon 2014; Van Zyl Smit 2010; Van Zyl Smit and Snacken 2009). In this regard, the main sociological and criminological literature downplays the very significant changes to prison structures induced by the European human rights law. The main reason of this underestimation is that these changes are related to the prison and judicial structures and are quite invisible as they do not directly affect interactions in prison. While these changes seem to be invisible from a pure and full interactionist perspective, they are massive and contribute to the renewal of prisons in Europe. First, prison policies and structures have particularly changed in many CoE countries through penal moderation (alternatives to prison sentences, see Snacken 2018), renovation and closure of old prisons and the building of new prisons and new psychiatric structures dealing with healthcare as well as new prison structures dealing with suicide prevention (Cliquennois, Snacken and van Zyl Smit 2021). These measures have contributed to tackle prison overcrowding and apply penal moderation and make some prisons more compliant with the right to dignity even though many violations still occur at national level (Snacken 2018). Second, the socio-professional profile of the prison staff has changed as the new recruited prison staff profile is dominated by lawyers on national and local level as an adjustment over time to the increasing influence of human rights on the prison world. In addition, as expected but overlooked by the main literature, the prison services charged with litigation activities grew over time in relation with the increase in litigation made by NGOs that push prisoners to complaint about human rights violations and their prison conditions. New trainings on prison law, administrative case law and human rights law and their European aspects have been set up over time for prison governors by some national prison administration schools. These new trainings are supposed to acculturate new and former prison governors to human rights issues in prison. Third, national judicial structures have also changed through the development of new domestic remedies (through the influence played by the ECtHR), domestic integration of the jurisprudence of the ECtHR and new investigation powers given to the judiciary under Articles 2 and 3 ECHR that obliges (according to the ECtHR) national authorities to conduct investigations into all deaths and torture (or inhumane and degrading treatments) in custody that are supposed to be formal, independent (in the sense that the investigators are not connected in any way to the officials involved in the death), impartial, prompt and effective.

In particular, one of the most overlooked change is related to public scrutiny, whether by individual citizens or the media, that can be exercised through the obligation of investigation into death in custody and breach of the right to dignity. This process would contribute to what some scholars have called "inverted panoptic (Cliquennois and de Suremain, 2018; Cliquennois and Snacken 2018), that is to say, the possibility for detainees, their relatives and society more generally to monitor and examine penitentiary practices. This reversal of the traditional view of prison (in which prisoners are monitored by prison officers), although not crystallised into the architecture of the prison system, may partly be to blame for the security excesses in the implementation of prison policies.

Some scholars could then consider such an approach to human rights law in prison to be naive, little realistic and too much optimistic. On the contrary, some socio-legal scholars have pointed out and much criticised the process of politicisation of the ECtHR and certain of its judgements in particular the more recent ones that grant a significant margin of appreciation to national States in the choice of penal and prison policies such as the right to vote for prisoners and the status of life sentences in the United Kingdom (Cliquennois, Snacken and van Zyl Smit 2021; Snacken and van Zyl Smit 2011).

Despite some political and national interferences, we can also notice a reinforcement of the influence of the Council of Europe, and the interactions between their organs have been observed over the last 20 years. The strengthening of these relationships has increased the pressure and control over national penal and prison administrations. Moreover and despite some limits, the positive and procedural obligations imposed by the ECtHR on the Member States have led to legal, administrative, judicial and practical changes such as the adoption of domestic penal and prison legislations enforcing the effective implementation of death prevention in custody, the provision of healthcare services, the assessment of prisoners' ability to serve custodial sentences and their right to apply for parole, limitations to overcrowding and improvements in conditions of detention, the right to effective remedies and compensation, the enhancement of rehabilitative programmes and the development of family visits. Nevertheless, two inquiries made by the Court on one problematic aspect of the case law with regard to the defence of prisoners' rights need to be recalled with the virtual absence of European control over sentencing procedures and access to measures of adjustment of penalties.

Importantly the book provides accounts of the main evolutions of the ECHR jurisprudence on prisoners' rights and how this European case law is being engaged within a range of nation states across Europe (including Western, Southern and Eastern countries). It focuses in particular on those countries that have been condemned by the ECHR for violations described by the European judge as deriving from structural/systemic issues pertaining to the national penitentiary system (pilot judgements, quasi-pilot judgements and judgements monitoring their executions), and requiring the development of effective redress mechanisms. Such countries include, in particular, Italy, France, Belgium and Romania whose detention conditions have been qualified as inflicting inhuman and degrading treatment, and which, in judgements rendered against them, have been ordered to implement a redress mechanism capable of dealing with such issues. Even though the Court has often recalled the importance of the principles of subsidiarity and the margin of appreciation in the penal and prison domains, the analysis of the ECHR jurisprudence shows the tendency of the Court to see in situations of prison overcrowding a circumstance limiting, in the name of the inviolability of the prohibition under Article 3 (right to dignity), the margin of appreciation given to the Member States.

Consequently, the book draws on penal and prison policies framed by the Strasbourg Court and bodies of the Council of Europe thanks to litigation efforts to illuminate and develop analysis about the significance of studying the national and local reactions to this influence of the European jurisprudence. Regarding the development of the ECHR and CoE control over penal and prison policies, we question whether the European case law has contributed to the shaping of prison policies and the creation of a monitoring and judicial review system based on human rights, which has forced national prison administrations to develop political, legal and organisational responses. In other words, is there any evidence that national Ministers of Justice and prison administrations are obliged to comply with human rights law? In this perspective, the book presents, on the one hand, the control and censure of penal policies and prisons by the ECtHR and the CoE bodies (thanks to litigation efforts undertaken by NGOs), and, on the other hand, the reactions and responses from the national prison administrations to this European case law.

In this respect, the book aims to clarify the European expectations of national authorities and to describe the various models existing in Europe, with a view to analysing their mechanisms and highlighting those that seem the most suitable. The book thus also studies the rights applicable in Italy, Germany, France, Ireland, the United Kingdom and Belgium. Consistent with such a perspective, the European national cases presented in the book have been selected in order to represent most important European countries in terms of human rights violations and ECHR jurisprudence (condemned by pilot judgements and landmark judgements), countries of the main European legal traditions (the Roman-law, Common-law and German-law systems) and a diversity of territories (Western, Southern and Eastern states) and political models (Liberal, Social-democratic, Corporatist, Mediterranean and Post-communist). In this manner, we show how these diverse legal and political legacies mediate the processes of European shaping and framing.

Consequently, the book outlines the development of the framing of penal and prison policies by the ECHR and will insist notably on the content of the obligations imposed progressively by the Strasbourg Court, the Luxembourg Court and bodies of the Committee of Ministers of the Council of Europe on national states. Importantly, we consider how these procedural obligations imposed by the Strasbourg Court could potentially impact and change penal and prison policies. This will be followed by three parts, each one presenting a set of particular aspect of this issue. The first part presents the main evolutions of the ECtHR and CJEU jurisprudence on the protection of prisoners' rights. The second part focuses on the effectiveness and ineffectiveness of human rights in prisons that face the ECtHR, the CoE Committee of Ministers, the European Committee for the Prevention of Torture and NGOs litigating the ECHR. The third and last part analyses the impacts of the ECtHR case law on national prison reforms and some curve and resistance opposed by some national countries to the ECtHR jurisprudence.

While this book is divided in three main parts, each chapter takes a similar approach in order to keep unity and coherence:

- An analysis of the procedural and substantial obligations imposed by the ECtHR and the Committee of Ministers.
- An account of the impacts of these obligations set up by the Court and CoE bodies on the penal and prison system in each country.

- An examination of how national countries react precisely to this European censure and in particular to the procedural obligations.
- An assessment of the effectiveness of the legislative, administrative and practical changes and responses to the European case law.

In Chapter 1 and first part of the book related to the main evolutions of the ECtHR and CJEU jurisprudence on the protection of prisoners' rights, Jean-Manuel Larralde and Gaëtan Cliquennois analyse the significance of the right to life that is enshrined by Article 2 ECHR and is presented as one "of the essential articles of the Convention which protects one of the fundamental core values of democratic societies and of the Council of Europe". Paradoxically, the interpretation of Article 2 (the right to life) by the ECtHR when defining national states liability in case of suicide of individuals within their jurisdiction has been overlooked by the literature on human rights to date. This is why Larralde and Cliquennois propose to analyse the case-law developments of the ECtHR based on Article 2 related to suicide and homicide (by co-detainees) prevention in places of detention (prisons and psychiatric hospitals) and their paradoxical effects on the prevention policies enacted by the States condemned by the Court. The ECtHR also sets a number of requirements and safeguards aimed at minimising the use of lethal force in prison. Larralde and Cliquennois first show that the jurisprudential philosophy to which the Court refers is marked by risk management and a narrow and synchronous conception of the suicide attempts of individuals. They then demonstrate that under the pressure exerted by the Committee for the Prevention of Torture and the national associations for the defence of the rights of detainees, the Court's judgements lead states to adopt suicide and homicide prevention policies marked by a rationality that is both actuarial (risk management) and punitive. The adoption of punitive measures can be seen as a perverse effect or a reversal of human rights and the right to life in particular. But this perverse effect seems partially offset by the possibility for the families of detainees and more broadly for citizens, judges, police and the media, through the investigative duties of member states of the Council of Europe, to exercise supervision, however small, on the prison system. It is precisely on this dialectic of human rights and this dualistic oscillation among risk management, punitivity and external control over places of detention that this first chapter is based.

In Chapter 2, Sonja Snacken starts with one of the great human rights challenges in prison matters of the last decades that is the prison population inflation afflicting many Council of Europe member states and its bad impacts on prisoners' rights. Both the European Committee for the Prevention of Torture and the ECtHR have found prison overcrowding under certain circumstances (the right to dignity protected by Article 3 ACHR) to result in inhuman and degrading treatment. In addition, prison overcrowding generates very poor and bad conditions of detention that hinder the right to legal assistance and to rehabilitation. The mechanisms behind this population inflation are well-known: an increased inflow of persons into detention, increased length of detention and/or restricted possibilities of early release. Research consistently illustrates that such developments are more related to national criminal and prison policies than to changes in crime rates. Its pilot judgements recognise the link between overcrowding and too severe penal policies, and recommend national governments to reconsider their penal legislation, policies and practices in accordance with other Council of Europe recommendations. In this regard, Sonja Snacken argues that more "moderate" penal policies, both quantitatively (detention rates) and qualitatively (preparing for reintegration), could and should be sustained by the Court through a more consistent interpretation of the legitimacy of deprivation of liberty under Article 5 ECHR.

In Chapter 3, Simon Creighton seeks to explore the concept of the "enforcement of sentences" and the relationship between the "ECHR" and the execution of prison sentences that have been lawfully imposed by domestic courts. The question of whether any such role does in fact exist remains confused particularly in the case of prisoners serving determinate sentences. This chapter contends that there has been a failure of the ECtHR to apply the developing broad principles of rehabilitation and resocialisation in a consistent manner, particularly in relation to determinate prison sentences and this failure runs the risk of weakening those principles. In this chapter, I will seek to explore the concept of the "enforcement of sentences" and the relationship between the ECHR and the execution of prison sentences that have been lawfully imposed by domestic courts. The question of whether any such role does in fact exist remains confused particularly in the case of prisoners serving determinate sentences. This chapter will contend that there has been a failure of the ECtHR to apply the developing broad principles of rehabilitation and resocialisation in a consistent manner, particularly in relation to determinate prison sentences and this failure runs the risk of weakening those principles. In particular, although it has been firmly established that the execution of life and indeterminate sentences is capable of raising fresh Article 5(4) issues, there are three further questions which require more structured and considered development by the Court: in what circumstances does the state have to guarantee the right to a review of a sentence – the "whole life sentence" issue? (1); What further guarantees must exist to ensure that a sentence is reducible both as a matter of law and practice (i.e.: both de jure and de facto reducibility)? (2); Whether these principles have any applicability to prisoners serving determinate sentences? (3).

In Chapter 4 that stands as the last development of the first part of the book, Leandro Mancano states that in the European Union (EU), the legal status of prisoners are still nearly exclusively governed by the law of the member states. However, as the reach of the EU's competences has expanded over the years, so have the situations in which individual rights can be affected by the Union, or by member states acting on the basis of EU law. This holds true for criminal law especially, where the body of EU law developed in substantive criminal law, judicial and police cooperation have together enhanced the effectiveness of law enforcement. The latter result, it goes without saying, has come with strings attached. A streamlined system of e.g. evidence gathering or surrender of suspects and convicted people across the EU has inevitably an impact on the person subject to those measures. That is even more so the case as many of the measures of cooperation between member states involve deprivation of liberty. There is no consolidated instrument that regulates the rights of prisoners. There are, nonetheless, different scenarios where EU law plays a relevant role for the treatment of persons who might be, are or were deprived of liberty. On that basis, the present chapter provides a critical overview of the EU's approach to deprivation of liberty in the context of criminal proceedings, by focusing on a series of core rights ensuing from – or impinged upon – the status of prisoners. Firstly, it provides an overview of the use of custodial penalties of EU substantive criminal law. Secondly, it moves on to consider rights and principles developed mostly in the context of judicial cooperation in criminal matters. These rights and principles are: the prohibition of inhumane treatments and the principle that penalties should aim to social reintegration. Thereafter, the chapter moves away from EU criminal law strictly understood and analyses the impact that detention can have on citizenship rights. The conclusions reveal the complex understanding of role and impact for custodial penalties in EU law and highlight strengths and weaknesses of the Union's approach in this area.

The second part of the book on the effectiveness and ineffectiveness of human rights in prisons that face the ECtHR, the CoE Committee of Ministers, the European Committee for the Prevention of Torture and NGOs litigating the ECHR starts with Chapter 5. Mary Rogan and Sophie van der Valk analyse and scrutinise the case of Ireland that has a long history as a member state of the Council of Europe and its supervisory mechanisms. Given the absence of ECtHR case law regarding Ireland, Rogan and van der Valk focus on the impact of the ECHR on domestic case law in relation to prisons alongside the activities of the CPT, as well as the influence of European standards on domestic law and policy. The authors also provide analysis of how European human rights protections are viewed by people in prison. They posit that the weak judicial European supervision of prison practices in Ireland derives in part from Irish legal culture's reluctance to use the Convention, as well as a general lack of prison litigation. Specifically, Rogan and van der Valk interestingly argue that the Council of Europe's framework for protecting rights in prisons as a whole must be considered when assessing the impact of European supervision on Ireland, especially in the absence of direct supervision by the Strasbourg Court, and that non-judicial supervision mechanisms have had some effect on domestic practice through standards, guidelines and soft law.

Chapter 6 deals with the implementation of ECtHR judgements in German prison law. While Germany is regularly considered a state with acceptably high standards of prisoners' rights, including their implementation in practice which are perceived to be mainly the result of the successful system of judicial review. The German judicial review allows prisoners to complain against any decision, action or omission to a judicial authority and – in case of final defeat – to draw an individual constitutional complaint to the Federal Constitutional Court. Nonetheless, Christine Graebsch reveals some significant shortcomings when taking a closer look at the practice of prisoners' rights. Some of the prevalent problems for their enforcement were also not recognised by the ECtHR. This applies equally to the dogmatic construction in the law of preventive detention that has been established by the Federal Constitutional Court. It partly aimed to avoid compliance with the ECtHR's case law. Against this backdrop, the resume about prisoners' rights in Germany is not as positive as by authors who focus on the theoretical benefits of German prison law and the majority of published decisions by the Federal Constitutional Court that are in favour of prisoners' rights. Before having a closer look at the relation between national law and the case law of the ECtHR in the case of preventive detention after the decision of the Grand Chamber in the case of Ilnseher v. Germany (Applications nos. 10211/12 and 27505/14), three decisions of the ECtHR dealing with prisoners' rights will be analysed in the context of national law. The analysis aims at assessing the impact of the ECtHR's case law on German prison law. It is inevitable to extend the analysis in two directions as compared to how it is usually done. It is by no means sufficient to simply conclude from the law in the books, a thorough analysis necessarily has to take into account the law in action as far as possible. Moreover, the extent to which the "human rights message" of ECtHR judgements is implemented into national law depends to a large degree on the depth of understanding the ECtHR itself could develop with respect to infringements of human rights within the respective national legal system.

In Chapter 7, Ciuffoletti and de Alburquerque put emphasis on the conduct of prison reforms and an assessment of the effectiveness of domestic remedies in Italy. As the recent doctrine has shown, the phenomenon of the prison boom has migrated from the United States to Europe, in less than a decade. To date, prison overcrowding is characterised by its endemic and structural nature in most European countries. The most effective judicial response to this phenomenon has been provided to date by the case law of the ECtHR. The phenomenon of prison overcrowding, in its European dimension, is therefore an excellent point of view of the ability of the European case law to produce responses that form a common narrative and force Member States, through substantive and procedural obligations, positive and negative obligations, to renegotiate the policies of protection of prisoners. In this analytical perspective, Italy stands out as one of the countries most affected by the phenomenon of prison overcrowding, with one peculiarity. In Italy, this phenomenon has historically been accompanied by the absence of a general judicial remedy capable of eliminating the violation in progress and compensating for the damage suffered. Ciuffoletti and de Alburquerque assume that it was only thanks to the European impulse that the dimension of detention was finally perceived as a perspective of rights and remedies in order to protect these rights in the Italian system. In this respect, the authors attempt to trace the lines of the Italian process of adaptation (and resistance) to the European case law on the protection of prisoners' rights. This process is not only normative, but also characterised by a critical reflection and a radical change in the specific normative ideology, which has so far supported the legal argumentation of Italian surveillance judges.

The case of France is analysed by Anne Simon and Isabelle Fouchard in Chapter 8. Considering the situation of distress that detainees may experience as a result of overcrowding and inhumane conditions of imprisonment, the question arises as to what legal remedies are available to challenge them. Within the scope of the prohibition of inhuman and degrading treatment, a number of requirements under the ECHR apply. Indeed, the national legal systems of the Member States must first of all recognise the violations of rights that have occurred and provide redress, but at the same time they must also ensure that persons deprived of their liberty are able to seek preventive remedies to put an end to the conditions constituting a prohibited form of treatment. The division of competences between the administrative and judicial orders, a specific feature of the French system, has resulted in a very uneven development of litigation in the field of imprisonment conditions that are contrary to human dignity and have led prisoners to "seek their judge" for a long time. Thanks to the advocacy of certain associations defending the rights of detainees (in particular International Prison Watch [IPW] French Section and A3D) and certain lawyers advocating for detainees' rights, awareness was raised of the limited means of remedies provided under French law in this area and, as a result, the ECtHR was finally able to rule on the issue. This led to a judgement against France at the beginning of 2020, which brought about profound changes in litigation in this area and put pressure on the French legislators.

The last chapter (Chapter 9) of the second part of the book scrutinises the Belgian case and in particular how Belgium has reacted to the European judicial review and monitoring. In this regard, Gaëtan Cliquennois and Olivia Nederlandt intend to examine the influence of pilot and quasi-pilot judgements rendered by the European Court on the Belgian prison services. Belgium is characterised by the weakness of its own national judicial (both judiciary and administrative) control over its prisons. Therefore, control over Belgian prisons is more and more exercised by the ECtHR and the Committee of Ministers which have extended the scope of their supervision to cover illegal detention, healthcare and insanity, prison overcrowding and poor conditions of detention. In this regard, Cliquennois and Nederlandt show that the ECHR judgements against Belgium have had various, but overall rather limited effects in issues such as: failing to provide adequate healthcare, and adequate living conditions for prisoners; poor prison conditions and insufficient prisoner psychiatric care. In addition, Belgium has refused to comply with ECHR case law in the field of domestic legal remedies available to prisoners. Nevertheless, the ECHR decisions have also contributed to the enactment of new policies which endeavour to grant alternative measures (to prison sentences) to offenders with the end goal of reducing prison overcrowding and prison population, the root cause of such problems.

The third and last part of the book starts with Chapter 10 that highlights the tensions and strains between reform and resistance in the Romanian penitentiary system. Cristina Dombeanu and Valentina Pricopie put emphasis on how prison staff perceptions and attitudes affect and influence the legal goal of detention. More precisely, Dombeanu and Pricopie examine prison staff perception in Romania from the perspective of a three dimensions model – legal (including the European legal framework), traditional and moral – to describe staff beliefs about the aims of imprisonment in relation to the practice of human rights in prison. Based on a survey with 289 staff members from 15 Romanian prisons, they show that the main pillars of their perception remain legal and security dimensions, while the moral dimension (including human rights) is more valorised at personal level than at the professional community level. These findings have some implications on how to conceive the European influence on domestic prison practices.

Chapter 11 also pinpoints specific resistance to the European judicial review and monitoring of national penal policies. In this respect, Rosaria Pirosa focuses on the assessment of the remedies in a particular Member State in the sense that a reading of the European Court case law against the United Kingdom shows that in the UK system the decisions of the ECtHR were not really enacted, no exception is made for the pilot judgements. Nevertheless, the theoretical framework to understand the real English set-up is not based on the view that the domestic reading of Convention rights is more circumscribed than in Strasbourg, because of the Member State concerned is deemed "particular", above all considering the approach of the European Court in relevant matters. Therefore, as Pirosa explains in detail, the relevant analytical tool can be found in the complex and strained relationship between the European Court and the United Kingdom as whole, especially after the withdrawal from the EU. This chapter avoids the category of the "dialogue between the Courts", because, in our opinion, it has not a proper epistemological scope and, in the specific case, it could lead the reader to misinterpret the main idea of the chapter. Concerning the life imprisonment, for example, the judiciary does not amount to a body monitoring the penal and prison policies in England and Wales, rather endorsing the political choices decided by the British government. Pirosa focuses on the English system through the core-issues of the whole life imprisonment, the right to vote and, in some aspects, the deaths in custody. These critical aspects can also be considered a strategic observatory to interpret the role of the ECtHR in the human rights protection system, given the "serious risk that the convention is applied with double standards".

Lastly, Chapter 12 deals with the specific case of Germany. Christine Morgenstern and Mary Rogan consider that the control of prisons and the protection of those in prison rest on two pillars: institutional oversight and prison monitoring by national and international bodies as the first pillar and individual complaints procedures, including the possibility to challenge prison decisions before a court as the second pillar. In this chapter, the authors concentrate on two aspects of this combined protection system in the German context. First, they look at prison litigation in Germany and highlight its overall impact on the prison system by introducing the legislative framework and analysing leading cases and recent case law. Second, the authors explore in how far its practice keeps the legislation's promise by looking at the individual prisoner's possibility to access the courts and find redress when their rights have been infringed.

Notes

1 Procedural obligations refer to the development of procedural requirements and its increased use of procedural-type review into which the Court looks at the quality, fairness and regulation of the decision-making processes of the national legislative, executive or judicial authorities to assess whether there has been a violation of the European Convention.

2 Pilot judgements, which were introduced in 2004, gather large group of identical and repetitive case deriving from systemic problems and the same root cause (the dysfunction under national law and administrative practices) of human rights violations. In this regard, pilot judgements allow the ECtHR to handle issues which repeatedly come before it, and to answer the structural or large-scale systemic breaches of the Convention caused by non-compliant legislation in certain Member States by ordering their governments to implement effective redress mechanisms and pass new legislation which is compliant with the Convention.

3 ECtHR, *Neshkov and others v Bulgaria*, 27 January 2015, 36, 925/10, 21, 487/12, 72, 893/12, 73, 196/12, 77, 718/12 and 9717/13 27; ECtHR, *Rezmives and Others v. Romania*, 25 April 2017, 61467/12 39516/13 48231/13; *Varga and Others v. Hungary*, 10 March 2015, 14097/12, 45135/12, 73712/12, 34001/13, 44055/13, and 64586/13; ECtHR, *Ananyev and others v. Russia*, 10 January 2012, 42732/12; ECtHR, *Torreggiani and others v. Italy*, 8 January 2013, 43,517/09; ECtHR, *W.D. v. Belgium*; 6 December 2016, 73,548/13; ECtHR, *Vasilescu v. Belgium*, 25 November 2014, 64,682/12.

4 Ibid.

5 ECtHR, *Vinter v. UK*, 9 July 2013, 66,069/09.

6 ECtHR, *Tanribilir v. Turkey*, 16 November 2000, 21422/93 ; ECtHR, *Keenan v. United Kingdom*, 3 April 2001, 27229/95 ; ECtHR, *Renolde v. France*, 16 October 2008, 5608/05; ECtHR, *Ketreb v. France*, 19 October 2012, 38447/09; ECtHR, *Sellal v. France*, 8 October 2015, 32432/13; ECtHR, *Slimani v. France*, 27 July 2004, 57671/00 ; ECtHR, *Isenc v. France*, 4 February 2016, 58828/13 ; ECtHR, *Shumkova v. Russia*, 14 December 2012, 9262/06 ; ECtHR, *De Donder and De Clippel v Belgium*, 6 December 2011, 8595/06 ; ECtHR, *Jeanty v. Belgium*, 31 March 2020, 82284/17.

7 ECtHR, *Gûlmez v. Turkey*, 20 May 2008, 16330/02.

8 ECtHR, *Vinter v. UK*, 9 July 2013, 66069/09; ECtHR, *Murray v. The Netherlands*, 26 April 2016, 10511/10 ; ECtHR, *Stafford v. UK*, 24 April 2002, 46295/99; *Clift v. UK*, 13 July 2010, 7205/07.

9 ECtHR, *Murray v. The Netherlands*, 26 April 2016, 10511/10.

10 ECtHR, *Thynne and others* v UK, 25 October 1990, 11,787/85.

11 ECtHR, *Gulay Cetin v. Turkey*, 5 March 2013, 44084/10.

12 ECtHR, *De Donder and De Clippel v Belgium*, 6 December 2011, 8595/06; *L.B. v. Belgium*, 2 October 2012, 22831/08; *Claes v. Belgium*, 10 January 2013, 43418/09; *Dufoort v. Belgium*, 10 January 2013, 43653/09; *Swennen v. Belgium*, 10 January 2013, 53448/10 ; *Rooman v. Belgium*, 31 January 2019, 18052/11; *Venken et al. v. Belgium*, 6 April 2021, 46130/14.

13 ECtHR, *Torreggiani and others v. Italy*, 8 January 2013, 43517/09, 46882/09, 55400/09, 57875/09, 61535/09, 35315/10 and 37818/10, § 50; *Vasilescu v. Belgium*, 25 November 2014, 64682/12, § 75; *Bamouhammad v. Belgium*, 17 November 2015, 47687/13, §§ 165–166.

References

Boyland, R. and Mocan, N. (2014). Intended and Unintended Consequences of Prison Reform. *Journal of Law, Economics and Organization*, 30, pp. 558–586.

Cartuyvels, Y. (2002). Réformer ou supprimer: le dilemme des prisons. In: O. De Schutter and D. Kaminski (eds.), *L'institution du droit pénitentiaire. Enjeux de la reconnaissance des droits aux détenus*. Bruxelles: Bruylant/LGDJ, pp. 113–132.

Chauvenet, A., Rostaing, C. and Orlic, F. (2005). *La violence carcérale en question*. Paris: Presses Universitaires.

Cliquennois, G. and de Suremain, H. (2018). *Monitoring Penal Policy in Europe*. Abingdon: Routledge.

Cliquennois, G. and Snacken, S. (2018). European and United Nations Monitoring of Penal and Prison Policies as a Source of an Inverted Panopticon? *Crime, Law and Social Change*, 70(1), pp. 1–18.

Cliquennois, G., Snacken, S. and Van Zyl Smit, D. (2021). Can European Human Rights Instruments Limit the Power of the State to Punish? – A Tale of Two Europes. *European Journal of Criminology*, 18(1), pp. 11–32.

Daems, T. and Robert, L. (2017). *Europe in Prisons. Assessing the Impact of European Institutions on National Prison Systems*. Palgrave McMillan: Camden.

Feeley, M. (2018). Privatizing Criminal Justice: An Historical Analysis of Entrepreneurship and Innovation in Daems. In: T. Vander Beken (ed.), *Privatising punishment in Europe?* Abingdon: Routledge.

Feeley, M. and Swearingen, V. (2004) The Prison Conditions Cases and the Bureaucratization of American Corrections: Influences, Impacts and Implications. *Pace Law Review*, 24(2), pp. 433–475.

Gottschalk, M. (2006). *The Prisons and the Gallows: The Politics of Mass Incarceration in America*. New York: Cambridge University Press.

Guetzkow, J. and Schoon, E. (2015). If You Build It, They Will Fill It: The Consequences of Prison Overcrowding Litigation. *Law and Society Review*, 49(2), pp. 401–432.

Herzog-Evans, M. (2012). *Droit pénitentiaire*. Paris: Dalloz.

Kaminski, D and de Schutter, O. (2002). *L'institution du droit pénitentiaire: enjeux de la reconnaissance de droits aux détenus*. Bruxelles: Bruylant/LGDJ.

Mary, P. (2013). *Les enjeux contemporains de la prison*. Brussels: Publications des Facultés Universitaires St-Louis.

O' Connell, C. and Rogan, M. (2022). Monitoring Prisons in Europe: Understanding Perspectives of People in Prison and Prison Staff. *Law and Social Inquiry*, pp. 1–31, https://doi.org/10.1017/lsi.2021.86

Piacentini, L. and Katz, E. (2016). Carceral Framing of Human Rights in Russian Prisons. *Punishment and Society*, 19(2), pp. 221–239.

Schoenfeld, H. (2010). Mass Incarceration and the Paradox of Prison Conditions Litigation. *Law and Society Review*, 44(3–4), pp. 731–768.

Simon, J. (2014). *Mass Incarceration on Trial: A Remarkable Court Decision and the Future of Prisons in America*. New York: The New Press.

Snacken, S. (2011). *Prisons en Europe, pour une pénologie critique et humaniste*. Bruxelles: Larcier.

Snacken, S. (2014). Les structures européennes de contrôle des administrations pénitentiaires. Le rôle et l'impact du Conseil de l'Europe et du Comité de Prévention de la Torture. *Déviance et Société*, 38(4), pp. 405–423.

Snacken, S. (2018). The European Court of Human Rights and National Penal Policies: Tackling Prison Population Inflation and Fostering Penal Moderation through Articles 3 and 5 of the Convention. *Revue Trimestrielle des Droits de l'Homme*, 14, pp. 56–66.

Snacken, S. and Van Zyl Smit, D. (2011). Shaping Penal Policy from above? The Role of the Grand Chamber of the European Court of Human Rights. In: A. Crawford (ed.), *International and Comparative Criminal Justice and Urban Governance, Convergence and Divergence in Global, National and Local Settings*. Cambridge: Cambridge University Press, pp. 168–190.

Snacken, S. and Van Zyl Smit, D. (2013). Distinctive Features of European Penology and Penal Policy-Making. In: T. Daems, D. Van Zyl Smit and S. Snacken (eds.), *European Penology*. Oxford: Hart, pp. 3–24.

Van Zyl Smit, D. (2010). Regulation of Prison Conditions. *Crime and Justice*, 39(1), pp. 503–563.

Van Zyl Smit, D. and Snacken, S. (2009). *Principles of European Prison Law and Policy: Penology and Human right*. Oxford: Oxford University Press.

PART I

EUROPEAN CASE LAW ON PRISONS

A Split Jurisprudence

1

THE RIGHT TO LIFE

Suicide and homicide prevention in prison

Jean-Manuel Larralde and Gaëtan Cliquennois

Introduction

The European Convention on Human Rights of 4 November 1950 (hereinafter "ECHR") does not have a visible internal structure and does not establish any real hierarchy of rights. The European Court of Human Rights (hereinafter "ECtHR") has stated for a very long time that the ECHR "must be read as a whole".[1] A more detailed reading of ECtHR case law, however, shows that this assumption is not entirely true, because the ECtHR has not hesitated to assert the pre-eminence and even the dominance of certain rights over other rights and a hierarchy of rights. This is the case of the right to life that is enshrined by Article 2 ECHR and presented as "one of the essential articles of the Convention which protects one of the fundamental core values of democratic societies and of the Council of Europe".[2] More generally, the ECtHR, on several occasions, has had the opportunity to recall "that the first sentence of Article 2 § 1 obliges the State not only to refrain from causing death voluntarily, but also to take the necessary measures to protect the lives of persons under its jurisdiction".[3] Detainees are, however, placed in a special position *vis-à-vis* this provision: while everyone obviously enjoys the right to life, including even those who are deprived of their liberty,[4] Article 2 allows the authorities of the State to inflict death, if it results "from a recourse to force made absolutely necessary", in particular to prevent the escape of a person lawfully detained, or to punish, in accordance with the law, a riot, insurrection or mutiny in a penal institution. However, these provisions are only exceptions to the general prohibition on public authorities to inflict death. Indeed, beyond any lethal action, national authorities have a general duty to protect persons deprived of their liberty.

Since the famous *Kudla v. Poland* judgement, respect for the human dignity of prisoners has become a conventional requirement, expressed by the need to

DOI: 10.4324/9780429317033-3

ensure "the health and the well-being of the prisoner (...) in an adequate manner, with regard in particular to the practical requirements of imprisonment and the required medical care more specifically".[5] The application of Article 2 to situations of unnatural deaths in detention[6] first triggers an obligation on the authorities to investigate. More specifically, "in all cases where a detainee dies under suspicious conditions and the causes of this death are likely to be linked to an action or omission by officials or public services, the authorities have an obligation to carry out a vast official and effective investigation ex officio".[7] This application of the so-called procedural aspect of the ECHR requires both the institutional and hierarchical independence of the investigators (who must be independent from the people who have committed such acts or omitted to act), reasonable measures in order to collect and exploit the evidence and finally sufficient diligence, effectiveness and promptness.[8] They must determine the cause of death and the circumstances surrounding the death. In addition, they must establish the liability of individuals or institutions for the death and must impose appropriate sanctions in the event of suicides that could have been prevented.[9] The aim of this investigation is clear for the ECtHR: "to ensure the effective application of the ECHR which protects the right to life and prohibits torture and inhuman or degrading treatment and punishment in cases where officials or bodies of the State are involved, and to ensure that they are held to account for the deaths and ill-treatment under their responsibility".[10] But the obligations arising from the application of Article 2 are not limited to this investigation.[11] They also (and above all) imply that measures be put in place to effectively avoid both suicides and other circumstances that have led to not only deaths in prison, such as violence committed by staff, but also other cases linked, for example, to non-existent or ineffective medical treatment, or even inadequate management of hunger strikes.[12]

The "necessary measures" imposed on the competent authorities constitute what is called in ECtHR case law "positive obligations", that is to say obligations to act, in order not to violate the very substance of a protected right, in this case to avoid deaths in detention. Following a casuistic approach, the ECtHR will therefore examine whether the measures taken to prevent the death of a detainee were sufficiently effective under Article 2. While the legal and socio-legal literature has recently paid some attention to the death of detainees,[13] it has quite neglected the analysis of the ECtHR jurisprudence, its philosophy and its impacts.[14] Such an analysis is important to understand which approach to suicide and death in custody the ECtHR has applied in its case law.

More precisely, ECtHR jurisprudence requires states to adopt effective measures to not only protect prisoners "against themselves" but also against their co-prisoners[15] (I). ECtHR case law also seeks to enforce adequate standards of care "in order to prevent fatal outcomes" (II). Finally, the ECtHR sets a number of requirements and safeguards aimed at minimising the use of lethal force in prison (III).

The protection of prisoners "against themselves" ... and against their co-prisoners

The protection of detainees at risk of suicide is an area for which the ECtHR has established and applied a clear approach in its case law, which can be found in particular in the Keenan judgement of 2001, in which the ECtHR ruled that "vulnerable persons",[16] including detainees, must be subject to "general measures and precautions (...) in order to reduce the risk of self-harm without encroaching on individual autonomy" and "the exact content and intensity of these measures must vary in accordance with the circumstances of the case".[17] Concretely, the task of the ECtHR is to "determine whether the authorities (...) knew or should have known that there was a real and immediate risk of suicide and, if so, whether they did all that they could reasonably be expected to do to prevent this risk".[18] Thus, faced with a detainee considered to be in a "critical condition", already observed during a previous placement in a disciplinary cell,[19] the *Renolde v. France* judgement stated that placing a prisoner at risk of suicide in a disciplinary cell cannot constitute an adequate measure, especially when other special protective measures could have been implemented correspondingly (such as strip-searching, which could have made it possible to find the belt with which the detainee hanged himself).[20] However, keeping a detainee suffering from a serious psychiatric illness in an ordinary cell may also violate Article 2.[21]

The ECtHR also considers that surveillance measures, even if they are reinforced, cannot in themselves constitute sufficient responses to prisoners at risk of suicide.[22] In this regard, a medical check-up, especially during the first day of imprisonment, is an important measure to be taken, which "may help to alleviate some of the anxiety experienced by all newly arrived detainees".[23] But if medical treatment is prescribed, it is incumbent on the authorities to ensure that such medical treatment is effective.[24] Faced with a prisoner's suffering from addictions that were known to the authorities, the establishment, from the start of detention, of drug treatments with special precautionary measures and of both pharmacological and psychological detoxification measures, could also be judged as adequate care, even though the prisoner may go on to commit suicide more than a year into his sentence.[25] Placing a prisoner in a secure solitary-confinement cell, with special surveillance every seven minutes, could also be considered relevant, as these measures were put in place "as soon as the risk of suicide is materialised".[26] In some particularly serious cases, it is the question of continued detention that must be raised.[27] In this regard, ECtHR case law does not question such permanent surveillance and even legitimises it. Then the ECtHR could contribute to reinforce the coercive approach to suicide applied by national prison authorities through special surveillance measures.

The physical constraints on at-risk detainees by limiting, or completely removing any opportunities for suicide, through placing them in secure cells and removing any objects that could be used to kill themselves, and through subjecting them to close suicide and medical observation, refers to a model of impeding or preventing suicide attempts. In these situations, the level of suicide risk is such that the national authorities are obliged to exercise particular and constant supervision of the detainees concerned. It is up to the national administrations to place high-risk detainees in secure cells with no sharp corners or fittings that could be used for suicide, to confiscate belts, shoelaces and any other objects that could be used for suicide,[28] and to exercise intensive surveillance with direct visual contact,[29] as well as daily medical supervision[30] with special attention to the signs and risks of self-harm.

The ECtHR seems to be aware of the limitations of this death avoidance model, for it notes the necessity of restricting its application by taking into consideration the principle of individual autonomy[31] and the proportionality, necessity and adequacy of the coercive measures imposed on suicidal psychiatric patients (taken under Article 2) and their compatibility with Articles 3, 5 and 8.[32] But rather than suicide prevention based on a process focused on long duration and a more holistic and reflexive paradigm (notably focused on the limits on coercive measures and their counter-effects), it seems that the ECtHR has chosen to rely on a narrow conception of suicide, where prevention is very close to its occurrence, to be compared with prevention of an attempted crime or even a "pre-crime" approach.[33] In this regard, the ECtHR considers attempted suicide to be one of the most significant risk factors for suicide. It hence applies a conception of suicide, characterised by the immediate intent to kill themselves and possibly materialised by attempted suicide, to predict suicide.

This approach focused on risk prediction is the result of the ECtHR's recourse to the insurance approach to its philosophy of segmentation of risks, which results in the application of an "act/commission" model aimed at preventing immediate risks that are easier to calculate.

The first feature of the approach adopted by the ECtHR is the specification of the procedure for the detection and segmentation of risks by national authorities, which reveals the Court's choice of priorities.[34] The criterion for triggering liability, namely awareness or prediction of suicide risks by the national authorities, implies adopting a policy for identifying and calculating such risks. In particular, the ECtHR requires the national authorities to detect the most-at-risk detainees, such as those with histories of suicide attempts, self-harm and psychiatric problems or those assigned to solitary confinement.

As the prison administration is not obliged to regard all detainees as potential suicide risks,[35] even though all detainees are in a vulnerable position,[36] the ECtHR expects detention authorities to conduct suicide risk assessments, especially of first-time detainees,[37] and those who have already self-harmed,[38] for whom the risk of suicide is very high. Detainees suffering from psychiatric problems (whose vulnerability must be taken into consideration by the national authorities[39]) are also considered to pose a high risk of suicide,[40] as well as those who are wrongly placed in ordinary prisons[41] and police custody or even in solitary confinement[42] and in disciplinary cells[43] without medical or psychiatric assessment and follow-up.[44]

The ECtHR only mentions personal risk factors (e.g. first offender, newcomer, history of self-harm, history of psychiatric problems) and particular zones of detention (e.g. cells for new detainees, solitary confinement cells) and other places of detention, for which risk calculation is relatively obvious. The ECtHR thus seems to have adopted an actuarial or insurance approach based on individual, topological and temporal risk factors, both as a model for assessing the liability of national governments and as the most effective means of preventing suicides among detainees.

This selection of risks is highly problematic. It largely ignores environmental and other more complex risk factors, such as population density and overcrowding, the punitive nature of certain detention regimes and the primacy of passive safety, such as architectural design and secure cells, at the expense of dynamic security based on positive interactions between staff and prisoners. The importance of these more complex factors is highlighted in the scientific literature on the wider factors that contribute to prison suicide. This literature, which has been ignored by the Strasbourg Court, has shown the influence of prison authorities on the repressive treatment of prisoners and the negative reaction of prisoners to such treatment. It has also highlighted the impact of other factors, such as the stigmatisation of suspects during police arrests and criminal trials, the new public oversight of detainees,[45] bullying and social isolation[46] and the "weight" of modern imprisonment.[47]The application of scientific research on suicide in prison would require focusing on increases in penal severity, the scale of punishments and confinement and its consequences for the deterioration of detention conditions as a result of prison overcrowding.[48] In summary, this approach has led the ECtHR to only require medical follow-up for detainees who attempt suicide and to focus with immediacy in a short-term manner on the physical surveillance of detainees with suicidal tendencies, to prevent them from attempting suicide.

But "Any suspected threat to life does not oblige (…) the authorities to take concrete measures to prevent its realisation".[49] The precautionary measures required by the ECtHR are always designed "so as not to impose an unbearable or excessive burden on the authorities, without losing sight of the difficulties that the police has in exercising their functions in contemporary societies", and to take into account "the unpredictability of human behaviour and the operational choices to be made in terms of priorities and resources".[50] Thus, in the Keenan judgement (cited above), the ECtHR did not accept the violation of Article 2 in the case of a young schizophrenic prisoner who committed suicide while placed in solitary confinement for disciplinary reasons, because prison officials adopted a "reasonable response" to the situation, including daily medical supervision and quarterly checks. In the same sense, the suicide in detention of an inmate suffering from schizophrenia, but for whom the disease was not accompanied by suicidal tendencies and for which no history or element of recent conduct could suggest autolysis, does not violate Article 2.[51]

The protection of detainees is not limited to effective suicide prevention. Indeed, the ECtHR also requests effective protective measures to be taken against the most violent detainees who are likely to commit criminal acts such as homicide. Thus, in the Paul and Audrey Edwards judgement of 2002, the applicants criticised the British authorities for not having protected the life of their son, murdered by a dangerous and mentally ill prisoner who had been placed in his cell while he was in pre-trial detention. The mental illness of the murderer was known to doctors, police and prosecutors (he had a history of violence sufficiently serious to justify his compulsory confinement) and the ECtHR found that this history should have been brought to the attention of the prison authorities. The dysfunctions led to placing a dangerous detainee in the cell of a fragile detainee and gave rise to a violation of Article 2 ECHR.[52]

The administration "throughout detention of adequate medical care capable of preventing a fatal outcome"[53]

Attacks on the life of persons deprived of their liberty can also refer to situations of failure of medical care. The Kudla judgement (*supra*) made care in detention one of the requirements of dignity. In fact, prison and health authorities have a "positive obligation to protect the life" of each prisoner. In this regard, the lack of appropriate care in this context can constitute a breach of the ECHR[54]: "the obligation to protect prisoners' lives also implies the obligation for the authorities to provide them with the necessary medical assistance to protect their lives".[55] According to the ECtHR, it was therefore a violation of Article 2 to simply have a detainee suffering from chronic hepatitis examined on the day before his death without adopting any of the measures recommended by practitioners.[56] The authorities were also considered to have failed in the case of a detainee suffering from multiple chronic diseases known to the prison authorities upon his arrival: stomach ulcer, gastritis and gastro-duodenitis. Operated on in hospital, his post-operative complications were insufficiently monitored.[57] In the ECtHR's view, adequate monitoring would have required blood transfusion systems which the prison hospital lacked. The ECtHR also requires the authorities to be proactive and to act with all necessary speed. This was not the case for a detainee suffering from a resistant form of tuberculosis who was not given access to laboratory tests in time, despite the tests being essential to establish the diagnosis and initiate adequate treatment.[58]

The much-publicised judgement in the *Magnitsky v. Russia* case is a striking example of a failure of care in detention leading to the death of a prisoner. The authorities did not take satisfactory measures to establish a diagnosis or to allow the prisoner to undergo surgery. The ECtHR considers that this lack of consultation fully contributed to his death. In addition, the prison authorities did not have the necessary facilities to take care of the prisoner and to take appropriate measures on the day of his death to address the emergency that had arisen.[59]

In addition, the issue of hunger strikes in detention and their management by the prison authorities has also led the ECtHR to set a number of requirements.[60] Hunger strikes have long been a technique of protest for detainees deprived of their freedom of expression and institutionalised means of action.[61] To a certain extent, hunger strikes can result in the death of prisoners. In order to avoid such tragic outcomes, the ECtHR has recognised the possibility for the authorities to resort to the imposition of forced feeding on prisoners on hunger strike[62] if three conditions are met: a proven therapeutic need, strict procedural guarantees and finally a course of the measure not exceeding the threshold of gravity of Article 3 ECHR.[63]

Control over lethal force used by national authorities

Regarding the use of force by public authorities, the ECtHR has always requested careful implementation, pointing out at the same time the necessary "vigilance", the reduction "to the minimum" of the endangerment of lives and the absence of "negligence" in the choice of measures taken.[64] In this perspective, the ECtHR takes into account the situation and the context, the danger to human life and bodily integrity and the risk that the use of force will generate victims[65] in order to hold that a violation of Article 2 ECHR has occurred, or not. Any use of force must therefore be "absolutely necessary" and "strictly proportionate to the legitimate aims" sought by the authorities.[66]

Concerning the more specific situation of prisoners, the ECtHR has initiated case law aimed at condemning the most violent behaviour by the authorities, *a fortiori* when these acts are likely to result in prisoners' death. In this regard, Article 2 holds that "the use of lethal force by the police may be justified in certain circumstances. However, Article 2 does not give them carte blanche".[67] Thus, the policeman, who, on leaving a criminal court hearing, shot dead a prisoner who had just escaped, did not comply with the ECHR. In fact, the ECtHR noted that the victim, who was handcuffed, was unarmed and that "nothing in his behaviour could suggest that he constituted a real threat to the policemen or to third parties". According to the ECtHR, it is therefore not "established that the situation made the use of lethal force absolutely necessary. Such use in these circumstances was therefore excessive and unjustified".[68] Similarly, a particularly violent intervention by the police in a hunger strike and prisoner protest against a reduction in cell size, where 12 prisoners were shot dead and 50 others were wounded, some by firearms, was also held by the Court to be in violation of Article 2.[69]

While recognising "the potential for violence that exists in a penal institution and the possibility that the disobedience of detainees will quickly degenerate into a mutiny, which may necessitate the intervention of the police", the ECtHR requires that such an operation be "prepared and carried out with all the necessary precautions, so as to reduce as much as possible the infringements of the prisoners' right to life".[70]

Among the main precautions to be taken is the creation of a precise legal framework and a "rigorous regulation" according to the vocabulary used by the ECtHR. The ECtHR has ruled that the failure of such regulation explains, in particular, the killing of 8 prisoners during a confrontation between about 30 prisoners at Diyarbakir prison in Turkey and the police.[71] Indeed, "members of the security forces must not be in the dark when exercising their functions, whether in the context of a prepared operation or a spontaneous operation: a legal and administrative framework must define the limited conditions under which law enforcement officials can use force and firearms, taking into account the international standards developed in this area".[72] The ECtHR has ruled that an appropriate legal and administrative framework is not sufficient in itself and must be completed with sufficient preparation for the operation, in the case of *Kavaklıoğlu and Others v. Turkey* (cited above) in which the authorities organised a large-scale operation[73] in which 8 detainees were killed and 65 others were injured in the ending of a mutiny in the Ulucanlar prison in Ankara. In the ECtHR's view, the lack of preparation for this operation led to the deaths and the violation of Article 2. Indeed, "the authorities should not have been satisfied with a framework that is as rudimentary as it is imprecise, making it practically inevitable the use of lethal force. In order to fulfil their obligation and to respect the right to life in particular, the authorities should have assessed with more caution the information at their disposal before directing the soldiers who were trained to kill 'terrorists' in particular, to use their firearms as soon as they thought they were facing enemies in the context of counter-terrorism action" (§ 203). Without considering the use of non-lethal means, and by failing to negotiate before any use of force, the police "did not deploy the necessary vigilance to ensure that any risk of putting life in danger would be minimised, and were negligent in the choice of measures taken before and after the operation" (§ 214).

The ECtHR has also often insisted on the positive obligation incumbent on the State "to train its police forces, and in particular its prison staff, in order to ensure a high level of competence and to prevent any treatment contrary to law and to the aforementioned provision".[74] This question of the competence of the officers is at the heart of the judgement in the *Tekin and Arslan v. Turkey* case (*supra*), in which it was the use of a dangerous immobilisation technique by prison officers that caused the death of a particularly (psychologically) vulnerable prisoner. The ECtHR, which considered that the force used was not necessary, also deplored the fact that "the lethal risk inherent in the use of a strangulation key was not mentioned during the training followed" by the officer, when "there is no doubt that such a measure could lead to asphyxiation of the person and was, therefore, potentially fatal".[75]

Conclusion

We have shown that the ECtHR's jurisprudence on suicide in places of detention is influenced by a concern for risk management and physically impeding suicide attempts. This logic draws on a particularly narrow conception of suicidal intent by the ECtHR, which is the opposite of a more holistic approach to suicide. The underpinning logic of the ECtHR jurisprudence has been translated in the member states of the CoE, many of which have been subject to hostile judgements from the ECtHR, into the actuarial management of suicide risks, supported by punitive measures of security constraint and segregation, applied not only to at-risk detainees but also to individuals who are wrongly thought to be at risk.[76] Certainly, the adoption of these measures can be seen as a perverse effect, or even a reversal, of human rights, in particular the right to life. This perverse effect has not been really offset by the opportunity given to the families of detainees and, more broadly, to citizens, judges, ombudsmen, the police and the media, through the obligation on member-state governments to investigate suicides in places of detention, to oversee prisons and police custody. These management strategies and the policies underlying them have failed, since suicide and self-harm rates in many prisons are rising. They reached their worst ever levels in 2016 in the UK[77] and remain extremely high and problematic in Belgium[78] and France.[79]

The negative impact on detainee suicide rates of upholding the right to life (guaranteed in Article 2 ECHR) is caused by the narrow approach to human rights adopted in much of the ECtHR jurisprudence and, in particular, by the failure to integrate the right to life with the right to dignity (Article 3 ECHR) and the right to privacy (Article 8 ECHR) into the ECtHR's case law on detainees' suicides. Except for the *Hiller* case, in which the ECtHR evoked the necessity of taking into account the proportionality and adequacy of the preventive measures for suicidal psychiatric patients (under Article 2) in relation to Articles 3, 5 and 8,[80] the lack of consideration of the right to dignity has meant that the Strasbourg Court has not taken into account the negative effects of such suicide prevention in places of detention. The rights to dignity and to privacy are breached by measures such as permanent video surveillance and frequent, intrusive suicide-watch rounds of prisoners at high risk, which have been adopted under the influence of the ECtHR jurisprudence. In practice, these coercive and even punitive measures override the medical and psychiatric care that theoretically constitutes a key part of the prevention policy promoted by both the ECtHR.

In this regard, the very narrow view of suicide adopted by the ECtHR and the negative effects of its jurisprudence on national suicide prevention policies call for a renewal of this jurisprudence, so that it relies not only on Article 2 ECHR. If the ECtHR were to adopt a more holistic approach to suicide in custody, this would imply taking into consideration the influence of prison authorities on the treatment of prisoners and the possible resistance of prisoners against such treatment; the impact of the stigmatisation of suspects during police arrests and criminal trials; the potentially negative impact of the new public oversight of prisons[81]; the weight of the prison and police systems architecture; bullying and social isolation[82]; the primacy of punishment and passive safety in some police and prison establishments[83]; and the negative effects of prison overcrowding on detainee suicides.[84] Most of these issues relate to Article 3 ECHR. Similarly, the use of a contextual and more holistic paradigm for suicide prevention would require focusing on the increase of penal severity and the scale of punishments, including the increased application of "life-trashing sentences" without any prospect of release in a near future and their consequences for feelings of hopelessness,[85] and on the deterioration of detention conditions and on prison overcrowding,[86] which also fall under Articles 3 and 5 ECHR.[87] In other words, Article 2 ECHR should be read and interpreted together with Articles 3, 5 and 8 ECHR with a view to finding more holistic – i.e. personal, contextual and systemic – explanations of suicide in custody.

Even though the jurisprudential approach to the right to life in prison adopted by the ECtHR has laid down a number of principles which aim at humanising places of detention, these judgements make it possible to implement the fundamental requirements formulated more than two centuries ago by François-Alexandre Frédéric de la Rochefoucald-Liancourt: "the prison is, for all, only a place of passage; (…) The society which only needs their detention, does not want and cannot want it to be painful to them; (…) Laws must ensure respect for humanity, even when they order punishment, and never suffer it to be degraded by inhumane and degrading treatment",[88] *a fortiori* when the treatment in question results in the death of the persons concerned because of the inaction or ineffectiveness of the authorities.

Notes

1 ECtHR, *Johnston and Others v. Ireland*, 18 December 1986, req. n° 9697/82, § 57.
2 See, inter alia, ECtHR *Ülüfer v. Turkey*, 5 June 2012, n° 23038/07, § 55. The ECtHR adds, moreover, that Article 2 "is one of the most fundamental provisions of the Convention, a provision which, in peacetime, does not allow any derogation under Article 15. With Article 3, it enshrines one of the fundamental values of the democratic societies making up the Council of Europe". ECtHR, *Cantaragiu v. Moldova*, 24 March 2020, n° 13013/11, § 28. For a general presentation of this provision, see the *Guide to Article 2 of the European Convention on Human Rights-Right to Life*, Strasbourg, Council of Europe, 31 August 2019, 50 pp.
3 ECtHR, *L.C.B.* v. *United Kingdom*, 9 June 1998, n° 23413/94, § 36; *Osman v. United Kingdom*, 28 October 1998, n° 23452/94, § 115.
4 As early as 1962, the European Commission of Human Rights recalled in its judgement *Ilse Koch v. Germany* that even though an applicant "is detained in execution of a sentence imposed on her for crimes perpetrated in breach of the most basic human rights (...) this circumstance does not however deprive her of the guarantee of the rights and freedoms defined in the Convention for the Protection of Human Rights and Fundamental Freedoms" (8 March 1962, n° 270/61).
5 ECtHR, *Kudla v. Poland*, 26 October 2000, n° 30210/96, § 94. See also *Naumenko v. Ukraine*, 10 February 2004, n° 42023/98, § 112.
6 But also in case of torture or inhuman or degrading treatment inflicted on prisoners under Article 3 ECHR. See, *inter alia*, ECtHR, *Perişan and Others v. Turkey*, 29 April 2010, n° 12336/03, § 100 and s. See also D. Roets, "L'obligation positive de punir les violences par les agents de l'administration pénitentiaire sur un détenu : l'absence d'instruction effective stigmatisée par la Cour européenne des droits de l'homme", *Revue de sciences criminelles et de droit pénal comparé*, 2020, p. 143 s.
7 ECtHR, *De Donder and De Clippel v. Belgium*, 6 December 2011, n° 8595/06, § 85.
8 *Paul and Audrey Edwards v. the United Kingdom*, Application No 46477/99, Merits, 14 March 2002 at para 70–73.
9 *Trubnikov v. Russia*, Application No 49790/99, Merits, 5 July 2005 at para 86–88.

10 ECtHR, *Kavaklıoğlu and Others v. Turkey*, 6 October 2015, n° 15397/02, § 271. When the breach of the right to life is not intentional, the accountability does not require criminal lawsuits. Civil, administrative and even disciplinary lawsuits may be sufficient in this particular case. ECtHR, Gagiu V. Romania, 24 February 2009, n° 63258/00, § 66.

11 See C. Madelaine, *La technique des obligations positives en droit de la Convention européenne des droits de l'homme*, PhD, Montpellier I, 2012, 673 pp.; *Guide to Article 2 of the European Convention on Human Rights-Right to Life*, Strasbourg, Council of Europe, 31 August 2019, p. 29.

12 The ECtHR has adopted a liberal approach to the applicant in such situations under Article 2 since it accepts applications lodged by the victims' relatives (such as the victim's parents). See Court ECtHR, *Kats and Others v. Ukraine*, 18 December 2008, n° 29971/04, § 94; *Karpylenko v. Ukraine*, 11 February 2016, n° 15509/12, § 73.

13 Daniel, 'Suicide-related litigation in jails and prisons: Risk management strategies' (2009) 15 *Journal of Correctional Health Care* 19; Hanser, 'Inmate suicide in prisons: An analysis of legal liability under 42 USC Section 1983' (2002) 82 *The Prison Journal* 459; Harris and Stanley, 'Exacerbating risks and diminishing rights for 'at-risk' prisoners' (2017) 18 *Criminology & Criminal Justice* 515; Huey Dye, 'Deprivation, importation, and prison suicide: Combined effects of institutional conditions and inmate composition' 38 *Journal of Criminal Justice* (2010); Liebling, *Suicides in Prison* (1992); Liebling, 'Vulnerability and prison suicide' (1995) 35 The *British Journal of Criminology* 173; Liebling, 'Prison suicide and prisoner coping' (1999) 26 *Crime and Justice* 283; Liebling, 'Suicides in prison: Ten years on' (2001) 138 *Prison Service Journal* 35; Liebling and Arnold, *Prisons and Their Moral Performance: A Study of Values Quality and Prison Life* (2004); Liebling, *The Role of the Prison Environment in Prison Suicide and Prisoner Distress. Preventing Suicide and Other Self-Harm in Prison* (2006); Sanchez, Fearn and Vaughn, 'Risk factors associated with near-lethal suicide attempts during incarceration among men in the Spanish prison system' (2018) 62 *International Journal of Offender Therapy and Comparative Criminology* 1452; Tartaro and Lester, *Suicide and Self-Harm in Prisons and Jails* (2009); Cliquennois and Chantraine, 'Empêcher le suicide en prison: origines et pratiques' (2009) 75 *Sociétés Contemporaines* 59; Cliquennois, 'Preventing suicide in French Prisons' (2010) 50 *British Journal of Criminology* 1023; Cliquennois and Champetier, 'A new risk management for prisoners: The emergence of a death-avoidance model' (2013) 17 *Theoretical Criminology* 397; Cliquennois and Herzog-Evans, 'European monitoring of Belgian and French prisons' (2018) 70 *Crime, Law and Social Change* 113; Aitken, 'Investigating prison suicides: The politics of independent oversight' (2021) *Punishment and Society* forthcoming https://doi.org/10.1177/1462474521993002

14 Murdoch, *The Treatment of Prisoners – European Standards* (2006); Tulkens, 'Les prisons en Europe. Les développements récents de la jurisprudence de la Cour européenne des droits de l'homme' (2014) 38 *Déviance et Société* 425; Rogan, 'Human rights approaches to suicide in prison: Implications for policy, practice and research' (2018) 6 *Health and Justice*.

15 According to the ECtHR, "*l'article 2 peut, dans certaines circonstances bien définies, mettre à la charge des autorités l'obligation positive de prendre préventivement des mesures d'ordre pratique pour protéger l'individu contre autrui ou, dans certaines circonstances particulières, contre lui-même*". ECtHR, *Tanribilir v. Turkey*, 16 November 2000, n° 21422/93, § 70.

16 ECtHR, *Trubnikov v. Russia*, 5 July 2005, n° 49790/99, § 68; *Taïs v. France*, 1 June 2006, n° 39922/03, § 84. According to the ECtHR, "*la vulnérabilité des détenus s'exprime spécifiquement au regard du suicide, le taux de suicides étant, en Belgique comme dans d'autres pays, nettement plus élevé dans la population carcérale que dans la population générale. Elle a du reste déjà souligné que toute privation de liberté physique peut entraîner, de par sa nature, des bouleversements psychiques et, par conséquent, des risques de suicide*". *De Donder and De Clippel v. Belgium*, 6 December 2011, n° 8595/06, § 75.

17 ECtHR, *Keenan v. UK*, 3 April 2001, n° 27229/95, § 92. See Rogan, M., "Human rights approaches to suicide in prison: Implications for policy, practice and research", *Health Justice*, 2018. Available at https://www.ncbi.nlm.nih.gov/pmc/articles/PMC6755609/; Cliquennois, G., (2018) 'La jurisprudence de la Cour européenne des droits de l'homme, son contenu et ses effets en matière de prévention du suicide' 51(2) *Criminologie* 86–108. Available at https://www.erudit.org/fr/revues/crimino/218-v51-n-2-crimino3961/1954236ar/

18 ECtHR, *Ketreb v. France*, 19 July 2002, n° 38447/09, § 75. However, "*dans le cas spécifique du risque de suicide d'une personne privée de sa liberté dans le cadre d'une procédure pénale, il n'y a une telle obligation positive*" to take effective measures for life protection "*que lorsque les autorités savent ou devraient savoir sur le moment qu'existe un risque réel et immédiat qu'un individu donné attente à sa vie*". ECtHR, *Robineau v. France*, 3 September 2013, n° 58497/11.

19 § 83. The ECtHR rejects the argument raised by the government on the lack of information on the applicant's health due to a structural issue. According to the Strasbourg judges, "*les difficultés, voire l'absence, de communication et de coordination entre le personnel pénitentiaire et les différents services médicaux appelés à intervenir auprès des détenus au sein de la maison d'arrêt – tels que l'UCSA et le SMPR –relèvent de la responsabilité des autorités internes*" (§ 83). On the issue of lack of function between prison services, see also ECtHR, *Isenc v. France*, 4 February 2016, n° 58828/13.

20 The ECtHR indeed ruled "*que le placement en cellule disciplinaire isole le détenu, en le privant de visites et de toute activité, ce qui est de nature à aggraver le risque de suicide lorsqu'il existe*". ECtHR, *Renolde v. France*, 16 October 2008, n° 5608/05, § 94 and 107.

21 ECtHR, *De Donder and De Clippel v. Belgium*, cited above, § 75.

22 ECtHR, *Isenc v. France*, cited above, § 44.

23 Ibid., § 45.

24 "La Cour considère que l'obligation d'assurer des soins médicaux appropriés à un détenu garantie par la Convention et confirmée par la jurisprudence serait vidée de tout sens si elle ne devait se limiter qu'à la prescription d'un traitement adéquat, sans s'assurer s'il a été correctement administré et suivi. Cette responsabilité est d'autant plus importante s'il s'agit de détenus avec des troubles mentaux". ECtHR, Jasińska v. Poland, 1 June 2010, n° 28326/05, § 77.

25 ECtHR, *Fabris and Parziale v. Italy*, 19 March 2020, n° 41603/13.

26 ECtHR, *Jeanty v. Belgium*, 31 March 2020, n° 82284/17, § 80. In this case, the prisoner did not die: while he tried to hang himself with his trousers, prison wardens prevent him from succeeding.

27 See *Renolde v. France*, cited above, § 98.

28 *Ketreb*, supra n° 49 at para 95; *Isenc v. France*, supra n° 53 at para 28.

29 *Keenan*, supra n° 32 at para 88.

30 *Gagiu v. Romania* Application N° 63258/00, Merits, 24 February 2009 at para 56–57.

31 *Keenan*, supra n° 32 at para 92.

32 *Hiller v. Austria* Application No 1967/14, Merits, 22 November 2016 at para 55.

33 Zedner, 'Pre-crime and post-criminology?' (2007) 11 *Theoretical Criminology* 261.

34 See Baldwin and Black, 'Driving Priorities in Risk-based Regulation: What's the Problem?' (2016) 43 *Journal of Law and Society* 565.

35 *Younger v. United Kingdom* Application No 57420/00, Merits, 7 January 2003.

36 *Salman v. Turkey* Application No 21986/93, Merits, 27 June 2000 at para 99.

37 *Isenc*, supra n° 53 at para 28 – on the basis of the recommendations made by the CPT in CPT/Inf/E (2002) 1-Rev. 2015.

38 *Keenan*, supra n° 32 at para 88.

39 Ibid. at para 94 and 111; *Renolde*, supra n 49 at para 84; *De Donder and De Clippel v. Belgium*, supra n° 46 at para 75 ; ECtHR, *Jeanty v. Belgium*, 31 March 2020, 82284/17.

40 *Shumkova v. Russia* Application n° 9262/06, Merits, 14 December 2012 at para 94.

41 *De Donder and De Clippel v. Belgium*, supra n° 46 at para 78.

42 *Renolde v. France*, supra n° 49.
43 *Ketreb*, supra n° 49.
44 Ibid. at para 92–94.
45 van Ginneken, Sutherland and Molleman, 'An ecological analysis of prison overcrowding and suicide rates in England and Wales, 2000–2014' (2017) 50 *International Journal of Law and Psychiatry* 76.
46 Liebling, 'Prison suicide and its prevention' in Jewkes (ed), *Handbook on Prisons* (2007); Liebling and Arnold, supra n° 13; Marzano et al., 'Prevention of suicidal behaviour in prisons. An overview of initiatives based on a systematic review of research on near-lethal suicide attempts' (2016) 37 *Crisis* 323.
47 Crewe, 'The depth of imprisonment' (2020) *Punishment & Society*. https://doi.org/10.1177/1462474520952153
48 van Ginneken, Sutherland and Molleman, supra n° 66; Opitz-Welke et al., 'Prison suicides in Germany from 2000 to 2011' (2013) 36 *International Journal of Law and Psychiatry* 386; Rabe, 'Prison structure, inmate mortality and suicide risk in Europe' (2012) 35 *International Journal of Law and Psychiatry* 222.
49 ECtHR, *Isenc v. France*, 4 February 2016, req. n° 58828/13, § 38. The ECtHR also ruled that "*ce qui concerne les détenus qui mettent, volontairement ou involontairement, leur propre vie en danger, la Cour rappelle que les autorités pénitentiaires doivent s'acquitter de leurs tâches de manière compatible avec les droits et libertés des individus concernés"*. ECtHR, *Keenan v. United Kingdom*, cited above, § 92; *Renolde v. France*, cited above, § 83. See on this aspect, L. Anelli, "Suicide: quand prévention rime avec coercition" 2018(101) *Dedans-Dehors* 24.
50 ECtHR, *Lykova v. Russia*, 22 December 2015, n° 68736/11, § 115.
51 ECtHR, *Sellal v. France*, 8 October 2015, n° 32432/13. See also *Trubnikov v. Russia* (cited above), in which the ECtHR rejects any violation of Article 2 in the case of a prisoner's suicide under psychiatric follow-up but for whom the medical reports highlighted an improvement of his behaviour and his approach to his previous suicide attempt. The medical reports also pointed out his consolidated mental health following his intense medical treatment (§ 75). According to the ECtHR, there is neither any violation of Article 2 for a prisoner who died of a drug overdose when the prison authorities demonstrated their fight against drug trafficking in prison through the adoption of measures judged to be sufficient. ECtHR, *Marro v. Italy*, 8 April 2014, n° 29100/07.
52 ECtHR, *Paul and Audrey Edwards v. United Kingdom*, 14 March 2002, n° 46477/99, § 60.
53 ECtHR, Gagiu v. Romania, 24 February 2009, n° 63258/00, § 55.
54 ECtHR, *Sakkopoulos v. Greece,* 15 January 2004, n° 61828/00; *Huylu v. Turkey*, 16 November 2006, n° 52955/99, § 58. The conviction of the state for violation of Article 2, however, only intervenes if the ECtHR is convinced by the existence of a direct causal link between the care provided and the death of the prisoner. See ECtHR, Răducu v. Romania*, 21 April 2009, n° 70787/01* ; *Gengoux v. Belgium*, 17 January 2017, n° 76512/11.
55 ECtHR, *Makharadze and Sikharulidze v. Georgia*, 22 November 2011, n° 35254/07, § 71.
56 ECtHR, *Gagiu v. Romania*, cited above.
57 ECtHR, Tarariyeva v. Russia, 14 December 2006, n° 4353/03, § 88.
58 ECtHR, *Makharadze and Sikharulidze v. Georgia*, cited above, § 90. The ECtHR reached the same conclusion in the judgement of *Karpylenko v. Ukraine*, 11 February 2016 (n° 15509/12) for a prisoner who died of AIDS and tuberculosis.
59 ECtHR, *Magnitsky v. Russia*, 27 August 2018, n° 32631/09 and 53799/12.
60 Which do not go so far as to oblige the authorities to systematically release a prisoner who is on hunger strike even if his state of health is seriously impaired. ECtHR, *Horoz v. Turkey*, 31 March 2009, n° 1639/03.

61 So for the death of Irish Republican Army activist Bobby Sands on 5 May 1981 in the Maze Prison after a 66-day hunger strike. Much more recently, Turkish lawyer Ebru Timtik died on August 27, 2020, after 238 days of hunger strike. Sentenced in 2019 to more than 13 years in prison for "belonging to a terrorist organisation", she demanded a fair trial.

62 But if the deterioration of the prisoner's health is caused by his refusal to accept treatment, the authorities do not have to bear the burden of such a deterioration. ECtHR, *Makharadze and Sikharulidze v. Georgia*, cited above, § 82.

63 ECtHR, 7 March 2013, *Rappaz v. Switzerland*, n° 73175/10. Prior to this decision, non-compliance with these three cumulative conditions had led the ECtHR to qualify as torture the forced feeding of a detainee without sufficient medical reason (handcuffed to a chair or to a heater, he was forced to undergo the insertion into the oesophagus of a rubber tube connected to a bucket containing a special nutritional mixture). ECtHR, *Nevmerjitski v. Ukraine*, 5 April 2005, n° 54825/00.

64 For all of these obligations, see ECtHR, *Andronicou and Constaninou v. Cyprus*, 9 October 1997, n° 25052/94, § 181.

65 Comm ECtHR, Decision on 6 October 1986 in the complaint n° 11257/84, *DR*, 49, p. 213; Decision on 10 July 1984, *Kathleen Steward v. United Kingdom, DR*, 39, p. 162; ECtHR, *McCann and Others v. United Kingdom* (GC), 27 September 1995, n° 18984/91, § 149.

66 ECtHR, *Tekin and Arslan v. Belgium*, 5 September 2017, req. n° 37795/13, § 97.

67 ECtHR, *Kavaklıoğlu and Others v. Turkey*, cited above, § 169.

68 ECtHR, *Ülüfer v. Turkey*, 5 June 2012, n° 23038/07, § 69 et 71.

69 ECtHR, *Songül İnce and Others v. Turkey*, 26 May 2015, n° 25595/08 et 34252/10; see also *Leyla Alp and Others v. Turkey*, 10 December 2013, n°. 29675/02.

70 ECtHR, *Ismail Altun v. Turkey*, 21 September 2020, n° 22932/02, § 73–74.

71 During the police operation, the police never attempted to use tear gas or other neutralising agents against the alleged rioters, who were immediately beaten with batons or sticks. The eight deaths were due to multiple injuries and fractures, including fractured skulls and ribs. ECtHR, *Perişan and Others v. Turkey*, 29 April 2010, n° 12336/03.

72 ECtHR, *Kavaklıoğlu and Others v. Turkey*, cited above, § 170.

73 With an intervention team of 211 soldiers and 59 officers, an auxiliary team comprising notably 50 soldiers and 9 officers, a commando troop, 4 special force squadrons and an unknown number of police officers.

74 ECtHR, *Tekin and Arslan v. Belgium*, cited above, § 95.

75 Ibid., § 105.

76 Bartlett, P. 'The Right to Life and the Scope of Control: Fernandes de Oliveira v. Portugal', *Strasbourg Observers*, 18 March 2019. Available at: https://strasbourgobservers.com/2019/03/18/the-right-to-life-and-the-scope-of-control-fernandes-de-oliveira-v-portugal/; Cliquennois, G., Snacken, S., and van Zyl Smit, D., 'The European human rights system and the right to life seen through suicide prevention in places of detention: Between risk management and punishment' *Human Rights Law Review* 2021, forthcoming.

77 National Audit Office, Report by the Comptroller and Auditor General, 'Mental Health in Prisons', 29 June 2017. Available at: https://www.nao.org.uk/wp-content/uploads/2017/06/Mental-health-in-prisons.pdf; No-Deportations, Incidents of Self-Harm requiring medical treatment in immigration detention, January to December 2019, January to December 2018. Available at: http://www.no-deportations.org.uk/Quarterly%20Asylum%20Stats/Self-Harm%202019.html; and http://www.no-deportations.org.uk/Quarterly%20Asylum%20Stats/Self-Harm%20 2018.html

78 Favril, et al., *Suicide in de Belgische gevangenissen: 2000–2016* (2017). Available at: https://www.academia.edu/33800995/Su%C3%AFcide_in_de_Belgische_gevangenissen_2000_2016 ; Favril, Vander Laenen and Audenaert, *Suïcidaal gedrag bij gedetineerden in*

Vlaanderen: prevalentie en samenhang met psychiste distress (2017). Available at: https://www.academia.edu/33801003/Su%C3%AFcidaal_gedrag_bij_gedetineerden_in_Vlaanderen_prevalentie_en_samenhang_met_psychische_distress

79 French Ministry of Justice, *Annual Report on Prisons* (2017). Available at: https://assets.publishing.service.gov.uk/government/uploads/system/uploads/attachment_data/file/630239/moj-annual-report-2016-17.pdf

80 *Hiller*, supra n° 77.

81 van Ginneken, Sutherland and Molleman, supra n° 66.

82 Liebling, supra n° 69; Liebling and Arnold, supra n° 13; Marzano et al., supra n° 67.

83 Liebling, supra n° 69.

84 van Ginneken, Sutherland and Molleman, supra n° 66.

85 Liebling, supra n° 69.

86 Opitz-Welke et al., supra n° 70; Rabe, supra n° 70.

87 Snacken, 'The European Court of Human Rights and National Penal Policies: Tackling Prison Population Inflation and Fostering Penal Moderation through Articles 3 and 5 of the Convention', in *La protection des personnes détenues en Europe/The protection of prisoners' rights in Europe, Actes de conférences – 21 April 2016, 14–15 June 2016 / Proceedings conferences – 21 April 2016, 14–15 June 2016, (2018)* 14 *Revue des Droits de l'Homme*, 56. Available at: https://journals-openedition-org.budistant.univ-nantes.fr/revdh/4230?file=1

88 F.-A. de La Rochefoucauld-Liancourt, "Plan de travail du comité de mendicité, en annexe de la séance du 6 juin 1790" (travail de l'Assemblée et productions du roi et des ministres), *Archives Parlementaires de la Révolution Française*, Année 1883, 16, p. 131. Available at: https://www.persee.fr/doc/arcpa_0000-0000_1883_num_16_1_7088_t1_0126_0000_5

References

Aitken, D., (2022) 'Investigating prison suicides: The politics of independent oversight' 24(3) *Punishment and Society* 477–497. doi:10.1177/1462474521993002

Anelli, L., (2018) 'Suicide: quand prévention rime avec coercition' 2018(101) *Dedans-Dehors* 24.

Baldwin, R. and Black, J., (2016) 'Driving priorities in risk-based regulation: What's the problem?' 43 *Journal of Law and Society* 565.

Bartlett, P. (2019) 'The Right to Life and the Scope of Control: Fernandes de Oliveira v. Portugal', *Strasbourg Observers*, 18 March 2019. Available at: https://strasbourgobservers.com/2019/03/18/the-right-to-life-and-the-scope-of-control-fernandes-de-oliveira-v-portugal/

Cliquennois, G. (2018) 'La jurisprudence de la Cour européenne des droits de l'homme, son contenu et ses effets en matière de prévention du suicide' 51(2) *Criminologie* 86–108. Available at https://www.erudit.org/fr/revues/crimino/218-v51-n-2-crimino3961/1954236ar/

Cliquennois, G., and Chantraine, G., (2009) 'Empêcher le suicide en prison: origines et pratiques' 75 *Sociétés Contemporaines* 59.

Cliquennois, G., and Prisons, (2010) 'Preventing suicide in French' 50 *British Journal of Criminology* 1023.

Cliquennois, G., and Champetier, (2013) 'A new risk management for prisoners: The emergence of a death-avoidance model' 17 *Theoretical Criminology* 397.

Cliquennois, G., and Herzog-Evans, M., (2018) 'European monitoring of Belgian and French prisons' 70 *Crime, Law and Social Change* 113.

Cliquennois, G., Snacken, S., and van Zyl Smit, D., (2021) 'The European human rights system and the right to life seen through suicide prevention in places of detention: Between risk management and punishment' 22 *Human Rights Law Review* 2022 ngab023.

Council of Europe, *Guide to Article 2 of the European Convention on Human Rights-Right to Life*, Strasbourg, Council of Europe, 31 August 2019, p. 29. Available at: https://inhak.adalet.gov.tr/Resimler/Dokuman/2432020134543Guide_Art_2.pdf

Crewe, B. (2020) 'The depth of imprisonment' *Punishment & Society* doi:10.1177/1462474520952153

Daniel, (2009) 'Suicide-related litigation in jails and prisons: Risk management strategies' 15 *Journal of Correctional Health Care* 19.

Favril, et al., (2017) *Suicide in de Belgische gevangenissen: 2000–2016*. Available at: https://www.academia.edu/33800995/Su%C3%AFcide_in_de_Belgische_gevangenissen_2000_2016

Favril, Van der Laenen and Audenaert, (2017), *Suïcidaal gedrag bij gedetineerden in Vlaanderen: prevalentie en samenhang met psychiste distress* (2017). Available at: https://www.academia.edu/33801003/Su%C3%AFcidaal_gedrag_bij_gedetineerden_in_Vlaanderen_prevalentie_en_samenhang_met_psychische_distress

French Ministry of Justice, (2017) *Annual Report on Prisons*. Available at: https://assets.publishing.service.gov.uk/government/uploads/system/uploads/attachment_data/file/630239/moj-annual-report-2016-17.pdf

Hanser, (2002) 'Inmate suicide in prisons: An analysis of legal liability under 42 USC Section 1983' 82 *The Prison Journal* 459.

Harris, and Stanley, (2017) 'Exacerbating risks and diminishing rights for 'at-risk' prisoners' 18 *Criminology & Criminal Justice* 515.

Huey Dye, M., (2010) 'Deprivation, importation, and prison suicide: Combined effects of institutional conditions and inmate composition' 38 *Journal of Criminal Justice* 796.

La Rochefoucauld-Liancourt, F.A. de, (1983) "Plan de travail du comité de mendicité, en annexe de la séance du 6 juin 1790" (travail de l'Assemblée et productions du roi et des ministres), In *Archives Parlementaires de 1787 à 1860 - Première série (1787–1799) Tome XVI - Du 31 mai au 8 juillet 1790*. Paris: Librairie Administrative P. Dupont, 1883. pp. 126–132. Available at: www.persee.fr/doc/arcpa_0000-0000_1883_num_16_1_7088_t1_0126_0000_5

Liebling, A., (1992) *Suicides in Prison*.

Liebling, A., (1995) 'Vulnerability and prison suicide' 35 *The British Journal of Criminology* 173.

Liebling, A., (1999) 'Prison suicide and prisoner coping' 26 *Crime and Justice* 283.

Liebling, A., (2001) 'Suicides in prison: Ten years on' 138 *Prison Service Journal* 35.

Liebling, A., (2006) *The Role of the Prison Environment in Prison Suicide and Prisoner Distress. Preventing Suicide and Other Self-Harm in Prison*.

Liebling, A., (2007) 'Prison suicide and its prevention' in Jewkes (ed), *Handbook on Prisons*. Collumpton: Willan Publishing.

Liebling, A., and Arnold, H., (2004) *Prisons and Their Moral Performance: A Study of Values Quality and Prison Life*.

Madelaine, C., (2012) *La technique des obligations positives en droit de la Convention européenne des droits de l'homme*, PhD, Montpellier I, 673 pp.

Marzano et al., (2016) 'Prevention of suicidal behaviour in prisons. An overview of initiatives based on a systematic review of research on near-lethal suicide attempts' 37 *Crisis* 323.

Murdoch, (2006) *The Treatment of Prisoners – European Standards*.

National Audit Office, Report by the Comptroller and Auditor General, 'Mental Health in Prisons', 29 June 2017. Available at: https://www.nao.org.uk/wp-content/uploads/2017/06/Mental-health-in-prisons.pdf

Opitz-Welke et al., (2013) 'Prison suicides in Germany from 2000 to 2011' 36 *International Journal of Law and Psychiatry* 386.

Rabe, (2012) 'Prison structure, inmate mortality and suicide risk in Europe' 35 *International Journal of Law and Psychiatry* 222.

Roets, D., (2020) 'L'obligation positive de punir les violences par les agents de l'administration pénitentiaire sur un détenu: l'absence d'instruction effective stigmatisée par la Cour européenne des droits de l'homme' 1 *Revue de sciences criminelles et de droit pénal comparé* 143 s.

Rogan, (2018) 'Human rights approaches to suicide in prison: Implications for policy, practice and research' 6 *Health and Justice*. Available at https://www.ncbi.nlm.nih.gov/pmc/articles/PMC6755609/

Sanchez, Fearn and Vaughn, (2018) 'Risk factors associated with near-lethal suicide attempts during incarceration among men in the Spanish prison system' 62 *International Journal of Offender Therapy and Comparative Criminology* 1452.

Snacken, (2018) 'The European Court of Human Rights and National Penal Policies: Tackling Prison Population Inflation and Fostering Penal Moderation through Articles 3 and 5 of the Convention', in *La protection des personnes détenues en Europe/The protection of prisoners' rights in Europe, Actes de conférences - 21 April 2016, 14–15 June 2016/Proceedings conferences - 21 April 2016, 14–15 June 2016, (2018)* 14 *Revue des Droits de l'Homme*, 56. Available at: https://journals.openedition.org/revdh/4230?file=1

Tartaro, and Lester, (2009) *Suicide and Self-Harm in Prisons and Jails*.

Tulkens, (2014) 'Les prisons en Europe. Les développements récents de la jurisprudence de la Cour européenne des droits de l'homme' 38 *Déviance et Société* 425.

van Ginneken, Sutherland and Molleman, (2017) 'An ecological analysis of prison overcrowding and suicide rates in England and Wales, 2000–2014' 50 *International Journal of Law and Psychiatry* 76.

Zedner, (2007) 'Pre-crime and post-criminology?' 11 *Theoretical Criminology* 261.

Cases ECtHR European Commission of Human Rights

ECtHR, 24 March 2020, *Cantaragiu v. Moldova*, n° 13013/11, § 28.

ECtHR, 31 March 2020, *Jeanty v. Belgium*, n° 82284/17, § 80.

ECtHR, 19 March 2020, *Fabris and Parziale v. Italy*, n° 41603/13.

ECtHR, 21 September 2020, *Ismail Altun v. Turkey*, n° 22932/02, § 73–74.

ECtHR, 27 August 2018, *Magnitsky v. Russia*, n° 32631/09 and 53799/12.

ECtHR, 5 September 2017, *Tekin and Arslan v. Belgium*, req. n° 37795/13, § 97; § 95.

ECtHR, 17 January 2017, *Gengoux v. Belgium*, n° 76512/11.

ECtHR, 22 November 2016, *Hiller v. Austria* Application No 1967/14, Merits, at para 55.

ECtHR, 11 February 2016, *Karpylenko v. Ukraine*, n° 15509/12, § 73.

ECtHR, 4 February 2016, *Isenc v. France*, n° 58828/13; § 38.

ECtHR, 6 October 2015, *Kavaklıoğlu and Others v. Turkey*, n° 15397/02, § 271; § 169; § 170.

ECtHR, 22 December 2015, *Lykova v. Russia*, n° 68736/11, § 115.

ECtHR, 8 October 2015, *Sellal v. France*, n° 32432/13.

ECtHR, 26 May 2015, *Songül İnce and Others v. Turkey*, n° 25595/08 et 34252/10.

ECtHR, 8 April 2014, *Marro v. Italy*, n° 29100/07.

ECtHR, 3 September 2013, *Robineau v. France*, n° 58497/11.

ECtHR, 7 March 2013, *Rappaz v. Switzerland*, n° 73175/10.

ECtHR, 10 December 2013, *Leyla Alp and Others v. Turkey*, n°. 29675/02.

ECtHR, 5 June 2012, *Ülüfer v. Turkey*, n° 23038/07, § 55; § 69 et 71.

ECtHR, 14 December 2012, *Shumkova v. Russia* Application n° 9262/06, Merits, at para 94.

ECtHR, 6 December 2011, *De Donder and De Clippel v. Belgium*, n° 8595/06, § 85.; § 75.

ECtHR, 22 November 2011, *Makharadze and Sikharulidze v. Georgia*, n° 35254/07, § 71; § 82; § 90.
ECtHR, 29 April 2010, *Perişan and Others v. Turkey*, n° 12336/03; § 100 and s.
ECtHR, 1 June 2010, *Jasińska v. Poland*, n° 28326/05, § 77.
ECtHR, 24 February 2009, *Gagiu V. Romania*, n° 63258/00, § 66, Merits, at para 56–57; § 55.
ECtHR, 31 March 2009, *Horoz v. Turkey*, n° 1639/03.
ECtHR, 21 April 2009, *Răducu v. Romania*, n° 70787/01.
ECtHR, 18 December 2008, *Kats and a. v. Ukraine*, n° 29971/04, § 94.
ECtHR, 16 October 2008, *Renolde v. France*, n° 5608/05, § 94 and 107; § 98; § 83.
ECtHR, 1 June 2006, *Taïs v. France*, n° 39922/03, § 84.
ECtHR, 16 November 2006, *Huylu v. Turkey*, n° 52955/99, § 58.
ECtHR, 14 December 2006, *Tarariyeva v. Russia*, n° 4353/03 § 88.
ECtHR, 5 July 2005, *Troubnikov v. Russia*, Application No 49790/99, Merits, at para 86–88; § 68.
ECtHR, 5 July 2005, *Trubnikov v. Russia*, n° 49790/99, § 68.
ECtHR, 5 April 2005, *Nevmerjitski v. Ukraine*, n° 54825/00.
ECtHR, 10 February 2004, *Naumenko v. Ukraine*, n° 42023/98, § 112.
ECtHR, 15 January 2004, *Sakkopoulos v. Greece*, n° 61828/00.
ECtHR, 7 January 2003, *Younger v. United Kingdom* Application No 57420/00, Merits.
ECtHR, 19 July 2002, *Ketreb v. France*, n° 38447/09, § 75.
ECtHR, 14 March 2002, *Paul and Audrey Edwards v. the United Kingdom*, Application No 46477/99, Merits, at para 70–73; § 60.
ECtHR, 9 October 1997, *Andronicou and Constaninou v. Cyprus*, n° 25052/94, § 181.
ECtHR, 3 April 2001, *Keenan v. UK*, n° 27229/95, § 92; § 88.
ECtHR, 26 October 2000, *Kudla v. Poland*, n° 30210/96, § 94.
ECtHR, 27 June 2000, *Salman v. Turkey* Application No 21986/93, Merits, at para 99.
ECtHR, 16 November 2000, *Tanribilir v. Turkey*, n° 21422/93, § 70.
ECtHR, 9 June 1998, *L.C.B.* v. *United Kingdom*, n° 23413/94, § 36.
ECtHR, 28 October 1998, *Osman v. United Kingdom*, n° 23452/94, § 115.
ECtHR, 27 September 1995, *McCann and Others v. United Kingdom* (GC), n° 18984/91, § 149.
ECtHR, 18 December 1986, *Johnston and a. v. Ireland*, req. n° 9697/82, § 57.
ECtHR, 6 October 1986, *Wolfgram v Germany*, in the complaint n° 11257/84, *DR*, 49, p. 213.
ECtHR, 10 July 1984, *Kathleen Steward v. United Kingdom*, APPLICATION/REQUÉTE N° 10044/82, DR, 39, p. 162.
ECtHR, 8 March 1962, *Ilse Koch v. Germany*, n° 270/61.

2

THE EUROPEAN COURT OF HUMAN RIGHTS AND NATIONAL PENAL POLICIES

Fostering quantitative and qualitative penal moderation through Articles 3 and 5 ECHR[1]

Sonja Snacken

Introduction

The European Court of Human Rights (ECtHR) consistently finds serious forms of prison overcrowding to violate Article 3 ECHR. Its pilot judgments recognize the link between overcrowding and too severe penal policies and recommend Governments to reconsider their penal legislation, policies and practices in accordance with other Council of Europe recommendations. This article argues that more "moderate" penal policies, both quantitatively (detention rates) and qualitatively (preparing for reintegration), could and should be sustained by the Court through a more consistent interpretation of the legitimacy of deprivation of liberty under Article 5 ECHR.

Prison overcrowding as a human rights issue under Article 3 ECHR

One of the great human rights challenges in prison matters of the last decades is the prison overcrowding afflicting many Council of Europe member states. The consequences of this overcrowding are well known: deteriorated living conditions, inadequate prison regimes, reduced safety for prisoners and staff, insufficient preparation for release. Both the European Committee for the Prevention of Torture (CPT) and the ECtHR have found prison overcrowding under certain circumstances to result in inhuman and degrading treatment. From its very beginning, the CPT considered that prison overcrowding can in itself constitute inhuman and degrading treatment, and the combination of overcrowding, inadequate sanitary facilities and insufficient activities for prisoners was systematically found to amount to such treatment (CPT 2nd General Report [CPT/Inf (92) 3] § 46;

DOI: 10.4324/9780429317033-4

CPT 11th General Report [CPT/Inf (2001) 16] § 13; van Zyl Smit, Snacken 2009). By contrast, the ECtHR before 2001 considered chronic forms of overcrowding to be "undesirable", but required violations of Article 3 ECHR to be deliberately imposed on the complainant. This changed with the case of *Dougoz v Greece* (6 March 2001), confirmed since by many cases concerning a wide range of European countries (see infra): the Court now accepts that the absence on the part of the state authorities of an intention to humiliate does not preclude a breach of Article 3 ECHR.

The mechanisms behind this prison overcrowding are also well known. They have been studied by academics (Zimring, Hawkins 1991; Snacken et al 1995; Tonry 2007; Lappi-Seppälä 2011; Snacken 2015) and taken up in policy papers and Recommendations by the Council of Europe. Overcrowding is the result of penal inflation: an increased inflow of persons into detention, the increased length of detention, restricted possibilities of early release, or a combination of such factors. All studies confirm there is no automatic relation between prison rates (the number of prisoners per 100,000 inhabitants) and (serious) crime rates, as penal policies determine the reaction to such crimes through legislation, prosecution, the use of remand custody, sentencing and early release.

The 1999 Recommendation concerning Prison Overcrowding and Prison Population Inflation R(99)22 of the Council of Europe's Committee of Ministers articulates five clear principles regarding how penal policies should tackle penal inflation:

a. Deprivation of liberty should be considered a last resort.
b. Expansion of prison capacity does not generally offer a lasting solution to prison overcrowding and should, hence, be an exceptional measure.
c. There should be provision for a coherent set of community sanctions and measures, leaving room for graduation according to severity, and public prosecutors and judges must be encouraged to apply them as much as possible.
d. Member states should consider decriminalizing certain offences or reclassifying them in order to avoid deprivation of liberty.
e. The factors contributing to prison overcrowding and to prison population inflation must be analysed in order to construct a coherent strategy. Such analysis must include a study of which offences produce long-term prison sentences, of priorities in the struggle against criminality, of the attitudes and concerns of the public, and of existing practices in sentencing.

Two decades later, these principles still stand strong. They have been further elaborated upon in subsequent Recommendations[2] and have been reaffirmed by the Committee of Ministers in its *White Paper on Prison Overcrowding* CM (2016)121: while recognizing different penal traditions and the public emotions that may accompany particular crimes and their punishment, it urges member states to fully adopt the principle of deprivation of liberty as a last resort and to reconsider their legislation and penal practices at all levels of the criminal justice system accordingly. It offers particular recommendations for decriminalization, the pretrial phase (discretionary prosecution, simplified procedures, out-of-court settlements such as mediation or diversion, alternatives for remand custody), the trial phase (reduce sentence length; foster community sanctions such as probation, treatment orders, mediation and combined sanctions) and the post-trial phase (emphasize resettlement).

The ECtHR has followed suit – at least partly. Faced with hundreds of recurring cases on prison overcrowding violating dignity under Article 3, it has increasingly resorted to pilot judgments, concluding that prison overcrowding results from structural problems relating to overly repressive penal policies. It has recommended Governments of countries as diverse as Italy, Russia, Romania, Moldavia, Hungary, Poland, Belgium and France[3] to take remedial measures, such as decriminalization of certain offences (e.g. drug offenses, illegal immigration), fostering community sanctions and measures including early release, resorting to shorter sentences and imposing shorter periods of, and alternatives to, remand custody. These pilot judgments have indeed led several Governments to amend their Penal Codes, reduce sentence length, and extend the use of community sanctions or early release (see Cliquennois et al 2021).

While these recommendations by the Court are broadly in line with the other "legal instruments" of the Council of Europe, I want to discuss two issues here:

1. the Court has a more ambivalent attitude towards *the* basic principle in those other legal instruments: applying *deprivation of liberty as a last resort*;
2. the Court has thus far mainly found overcrowding to violate dignity through poor material conditions; although it recognizes *reintegration* as an equally important aim of imprisonment as retribution and deterrence, it fails to apply the consequences of this aim to *prison regimes* in general.

Both issues relate to the Court's interpretation of the requirements for legitimacy of deprivation of liberty under Article 5 ECHR. They also relate to the penological concept of "penal moderation" as a public philosophy of punishment offering "a convincing rationale for radically reducing the harshness and scale of the penal system", which is explicitly linked to dignity (Loader 2010: 352). I will argue that a more consistent interpretation of Article 5 ECHR would support penal moderation both in its *quantitative* (detention rates) and *qualitative* meaning (preparing for reintegration) and would be more in accordance with the protection of dignity, which lies at the core of the ECHR.

Quantitative penal moderation: legitimacy of the decision to imprison and of sentence length

The key purpose of Article 5 is to prevent arbitrary or unjustified deprivations of liberty (*McKay v. the United Kingdom* [GC] 3 October 2006, § 30). The Court has emphasized on several occasions that the right to liberty and security is of the highest importance in a "democratic society" within the meaning of the Convention (*Medvedyev and Others v. France* [GC], 29 March 2010, § 76; *Ladent v. Poland*, 18 March 2008, §45). It follows that only a narrow interpretation of the exceptions stated in Article 5 §1 is consistent with the aim of that provision (*Medvedyev and Others v. France* [GC], 29 March 2010, § 78).

Analysis of the case-law of the Court shows, however, that the principles of proportionality and non-arbitrariness are applied differently to the different types of deprivation of liberty mentioned in Article 5 §1 a–f. The requirement to use *imprisonment as a measure of last resort* and the obligation to look for other, less stringent measures is enforced more strictly for Article 5§1 b, c, and f than for Article 5§1 a which relates to imprisonment after conviction.

An arrest aiming at the *fulfilment of an obligation* (Article 5§1, b) will only be acceptable in Convention terms if the obligation prescribed by law cannot be fulfilled by milder means (*Khodorkovskiy v. Russia*, 31 May 2011, § 136). The principle of proportionality further dictates that a balance must be struck between the importance in a democratic society of securing the immediate fulfilment of the obligation in question, and the importance of the right to liberty (*Saadi v. the United Kingdom* [GC], 2008, § 70).

The case-law of the Court shows an important evolution in respect to *remand custody* (Article 5§1, c). In *Bouchet v France* (20 March 2001), the Court found no violation of Article 5§1c in a case where the public prosecutor had successfully appealed against a decision of an investigating judge to release a suspect under an alternative measure of judicial supervision (*contrôle judiciaire*) after he had been in custody for two and a half months. The arguments of the investigating judge, that a *contrôle judiciaire* could attain the same aims, and of an expert psychiatrist that a further incarceration would be detrimental for the psychological health of the suspect, were rejected at the level of the Appeal Investigating Court and of the Court of Assizes. The suspect remained in remand custody for 17 months for the alleged rape of his girlfriend, for which he was subsequently acquitted by the Court of Assizes. The ECtHR found that the deprivation of liberty was sufficiently justified by the seriousness of the offence, the psychological state of the suspect, and the vulnerability of the victim. In a dissenting opinion however, Judges Tulkens, Loucaides and Bratza argued that "the legality of the remand custody should be examined in the light of all the options available to the State, which must choose the measure that infringes the least upon the rights of the suspect. The right to freedom and security, guaranteed in a democratic society by Article 5 of the Convention, means that only those deprivations of liberty which are strictly necessary are acceptable". This dissenting opinion gradually became the Court's stance on this issue, requiring judicial authorities to apply the strict proportionality test and consider other less stringent measures before deciding on remand custody (*Kudla v. Poland* [GC], 26 October 2000, §§ 110–111; *McKay v. the UK* [GC], 3 October 2006, §§ 41–45; *Ladent v Poland,* 18 June 2008, § 55; *Ambruszkiewicz c. Pologne,* 23 October 2006,§31). In *Idalov v. Russia* (GC) (22 May 2012, §§ 140–148) the Court even criticized the essential reliance on the gravity of the offence and the use of stereotypes when prolonging a remand custody.

The strict proportionality test and the principle of the use of imprisonment as last resort is also applied in cases concerning *detention to prevent unauthorized entry into a country* (Article 5 §1, f). In *Saadi v. the United Kingdom* (GC, 29 January 2008n §70) the court emphasized that "*The detention of an individual is such a serious measure that it is justified only as a last resort where other, less severe measures have been considered and found to be insufficient to safeguard the individual or public interest which might require that the person concerned be detained*".

A different approach is applied however towards *detention after conviction* (Article 5 § 1, a). In *Saadi v. the United Kingdom* (GC) (29 January 2008, §71), the Court explains that "*The Court applies a different approach towards the principle that there should be no arbitrariness in cases of detention under Article 5 § 1 (a), where, in the absence of bad faith or one of the other grounds set out in paragraph 69 above, as long as the detention follows and has a sufficient causal connection with a lawful conviction, the decision to impose a sentence of detention and the length of that sentence are matters for the national authorities rather than for the Court under Article 5 § 1*".

Contrary to the other forms of deprivation of liberty, where the Court reiterates that penal practices should not only be in accordance with national legislation but also with the Court's interpretation of the ECHR, imprisonment after conviction is left almost exclusively to the national authorities. Only in exceptional cases, for example where the refusal to grant probation or a fine was based on discrimination (Article 14 ECHR), would the imposition of a sentence of imprisonment be found to violate article 5§1 (*Aleksandr Aleksandrov v. Russia*, 27 March 2018). This may be understandable in view of the large differences existing between penal practices in the member states of the Council of Europe. However, this does not explain why the strict proportionality test applied to all other forms of deprivation of liberty is omitted here.

Arguments in favour of a consistent and strict application of the principles of proportionality and non-arbitrariness to all forms of deprivation of liberty

Different arguments plead against this distinction between imprisonment following conviction and the other reasons for deprivation of liberty under Article 5 §1.

The right to liberty is one of the most fundamental rights and deserves full protection

This is explicitly recognized by the Court itself, including, as shown above, with regard to decisions on remand custody. In its latest Guide on the interpretation of Article 5, updated on 31 August 2020 (European Court of Human Rights 2020), the Court remains ambivalent. On the one hand, §48 states "*Moreover, authorities should consider less intrusive measures than detention (Ambruszkiewicz v. Poland, § 32)*", which despite the reference to a case concerning remand custody could be interpreted as applicable to all cases under Article 5. On the other hand, §53 still reiterates that "*Matters of appropriate sentencing fall in principle outside the scope of the Convention. It is not the role of the Court to decide what is the appropriate term of detention applicable to a particular offence*".

The Convention is a "living instrument"

The Court has emphasized on several occasions that the Convention is a "living instrument" (*Selmouni v France* [GC], 28 July 1999 § 101) and that evolution in the case law of the Court is necessary taking into account (i) the other "legal instruments" of the Council of Europe; and (ii) developments in member states' national policies.

Other Council of Europe "legal instruments"

In its dynamic interpretation of the Convention, the Court increasingly refers to the CPT standards and reports and to the Recommendations by the Committee of Ministers as the "legal instruments" of the Council of Europe (see e.g. *Dickson v United Kingdom* [GC], 4 December 2007, § 28; *Vinter v United Kingdom* (GC), 9 July 2013). As mentioned above, these legal instruments display a large consensus on *always* using imprisonment as a last resort, including at the level of sentencing. Its application should be avoided as much as possible through the use of alternative sanctions and measures. The use of community sanctions and measures should be promoted (Rec (2000) 22 on improving the implementation of the European rules on community sanctions and measures) and fosters social inclusion and community safety (Rec (2010) 1 on the Council of Europe Probation Rules). Moreover, it is recognized that the detrimental effects of imprisonment increase with the length of the sentences (Rec (2003) 23 on the Management of life sentence and other long-term prisoners), and that conditional release should be promoted as a way to reduce the risk of recidivism while simultaneously reducing the length of imprisonment (Rec (2003) 22 concerning conditional release).

These "legal instruments" hence do not distinguish between the different forms of deprivation of liberty, and do not justify the Court's differentiation between remand custody, where a strict proportionality test is required, and imprisonment following conviction, where a much looser proportionality principle is applied. On the contrary, they recognize that the harm imposed on the prisoner is similar, and because of this detention harm, both forms of deprivation of liberty in the penal realm require authorities to foster the prisoner's reintegration. Indeed, where reintegration under the former 1987 European Prison Rules was limited to sentenced prisoners, Basic Principle 6 of the 2006 European Prison Rules clearly states that "*All detention shall be managed so as to facilitate the reintegration into free society of persons who have been deprived of their liberty*".

This former distinction – based on the fact that remand prisoners being presumed innocent, they could not be subjected to programmes aiming at their "rehabilitation" – is further diminished by the principle that even sentenced prisoners are sent to prison "*as punishment, not for punishment*" – the famous adage of Alexander Paterson, the English Prison Commissioner between 1922 and 1946, which has since become an internationally recognized principle (van Zyl Smit, Snacken 2009: 81).

National penal policies

The evolution in the national policies of the member states of the Council of Europe is another important criterion for the Court when assessing the dynamic interpretation of the Convention (cf. *Hirst v UK* (no 2) [GC], 6 October 2005 on the right to vote for prisoners).

All European countries have now established community sanctions and probation services (van Kalmthout, Durnescu 2008; CM Rec (2010) 1 on the Council of Europe Probation Rules). We can conclude that current European penal systems are characterized by a variety of sanctions, including fines, community sanctions and deprivation of liberty, offering sentencing judges a choice, especially in the lower and medium range of seriousness of the crimes committed.

Similarly, all European systems provide for some form of conditional release, although their legal framework and practical application varies (van Zyl Smit, Snacken 2009). Where some countries do not allow conditional release for life sentence prisoners, the Court has steadily evolved towards recognizing that a life sentence without a *de facto and de jure* possibility of parole violates human dignity under Article 3 (*Vinter v UK* (GC), 9 July 2013).

As far as the length of sentences is concerned, the picture is more blurred. While we mentioned above reductions in sentence length in some countries in order to tackle prison overcrowding, penal policies are often characterized by bifurcation: the introduction of community sanctions and measures at the lower end of the penal scale while reinforcing punitive levels at the upper end. This may even result from international obligations, such as the European Union's legislation and Court of Justice case law emphasis on "effective, proportionate and dissuasive" sanctions, in which effectiveness is understood as aiming at retribution and deterrence (Baker 2013; Martufi 2019; Cliquennois et al 2021). Here, the ECtHR's recognition that imprisonment is inherently humiliating could offer a stronger countervailing argument.

Imprisonment as inherent humiliation

A third argument why the Court should apply a strict proportionality test to all subsections of Article 5 §1 without distinction is its own repeated recognition, when assessing violations of Article 3, that imprisonment constitutes a form of "*inherent humiliation*" and entails an "*unavoidable level of suffering inherent in detention*" (e.g. *Tyrer v. UK,* 25 April 1978, § 30; *Costello-Roberts v. UK,* 25 March 1993, § 30; *Dougoz v. Greece,* 6 March 2001, § 46) (see also Tulkens, van de Kerchove 2006). The Court therefore imposes a higher threshold before admitting a violation of Article 3. Although the Convention in 1950 did not explicitly mention "human dignity", the Court uses the concept repeatedly in its case-law, especially when dealing with the core rights of Articles 2, 3, and 4. And given the explicit reference to "*the inherent dignity of all human beings*" in the Preamble of Protocol 13 to the Convention on the abolition of the death penalty, it has been argued that "*apparently dignity had by 2002 entered the normal vocabulary of the European Convention system*" (McCrudden 2008; Costa 2013; Buyse 2016[4]). Article 1 of the EU Charter of Fundamental Rights (2000) equally states "*Human dignity is inviolable. It must be respected and protected*". We could then argue that European member states have a positive obligation to protect human dignity and to limit humiliation – and hence imprisonment – as much as possible, both in its imposition and in its duration.

Applying the strict proportionality test to Article 5 §1 (a)

Limiting imprisonment refers to two strategies, which are directly linked to the mechanisms behind penal inflation and prison overcrowding: (i) the choice between deprivation of liberty and a non-custodial sanction or measure at the level of sentencing; (ii) the length of the imposed deprivation of liberty and the possibility of early release.

Choice between deprivation of liberty and community sanctions

The Court recognizes the "inherent humiliation" of punishment in general and of imprisonment in particular. It has never defined what the "inherent humiliation" of deprivation of liberty entails. We can only derive from its case-law concerning Article 3 what it considers to be an "acceptable" or "unacceptable" level of humiliation. I have tried earlier to make the basic humiliation resulting from deprivation of liberty more explicit by referring to the definition of "dignity" by the Belgian philosopher Leo Apostel (1987), as "*the recognition of the individual and social identity; the possibility to choose, decide and act autonomously*". An additional argument should be the increased evidence of the harms suffered by the families of prisoners, including their children, by the sole fact of the imprisonment of their partner or parent (Murray, Farrington 2008). As the Court explained in *Dickson v UK,* (GC) 4 December 2007, on the refusal of artificial insemination, family members should not be punished for the deeds committed by the offender.

It is increasingly recognized that community sanctions also present "*pains of probation*" which may challenge fundamental human rights (Durnescu

2011): deprivation of autonomy; deprivation of private or family life; deprivation of time; financial costs; stigmatisation effects of the probation supervision; the forced return to the offence; and living under the threat of imprisonment. Compared to imprisonment, community sanctions represent different "*degrees of freedom*" (van Zyl Smit 1994), which hence entail different degrees of humiliation. Choosing the lowest degree of humiliation possible would therefore mean to avoid imprisonment whenever possible and to favour fines or community sanctions when sentencing.

The application of the strict proportionality test to Article 5 §1 (a) could then result in a *procedural safeguard* through which the Court imposes on the states the burden of proof that no other sanction than deprivation of liberty is sufficient (see Snacken 2006) – as it does with the protection of other fundamental rights for prisoners. When doing so, it should ensure (as it does for remand custody) that stereotyped formulae such as the mere reference to the gravity of the offence and the criminal record are insufficient proof of such necessity (*Idalov v. Russia* (GC), 22 May 2012, §147).

Length of sentences

As deprivation of liberty is inherently humiliating, limiting its duration as much as possible seems another logical consequence of the duty to protect human dignity. However, monitoring the length of sentences imposed by national courts according to national legislation is difficult for the ECtHR, given the very large variations between member states. Although it has been demonstrated that more severe sentences have no impact on crime rates (Lappi-Seppälä 2011; Tonry 2014), and countries would not suffer more criminality if they all applied, for example, moderate Scandinavian sentencing practices, it would probably be very difficult to find a consensus on this issue amongst member states and judges of the Court.

The European "legal instruments" display a much higher consensus though on the usefulness of early release mechanisms, which shorten the length of the sentences imposed by the courts. The Rec (2003) 23 on the management of life and other long-term sentences, Rec (2003) 22 concerning conditional release and CM Rec (2010) 1 on the Council of Europe Probation Rules all emphasize the importance of conditional release as an important instrument to reduce the risk of recidivism and foster community safety. Of course, from the point of view of proportionality, conditions should only be imposed when necessary to attain these aims (van Zyl Smit et al 2015).

The Court has gradually evolved into recognizing a right for life-sentence prisoners to be considered for parole through a fair procedure, considering a life sentence without a *de iure and de facto* possibility of parole to violate human dignity under Article 3 (*Vinter v UK* (GC), 9 July 2013; *Trabelsi v Belgium*, 4 September 2014). This follows its increased recognition of reintegration as a fundamental aim of the implementation of a prison sentence (*Mastromatteo v Italy*

[GC], 24 October 2002; *Dickson v UK* [GC], 4 December 2007; *Maiorano v Italy*, 15 December 2009). Although the Court has not yet followed the other Council of Europe legal instruments in advocating early release mechanisms for all prisoners, its reliance on these instruments in other penal matters abode a possible further evolution in its case-law in this regard.

I have so far mainly discussed the opportunities for the Court to foster penal moderation in a *quantitative* sense, by aiming for "less" imprisonment. A similar exercise is required concerning the Court's emphasis on reintegration as an important instrument for a more *qualitative* dimension to moderate penal policies.

Qualitative penal moderation: legitimacy of the manner of implementing deprivation of liberty, reintegration and prison regimes

Article 5 ECHR offers the framework for the question of legitimacy of deprivation of liberty not only from the point of view of the (strict) principle of proportionality, but also from the principle of non-arbitrariness of the decision linked to its manner of implementation.

The Court has made it very clear in its assessments of Article 5 §1, d and e concerning deprivation of liberty imposed on juveniles and on mentally ill persons, that in order to be legitimate there must be a necessary link between the purpose of the detention and the manner of its implementation. Belgium was found to violate this requirement in the 1980s with regard to the imprisonment of juvenile offenders without any educational purpose (*Bouamar v Belgium,* 29 February 1988) and was repeatedly found to violate this condition with regard to its detention of mentally ill offenders without adequate psychiatric treatment (23 violations, starting with *Aerts v. Belgium,* 30 July 1998, and resulting in the pilot judgment *W.D. v. Belgium,* 6 September 2016).

A consistent application of this principle to sentenced prisoners then implies that a prison regime not aiming at their reintegration is illegitimate under Article 5 §1 (a).

Indeed, the Court has increasingly emphasized that reintegration/rehabilitation of prisoners is as important an aim of punishment as retribution and deterrence. It is linked to human dignity and to other individual rights for prisoners, such as the right to family contacts (*Khoroshenko v. Russia,* 30 June 2015); to start a family (*Dickson v United Kingdom*, 4 December 2007); to life-sentence prisoners having a realistic prospect of release (*Vinter v United Kingdom*, 9 July 2013) (van Zyl Smit, Snacken 2009; Martufi 2019). If legitimacy under Article 5 §1 requires a necessary link between the purpose of the detention and the manner of its implementation, then prison regimes for all (sentenced) prisoners should foster their reintegration.

This is not in contradiction with the fact that a sentence of imprisonment also aims at retribution (*Sawoniuk v United Kingdom*, 29 May 2001; *V United Kingdom*, 16 December 1999), deterrence (*M C v Bulgaria,* 4 December 2003; *Öneryldiz v Turkey*, 30 November 2004) or incapacitation (*Weeks v United Kingdom*, 2 March 1987). Following the internationally recognized principle that convicted prisoners are sent to prison "*as punishment and not for punishment*", the deprivation of liberty is in itself sufficient retribution, and hence doesn't offer a framework for the content of a prison regime (see Rule 102.2 European Prison Rules). Similarly, research ascertains that deterrence is not dependent on the length or the conditions of imprisonment, but on the perceived risk of apprehension (von Hirsch et al 1999). Deterrence is hence not influenced by the elaboration of a prison regime aiming at reintegration. Even preventive detention aiming at incapacitation of "dangerous" offenders requires "*the necessary means, such as suitable therapy, to demonstrate that he or she was no longer dangerous*" (*Klinkenbuß v. Germany*, 25 February 2016, § 47).

That leaves reintegration as a major purpose offering guidance as to the manner in which sentences of imprisonment should be implemented.

How should a regime aiming at reintegration look like? Several of the Council of Europe Recommendations describe such a regime. Rules 102–107 of the European Prison Rules mention individual sentence plans; a systematic programme of work and education, including skills training, designed to enable prisoners to lead a responsible and crime-free life; a system of prison leaves as an integral part of such a regime. Rec (2003) 23 on the management of life sentence and other long-term prisoners elaborates six main principles: individualization, normalization, responsibility, safety and security, non-segregation and progression. Rec (2003) 22 on conditional release emphasizes the importance of a gradual return to society through appropriate pre-release programmes; encouraging prisoners to take part in educational and training courses that prepare them for life in the community; specific modalities such as semi-liberty, open regimes or extra-mural placements; the importance of prisoners' maintaining, establishing or re-establishing links with their family and close relations, and of forging contacts with services, organisations and voluntary associations that can assist conditionally released prisoners in adjusting to life in the community through various forms of prison leave.

So far, this obligation of the States to promote resocialisation has been recognized by the Court most explicitly in the case of life-sentenced prisoners, as this sentence must be reducible under Article 3, but with reference to "convicted prisoners" in general (*Murray v the Netherlands* (GC), 26 April 2016): "*Notwithstanding the fact that the Convention does not guarantee, as such, a right to rehabilitation, the Court's case-law thus presupposes that convicted persons, including life prisoners, should be allowed to rehabilitate themselves*" (§103). It considers "*that even though States are not responsible for achieving the rehabilitation of life prisoners (.), they nevertheless have a duty to make it possible for such prisoners to rehabilitate themselves. Were it otherwise, a life prisoner could in effect be denied the possibility of rehabilitation, with the consequence that the review required for a life sentence to be reducible, in which a life prisoner's progress towards rehabilitation is to be assessed, might never be genuinely capable of leading to the commutation, remission or termination of the life sentence or to the conditional release of the prisoner*" (§104).

The Court then refers to individualized sentence programmes "*that will encourage the sentenced prisoner to develop himself or herself to be able to lead a responsible and crime-free life* (§103). Importantly, a State will only have complied "*with its obligations under Article 3 when it has provided for conditions of detention and facilities, measures or treatments capable of enabling a life prisoner to rehabilitate himself or herself*" (§111).

If the Court takes the aim of reintegration seriously for all prison sentences, then this reasoning must be enlarged to Article 5 as well.

Conclusion: from prison overcrowding to penal moderation as a human rights issue

In this contribution, we have moved from prison overcrowding as a human rights issue to penal moderation as a human rights issue. The Court has gradually recognized the obligation by states to consider other, less stringent alternatives than deprivation of liberty, except for imprisonment after conviction. Our arguments for abandoning this exception for Article 5 §1 (a) relate to the stance of all other European legal instruments in this regard, and the recognition by the Court that imprisonment is inherently humiliating. The application of a strict principle of proportionality and non-arbitrariness should restrict the use of imprisonment, reduce its length and guarantee that prison regimes aim at reintegration.

I would like to end by citing Françoise Tulkens, former judge in the ECtHR: "*(.) can we continue to admit that punishment necessarily entails humiliation and suffering? I think not (.). Just as the right to life now prohibits death penalty, I think one day the right to liberty will preclude imprisonment as punishment* » (Tulkens 2008: 9–10; my translation).

Notes

1 This chapter is a reworked version of Snacken S (2018) The European Court of Human Rights and National Penal Policies: Tackling Prison Population Inflation and Fostering Penal Moderation through Articles 3 and 5 of the Convention, in: The protection of prisoners' rights in Europe, Actes de colloque, *Revue des Droits de l'Homme*, 14: 56–66. I thank the publishers for granting permission to build on my previous article.

2 Rec (2003)22 on parole; Rec (2006)2 on the European Prison Rules; Rec (2006)13 on the use of remand custody; Rec (2010)1 on the Council of Europe Probation Rules; Rec (2012)12 on foreign national prisoners; Rec (2014)3 on dangerous offenders; Rec (2014)4 on electronic monitoring; Rec (2017)3 on the European Rules on community sanctions and measures.

3 See *Torreggiani a.o v Italy* 8 January 2013; *Stella a.o. v. Italy* 16 September 2014; *Ananyev a.o. v. Russia*, 10 January 2012; *Ciorap v. Moldova* 19 June 2007; *Rezmives a.o. v. Romania* 25 April 2017; *Varga a.o. v. Hungary* 10 March 2015; *Neshkov a.o. v. Bulgaria* 27 January 2015; *Sikorski v. Poland* 22 October 2009; *Orchowski v. Poland* 22 October 2009; *Vasilescu v. Belgium* 25 November 2014; *Bamouhammad v. Belgium* 17 November 2015; *J.M.B. and others v. France* 30 January 2020.

4 The author found in the case-law database (halfway October 2016) 876 cases including a reference to human dignity.

References

Apostel A (1987) Beschikken over lijf en leven: een wijsgerig standpunt, in L Apostel, P Devroey, H Cammaer (eds), *Beschikken over Lijf en Leven. Ethische vragen rond vrijheid en geborgenheid*, Leuven: Acco.

Baker E (2013) The Emerging Role of the EU as a Penal Actor, in T Daems, D van Zyl Smit, S Snacken (eds), *European Penology?*, Oxford: Hart.

Buyse A (2016) *Dignified Law: The Role of Human Dignity in European Convention Case-Law*, keynote 11 October 2016, Utrecht University; http://echrblog.blogspot.be/2016/10/the-role-of-human-dignity-in-echr-case.html (30 October 2017).

Cliquennois G, Snacken S, van Zyl Smit D (2021) Can European human rights instruments limit the power of the state to punish? – A tale of two Europes, *European Journal of Criminology*, 18/1: 11–32.

Costa J P (2013) Human Dignity in the Jurisprudence of the European Court of Human Rights, in C McCrudden (ed), *Understanding Human Dignity – Proceedings of the British Academy*, Oxford: Oxford University Press, vol. 192, 393–402.

Durnescu I (2011) Pains of probation: Effective practice and human rights, *International Journal of Offender Therapy and Comparative Criminology*, 55/4: 530–545.

European Court of Human Rights (2020) *Guide on Article 5 of the European Convention on Human Rights – Right to Liberty and Security*, Updated 31 August 2020; https://www.echr.coe.int/documents/guide_art_5_eng.pdf (1 December 2020).

Lappi-Seppälä T (2011) Explaining imprisonment in Europe, *European Journal of Criminology*, 8/4: 303–328.

Loader I (2010) For penal moderation. Notes towards a public philosophy of punishment, *Theoretical Criminology*, 14/3: 349–367.

Martufi A (2019) The paths of offender rehabilitation and the European dimension of punishment: New challenges for an old ideal, *Maastricht Journal of European and Comparative Law*, 25/6, 672–688.

McCrudden C (2008) Human dignity and judicial interpretation of human rights, *The European Journal of International Law*, 19/4: 655–724.

Murray J, Farrington D P (2008) The effects of parental imprisonment on children, *Crime and Justice*, 37: 133–206.

Snacken S (2006) A reductionist penal policy and European human rights standards, *The European Journal on Criminal Policy and Research*, 12: 143–164.

Snacken S (2015) Punishment, legitimate policies and values: Penal moderation, dignity and human rights, *Punishment & Society*, 17: 397–423.

Snacken S, Beyens K, Tubex H (1995) Changing prison populations in Western Countries: fate or policy?, *European Journal of Crime, Criminal Law and Criminal Justice*, 1: 18–53.

Tonry M (2007) Determinants of penal policies, *Crime and Justice*, 36/1: 1–48.

Tonry M (2014) *Why Crime Rates Are Falling throughout the Western World*, University of Minnesota Law School, Legal Studies Research Paper Series, No. 14–41.

Tulkens F (2008) Préface, Philippe Landenne, in *Peines en prison. L'addition cachée*, Bruxelles: Larcier. Crimen.

Tulkens F, van de Kerchove M (2006) La nature et les contours de la peine. Regards croisés sur la jurisprudence interne et internationale, in M Born, F Kéfer, A Lemaître (eds), *Une criminologie de la tradition à l'innovation. En hommage à Georges Kellens*, Bruxelles: Larcier, 454–474.

van Kalmthout A M, Durnescu I (2008) *Probation in Europe*, Nijmegen: Wolf Legal Publishers/CEP.

van Zyl Smit D (1994) Degrees of freedom, *Criminal Justice Ethics*, 13/1: 31–38.
van Zyl Smit D, Snacken S (2009) *Principles of European Prison Law and Policy. Penology and Human Rights*, Oxford: Oxford University Press.
van Zyl Smit D, Snacken S, Hayes D (2015) 'One cannot legislate kindness': Ambiguities in European legal instruments on non-custodial sanctions, *Punishment & Society*, 17/1: 3–26.
Von Hirsch A, Bottoms A E, Burney E, Wikström P-O (1999) *Criminal Deterrence and Sentence Severity*, Oxford: Hart.
Zimring F E, Hawkins G J (1991) *The Scale of Imprisonment*, Chicago: University of Chicago Press.

3

THE EXECUTION OF PENALTIES IN THE JURISPRUDENCE OF THE EUROPEAN COURT OF HUMAN RIGHTS

Simon Creighton

Introduction

In this chapter, I will seek to explore the concept of the "enforcement of sentences" and the relationship between the European Convention on Human Rights ("ECHR") and the execution of prison sentences that have been lawfully imposed by domestic courts. The question of whether any such role does in fact exist remains confused particularly in the case of prisoners serving determinate sentences. This chapter will contend that there has been a failure of the European Court of Human Rights ("the Court") to apply the developing broad principles of rehabilitation and resocialisation in a consistent manner, particularly in relation to determinate prison sentences, and this failure runs the risk of weakening those principles.

In seeking to identify whether there are any underlying principles engaging fundamental rights that are capable of cross-jurisdictional application, it is necessary to look back to the genesis of judicial oversight of indeterminate sentences to try and draw out the themes that have mandated the application of the Convention in place of deference to domestic law. I will predominantly examine the decisions of the Court as the expression of the rights that have been afforded judicial recognition. It is important, therefore, to note that the use of the term "enforcement" in this context may be considered to pre-suppose that there are, as a matter of fact, laws, regulations or social norms that are capable of being engaged. A more neutral expression, such as the "supervision of sentences", may better reflect the history of this jurisprudence but it is my contention that international law and human rights standards now recognise that the components of prison sentences extend beyond simple containment and punishment and are capable of bringing into play a range of rights that address the execution and administration of the length of the sentence as well as the treatment of individuals during that sentence.

DOI: 10.4324/9780429317033-5

The starting point of ECHR case law was that any domestic law prison sentence – whether determinate or indeterminate – does not raise any new questions under the Convention providing the sentence itself complies with the procedural and substantive safeguards of Articles 5(1)(a) and 6 at the time it was imposed. This contrasted with other forms of detention that do not follow a conviction, such as the detention of persons of unsound mind pursuant to Article 5(1)(e) where the right to have a periodic review of the necessity for continuing detention was recognised.[1] The correctness of this approach was called into question in the *Van Droogenbroeck v Belgium*[2] decision and for the first time, raised questions about the interplay of Articles 5(1) and 5(4) in respect of the enforcement of sentences. The case concerned the powers of the Belgian Ministry of Justice to detain a recidivist for a period of up to 10 years. The Court explained that the order for detention did not involve a violation of Article 5(1):

> On this point the Court, like the Commission, confines itself to observing that in Belgium—as in other Contracting States—it is traditional for the execution of sentences and other measures pronounced by criminal courts to fall within the province of the Minister of Justice. The Court sees no reason to doubt that the Minister was, by virtue of the general principles of Belgian public law concerning the attribution and the allocation of powers, an appropriate authority to act in Mr van Droogenbroeck's case.[3]

However, in an apparent departure from previous case law, the Court found that the lack of further independent review of the ongoing necessity for detention was a breach of Article 5(4), noting that the purpose of imprisonment in this case was not purely punitive but "*also to provide the executive with an opportunity of endeavouring to reform the individuals concerned*".[4] The underlying basis for this finding – that the grounds upon which the sentence was originally imposed might be subject to change – was to form the foundation stone of the analysis that Article 5 does have a role to play in the execution of sentences and was subsequently examined in greatest detail in relation to indeterminate sentences imposed in the United Kingdom.

The United Kingdom proved to be such fertile ground for testing the boundaries of this analysis precisely because of its attachment to the use of a wide variety of indeterminate sentences. A succession of cases, starting with *Weeks v United Kingdom*[5] established a core principle in respect of life and indeterminate sentences. In circumstances where an indeterminate sentence is imposed, it must be assumed that the rationale for detention might change over the years and thus any fresh decision about the legality of detention must comply with the procedural safeguards of Article 5(4). The time at which the safeguards of Article 5 would be re-engaged would be at the end of the tariff or punitive period and on the occasion of any re-detention following release. It was for domestic law to decide when that point was reached, providing that the sentencing decision had been made in accordance with Article 6. This principle was summarised in *Weeks* in the following terms:

> (a) The requisite judicial control of the lawfulness of the detention under national law and the Convention was not incorporated in the original conviction, as new issues affecting its lawfulness might arise in an ensuing period of detention. Given the particular nature of the reasons warranting an indeterminate sentence the applicant was entitled to such a review at the moment of any return to custody and also at reasonable intervals during the course of the imprisonment.
>
> *56–58*

This essentially represents the key breakthrough made by the Court in respect of their comprehension of when the Convention has a role to play in the execution of domestic sentences. It is noteworthy that the series of cases which decided this issue demonstrated that the Convention is a living instrument, adjusting to both developments in domestic law and also to wider international standards. Thus, in 1992, the case of a prisoner convicted of murder who had received a mandatory life sentence was held not to engage Article 5(4) on the basis that under domestic law, the conviction and sentence authorised lifelong punitive detention and so no new issues could arise under the Convention.[6] However, less than a decade later, when faced with the reality of a case where a prisoner serving an identical sentence had been released and recalled to custody, the Court noted that:

> After the expiry of the tariff, continued detention depends on elements of dangerousness and risk associated with the objectives of the original sentence of murder. These elements may change with the course of time, and thus new issues of lawfulness arise requiring determination by a body satisfying the requirements of Article 5(4). It can no longer be maintained that the original trial and appeal proceedings satisfied, once and for all, issues of compatibility of subsequent detention of mandatory life prisoners with the provisions of Article 5(1) of the Convention.[7]
>
> *emphasis added*

Although it has been firmly established that the execution of life and indeterminate sentences are capable of raising fresh Article 5(4) issues, there are three further questions which require more structured and considered development by the Court:

1. In what circumstances does the state have to guarantee the right to a review of a sentence – the "whole life sentence" issue?
2. What further guarantees must exist to ensure that a sentence is reducible both as a matter of law and practice (i.e.: both *de jure* and *de facto* reducibility)?
3. Whether these principles have any applicability to prisoners serving determinate sentences?

The "whole life sentence issue"

Given the relatively small number of prisoners serving irreducible whole life terms and the small number of countries that impose such sentences, it is necessary to consider what issues these sentence raise that are so critical to the debate.[8] The Grand Chamber judgement in *Vinter v United Kingdom*[9] arguably contained the first comprehensive analysis of the *purpose* of a prison sentence. In seeking to address the purpose of imprisonment, it has allowed for a tentative judicial analysis as to how those sentences must be executed by the domestic authorities, with implications not just for the formal release mechanisms that are necessary but also for the practical measures that must be put in place to make release attainable. This necessarily entails the possibility of resocialisation and progression during the sentence itself.

Vinter built upon the Court's findings in *Dickson v United Kingdom*,[10] a case concerning the right of a prisoner serving a life sentence to access artificial insemination. This judgement explicitly recognised that rehabilitative rights do exist even during the punitive phase of a prison sentence. When addressing the objectives of a prison sentence, the Court made direct reference to the concepts of "resocialisation" and articulated the "progression principle":

> D. The objectives of a sentence of imprisonment
>
> 28. Criminologists have referred to the various functions traditionally assigned to punishment, including retribution, prevention, protection of the public and rehabilitation. However, in recent years there has been a trend towards placing more emphasis on rehabilitation, as demonstrated notably by the Council of Europe's legal instruments. While rehabilitation was recognised as a means of preventing recidivism, more recently and more positively, it constitutes rather the idea of re-socialisation through the fostering of personal responsibility. This objective is reinforced by the development of the "progression principle": in the course of serving a sentence, a prisoner should move progressively through the prison system thereby moving from the early days of a sentence, when the emphasis may be on punishment and retribution, to the latter stages, when the emphasis should be on preparation for release.

The formal breakthrough in *Vinter* was to import these principles into the length of the sentence itself by finding that a lifelong punitive sentence with no prospect of release breaches Convention rights as it fails to incorporate the concepts of resocialisation and rehabilitation. This is unquestionably a critical juncture. The development of the law from the circumscribed view of the role of the ECHR in the supervision of domestic sentences as expressed in *Wynne* is unquestionable. However, one criticism that can be made of the *Vinter* judgement is the failure to properly explore the requirements of Article 5 in this context, and to analyse the problem solely through the lens of Article 3. This may be a hangover from the somewhat confused reasoning on Article 5 in *Kafkaris v Cyprus*,[11] or it may be explicable as reluctance on the part of a supra-national court to become too didactic. Whatever the explanation for this approach, it does leave a vacuum at the heart of the analysis.

The reluctance of the Grand Chamber to examine the requirements of Article 5 in this context has meant that subsequent judgements seeking to apply *Vinter* to the specific workings of individual jurisdictions have increasingly been reduced to a mechanistic analysis of the workings of compassionate release schemes and pardons in domestic law, thus avoiding any real clarity about the overarching principles.[12] This was most graphically illustrated in the Grand Chamber's decision in *Hutchinson v United Kingdom*[13] where the Grand Chamber decided that the power of compassionate release they had previously found to be inadequate in *Vinter* was now sufficiently robust to prevent a breach of Article 3 as it would have been interpreted in accordance with the requirements of the earlier judgement. The paradox was noted in two dissenting opinions.[14]

Leaving aside the potential crisis in legitimacy that the judgement creates, it also unearths a more far-reaching problem in respect of the real ambit of the Convention in the enforcement of sentences as was illustrated by the case of *Murray v The Netherlands*.[15] To a large extent, *Murray* represents the current high watermark of the Court's role in enforcing sentences. The critical departure from previous judgements was the finding that sentences must be reducible both *de jure* and *de facto* and this includes providing prisoners with the opportunity to rehabilitate themselves. However, that conclusion was once again reached through the Article 3 route, leaving open the question of what enforcement means in practice. In order to understand how this line of reasoning has obscured the Court's potential role, it is necessary to look back a decade to the dissenting judgement of Judge Costa in *Léger v France*.[16] Judge Costa was more precise in his approach to the problem, focussing on the requirements of Article 5 rather than Article 3. He made it clear that even if parole, or the "right to early release", is not characterised as a right in domestic law, it must be subject to the supervision of the ECHR otherwise it runs the risk of arbitrariness. He was also cognisant of the fact that this meant that the principles would apply with equal force to prisoners serving determinate sentences. The importance of his observations requires them to be repeated in full:

> Before considering whether the applicant's continued detention was lawful, I need to dismiss two objections which occurred to me and caused some hesitation in my mind. Firstly, is the Court not running the risk of acting as a court of third or fourth instance if it reviews domestic judgements refusing an application for release on licence? Secondly, and more importantly, does the fact that parole is not a right allow the national authorities a discretionary power not amenable to review at European level?
>
> .... I ultimately consider, for two reasons, that our Court has the right and duty to review decisions by such courts. Firstly, with regard to Article 5, which to a certain extent departs from the subsidiarity principle, the Court

> has always held that, since deprivation of liberty is compatible with the Convention only if it complies with domestic law, it is required to review such compliance itself without simply leaving the matter to the national courts.
>
> .... Should the Court then of its own motion construct a theory to the effect that decisions on parole are both discretionary and unreviewable? I would be reluctant to do so, not only because there are already instruments laying down procedures and criteria for granting or refusing release (the fact that no such right exists means only that it will not automatically be granted to anyone who requests it, and not that it can be refused arbitrarily), but also because the right to liberty is too essential for our Court to make "real" life imprisonment an automatic and unreviewable process. I would add, lastly, that if the purpose of the legislation was to increase the role of the courts in dealing with applications for release, it would be ludicrous for the European Court of Human Rights to fly in the face of this trend by refusing to review the relevance, adequacy and lack of arbitrariness of the grounds on which the appropriate courts' decisions were based.
>
> .... In my opinion, there is unfortunately no such thing as zero risk, but if we take that approach, then we should never release prisoners on licence: life sentences would always be served for a whole-life term, and determinate sentences would always be served in full. Potential victims would perhaps be better protected (except where prisoners escaped) – but would transforming prisoners into wild beasts or human waste not mean creating further victims and substituting vengeance for justice?[17]

The right to rehabilitation in practice

Although there remain reservations about the practical implications of the prohibition on irreducible whole-life sentences, this jurisprudence does have important consequences for the wider principles of rehabilitation and resettlement for those serving custodial sentences. Consistently with its judgement in *Dickson v United Kingdom*, in *Khoroshenko v Russia*,[18] the Court reiterated that *"the emphasis on rehabilitation and reintegration has become a mandatory factor that the member states need to take into account in designing their penal policies"* and therefore the *"regime and conditions of a life prisoner's incarceration cannot be regarded as a matter of indifference in that context"*.

The extent to which post-conviction intervention in the supervision of a life sentence is mandated by the Convention was tested further in *Viola v Italy (No 2)*.[19] The relevant domestic legislation made release contingent upon co-operation with the judicial authorities and in fact denied access to rehabilitative measures while such co-operation was withheld. Although this was framed as a matter of choice for the individual, the Court expressed doubts as to whether this was a genuine matter of choice and the questioned relevance that it had to an assessment of whether that individual still represented a danger to society.

By acting as an insuperable barrier, it prevented a genuine examination of the extent to which detention continues to be justified on penological grounds and so was incompatible with Article 3. The judgement therefore seeks to further embed the duty of resocialisation and rehabilitation within the practical framework of the sentence, albeit in the context of Article 3 rather than through the application of Article 5 with the attendant procedural safeguards.

The problem of rooting these broad principles into concrete procedural safeguards was illustrated by the contrasting Court decisions in *James v United Kingdom*[20] and *Kaiyam v United Kingdom*.[21] The Court had to grapple with cases arose in the United Kingdom introducing a new mandatory sentence of indefinite detention for public protection ("IPP"). IPP was created by the Criminal Justice Act 2003 and implemented for offences committed after 4 April 2005 (Ministry of Justice 2011). The purpose was to create a sentence permitting the indefinite detention of persons deemed to be dangerous but whose offence was not serious enough to merit a life sentence. It was available for a range of over 150 offences, for offences as minor as affray. In practice, the sentence is indistinguishable from a life sentence and is subject to the same statutory provisions regarding the fixing of the tariff and release as all other life sentences. During the sentence, they would be expected to undertake work to reduce the risk they posed with release at the discretion of the Parole Board. The impact on the number of prisoners serving indeterminate sentences was profound, and by 31 March 2011, the number of people serving this sentence stood at 6,550.[22] The problem that this created was compounded by the relatively short length of the tariffs imposed when compared to life sentences, with the vast majority having tariffs of under 4 years (Ministry of Justice 2011).[23]

The UK Government belatedly recognised the faults with this system and gradually imposed more stringent criteria for its imposition before finally abolishing it in December 2012.[24] However, in the meantime, the British prison system had become overloaded with prisoners who are all required to prove they no longer pose a risk to the public to secure their release. In the view of Her Majesty's Chief Inspector of Prisons (Inspectorate of Prisons 2016):

> Failures in the criminal justice and parole systems have resulted in far too many people with IPP sentences being held in prison for many years after their tariff has expired. They have been denied the opportunity to demonstrate whether they present a continuing risk to the public, or to have this properly assessed. IPP sentences have not worked as intended and the current situation in which many prisoners find themselves is clearly unjust.[25]

In *James v United Kingdom*,[26] the Court held that following the expiry of the tariff and until steps were taken to progress IPP prisoners him through the prison system with a view to providing access to appropriate rehabilitative courses, detention was arbitrary and therefore unlawful within the meaning of Article 5(1). This analysis was only partly accepted by the domestic courts. The Supreme

Court in the United Kingdom accepted that it is implicit in the scheme of Article 5 that the state has a duty to provide a reasonable opportunity to a prisoner for rehabilitation and to demonstrate that the risk posed to the public is no longer unacceptable. But that duty cannot be brought within the express language of either Article 5(1)(a) or Article 5(4). A duty to facilitate release can only be implied as part of the overall scheme of Article 5 as an *ancillary* duty not affecting the actual lawfulness of the detention. Where this duty has been breached, the appropriate remedy is not a release but an award of damages for legitimate frustration and anxiety.[27]

This analysis fell to be reconsidered by the Court.[28] Although the Court considered that the development of an ancillary Article 5 duty in domestic law was less stringent than their own analysis that detention could become arbitrary under Article 5(1)(a) absent the provision of appropriate rehabilitation opportunities, the application of this principle to the facts made the scope of this remedy questionable. For example, in one of the cases considered by the Court, a delay of 18 months in making an essential course available to a prisoner after the expiry of his tariff was not considered to breach his Convention rights, even though this delay had been deemed unlawful in domestic law.

There remains a distinct lack of clarity about the meaning of *de facto* reducibility of a life sentence once the punitive period has been served. It is disconcerting that a finding in domestic law of unlawful delay does not cross the threshold of illegality applied by the Court and it is troubling that domestic courts have had to bridge this gap by developing a theory of an ancillary Article 5 duty: a duty that does not create an enforceable right to release even when detention runs the risk of being arbitrary, but which instead creates a justiciable right to access rehabilitative courses and a right to compensation. The difficulty with domestic law seeking to bridge this gap is that it runs ahead of the Convention jurisprudence, making those rights vulnerable to erosion. This is the situation that is currently facing prisoners serving determinate sentences.

Determinate sentences

The progressive intervention of the Court into the execution of indeterminate sentences has not yet been followed in determinate sentences. The long-standing view expressed by the Court is most succinctly expressed contained in the admissibility decision in *Ganusaukus v Lithuania*[29] where it was confirmed that for the purposes of Article 5, the criminal conviction and sentence provide authority for detention for the entire duration of the sentence:

> The Court recalls that the Convention does not confer, as such, a right to release on licence or require that parole decisions be taken by or subject to review by a court. A penalty involving deprivation of liberty which the offender must undergo for a period specified in the court decision is justified at the outset by the original conviction and appeal proceedings

> (see, mutatis mutandis, the Van Droogenbroeck v. Belgium judgement of 24 June 1982, Series A no. 50, pp. 21-22, §§ 39–40). In the present case, the order for the applicant's conditional release did not in any way affect the validity of the trial court's judgement and the subsequent appeal procedures by which the applicant was convicted and sentenced to six years' imprisonment. Nothing indicates that the causal link between the conviction and the re-detention was broken ...[30]

This approach was followed in *Brown v United Kingdom*[31] in the context of a determinate sentence prisoner who had been released and recalled to custody. A distinction was drawn between prisoners serving indeterminate sentences, whose detention is based on risk alone in the post-tariff phase, and those serving determinate sentences where "*detention is again governed by the fixed term imposed by the judge conforming with the objectives of that sentence and thus within the scope of Article 5(1)(a) of the Convention*".[32] These cases have reiterated that for all determinate sentences, all of the protections of Article 5 are incorporated into the original sentence. Thus, whatever regimes may be in place for release, whether discretionary or mandatory, and irrespective of whether release has actually taken place, there can be no re-engagement of Article 5 at any point before the entire sentence expires.

This analysis of the applicability of Article 5 can be seen to be in direct conflict with the reality of many domestic release schemes. For example, in the United Kingdom, there has been a statutory and automatic right to release from a determinate sentence, subject to a supervisory licence, since 1992.[33] A failure to release at this statutory date was held to amount to false imprisonment and a breach of Article 5(1)(a) by the domestic courts.[34] The inevitable consequence of such a finding was that a recall to custody following statutory release was held to re-engage Article 5.[35] However, relying on these earlier decisions of the Court, the Supreme Court of the United Kingdom halted the advances that had been made in domestic law in the case of *Whiston v Secretary of State for Justice*.[36] The majority of the Supreme Court considered that there had been no proper explanation for domestic law to have departed from *Ganusauskas* and *Brown*. They considered that the Strasbourg Court might want to reconsider its jurisprudence, but the domestic courts should not outstrip it when seeking to interpret Convention rights.

The analysis – both in the United Kingdom and in Strasbourg to that point – was lacking in several respects and in any event may no longer be compatible with other developments in the Court's case law. In *Del Rio Prada v Spain*,[37] the Court examined an adjustment to a life sentence and found that there had been a violation of Article 7 but went on to find there had been a violation of Article 5(1). In reaching this conclusion, the judgement notes that:

> The causal link required under [Article 5(1)(a)] might eventually be broken if a position were reached in which a decision not to release, or to redetain a person, was based on grounds that were inconsistent with the objectives of the sentencing court, or on an assessment that was unreasonable in terms

> of those objectives. Where that was the case a detention that was lawful at the outset would be transformed into a deprivation of liberty that was arbitrary and, hence, incompatible with art.5.[38]

This approach as adopted by the Court in *Etute v Luxembourg*[39] concerned a prisoner who had had the benefit of conditional release under Article 100 of the Luxembourg Criminal Code. It is relevant that Article 100 confers a power of release (exercisable by the state general prosecutor) during the course of a determinate sentence, and that where conditional release is later revoked, the individual serves the remainder of the custodial term outstanding from the date of the conditional release. The key passage of the judgement appears to be in direct conflict with the earlier admissibility decisions insofar as it recognises that a new issue can arise during the currency of a determinate sentence:

> The applicant's re-incarceration with effect from 4 November 2015, for the purpose of serving the portion of sentence remaining at the time when he was released subject to conditions, depended on a new decision, namely that to cancel the conditional release. This decision specifically arose from the observation that the Applicant was no longer respecting the conditions attached to his conditional release, namely not to commit a new offence and to stop frequenting places where drugs were present .... In these circumstances, the Court considers that the question concerning respect of the conditions imposed on the applicant under the conditional release was crucial in determining the legality of his detention from 4 November 2015. The Court considers that this is a new question regarding the re-incarceration following cancellation of the conditional release. The internal court order should therefore allow the applicant access to a judicial appeal that satisfies the requirements of Article 5(4) of the Convention to resolve this question.[40]

Regrettably, the judgement failed to confront the apparent departure from the previous settled position of the Court, a point that was noted in the two concurring opinions of Judges Kuris and Pinto de Albuquerque. Although this undoubtedly represents a step forward, the absence of any definitive examination by the Court of the application of Article 5 to determinate prison sentences raises three concerns that require further exploration. First, it ignores the application of Article 5(4) after a statutory decision to release has taken place. As *Etute* appears to acknowledge, if domestic law creates an enforceable Article 5(1) right to liberty at a certain point of the sentence, it is difficult to see how subsequent decisions to re-detain do not, at the very least, engage Article 5(4) and has the potential to engage Article 5(1)(a) for precisely the same reasons as set out in *Weeks* and *Stafford* above.

Second, the assumption that the entire determinate sentence is punitive, no matter how long the sentence may be, effectively disregards the progression and resocialisation principles that have been articulated in the context of indeterminate sentences. A prisoner serving a discretionary life sentence has the protection of both Article 5(4) and Article 5(1)(a) as soon as the tariff period expires, whereas a prisoner serving an equivalent determinate sentence for the same offence has no such protection at any point simply because the sentence has an end point. It is also difficult to see how it can be consistent with *Clift v United Kingdom*[41] where the European Court of Human rights held that a prisoner serving a determinate sentence was the subject of discriminatory treatment under Article 14 as he was required to satisfy a more stringent release test than a life-sentenced prisoner, even though parole in his case only fell within the ambit or Article 5 rather than directly engaging an Article 5 right.

Finally, if Article 5 has no role to play in the execution of these sentences, it is unclear how the wider purposes of imprisonment as articulated in the resocialisation principle can ever be brought to bear through judicial intervention. Even the attempts to develop these principles in domestic law, such as the ancillary Article 5 duty identified by the Supreme Court of the United Kingdom for IPP prisoners will have no application.

Conclusions

The role of Court in maintaining the Convention's status as a living instrument has come under increased scrutiny, not least by its own judicial members, through the debate on the status of Article 5 in the execution of sentences. Although the Court has commenced the task of analysing the contemporary purpose and components of a prison sentence, this has primarily been achieved through the obligations and duties of Article 3. It appears that for the time being, the case of *Kafkaris*[42] has imposed a temporary block on establishing any comprehensive analysis of these duties under Article 5.

The problem in this diversionary approach is that it risks undermining the development of *de facto* rights as opposed to *de jure* rights. This tension is demonstrated by the ongoing debate about the meaning of an irreducible life sentence but is possibly felt most acutely by those prisoners serving determinate sentences as it remains the case that there is still no real judicial recognition that the Convention has a role to play in the execution of their sentences. Judge Costa foreshadowed this issue when he grappled with the role of the Court in developing this area law in a progressive fashion. It is a sentiment that has been developed further in the dissenting opinion of Judge Pinto de Albuquerque in *Murray*:

> The logical conclusion to be drawn from the above set of Convention principles is that, if a parole mechanism must be available to those convicted of the most heinous crimes, a fortiori it must be available to other prisoners. It would fly in the face of justice if offenders convicted of less serious offences could not be paroled whenever they are apt to reintegrate society, while such an opportunity would be afforded to offenders convicted of more serious crimes. Thus, in principle, the Convention guarantees a right to parole to all prisoners.

The ongoing challenge for the Court is to ensure that Convention rights are "practical and effective" rather than "theoretical or illusory". In respect of the execution of prison sentences, it does appear that the Court is beginning to lag behind the requirements of international human rights instruments and other jurisdictions. For example, Recommendation 2003(23) of the Council of Europe on conditional release (parole), which is specifically made applicable to the release of life-sentenced prisoners by paragraph 34 of the Recommendation 2003(22) on the management of life sentence and other long-term prisoners, contains procedural requirements that should apply to all forms of conditional release. These include the setting of minimum periods (paragraph 16), prompt procedures when these periods have been served (paragraph 17) and clear criteria for consideration (paragraph 18). Further detailed procedural safeguards for decisions on granting conditional release are set out in paragraphs 32–36 of Recommendation 2003(23). Furthermore, Article 110(3) of the Rome Statute provides for a review of life-sentenced prisoners after 25 years and is underscored by Article 110(4) and (5) of the Statute and Rules 223 and 224 of the International Criminal Court's Rules of Procedure and Evidence that set out detailed procedural and substantives guarantees which should govern that review. The criteria for reduction include, inter alia, whether the sentenced person's conduct in detention shows a genuine dissociation from his or her crime and his or her prospect of resocialisation (see Rule 223(a) and (b)). Finally, the Mandela Rules, as updated in 2015, make it clear that:

> The purposes of a sentence of imprisonment or similar measures deprivative of a person's liberty are primarily to protect society against crime and to reduce recidivism. These purposes can be achieved only if the period of imprisonment is used to ensure, so far as possible, the reintegration of such persons into society upon release so that they can lead a law-abiding and self-supporting life.[43]

These international and European instruments demonstrate a consensus that life-sentenced prisoners must have a realistic prospect of release and that the review mechanism governing their release must be foreseeable and accessible; it must apply clear criteria in order that sentence planning and progression may be directed towards it and it must take place at a specified time (often held to be 25 years after the date of the imposition of the sentence) and at regular intervals thereafter.

This fundamental penological issue does create challenges for a supra-national court when seeking to ensure that both domestic legal traditions and the margin of appreciation are respected. However, it is a challenge that is being addressed in other jurisdictions. By way of example, in holding that irreducible life sentences violate the Zimbabwean Constitution, their Constitutional Court has expressed most clearly that the traditional approach of *lex talionis* is an "archaic retributive approach" which has now been replaced by the principle of social reintegration.[44] It remains to be seen whether this is a challenge that can be met by the Court, while Article 5 remains at the sidelines rather than centre stage.

Notes

1 See, for example, *Winterwerp v The Netherlands* (1979–1980) 2 EHRR 387.
2 (1982) EHRR 443.
3 ibid, paragraph 41.
4 ibid, paragraph 47.
5 (1988) 10 EHRR 293.
6 *Wynne v United Kingdom* (1993) 15 EHRR CD16: the guarantee of Article 5(4) was satisfied by the original trial and appeal proceedings and confers no additional right to challenge the lawfulness of continuing detention or re-detention following revocation of the life licence.
7 *Stafford v United Kingdom* (2002) 35 EHRR 32.
8 Judge Paolo Pinto de Albuquerque described it as the "*most important penological issue on the European agenda today*" in a speech to the Associazone Italiani dei Constitutionalista on 29 May 2015.
9 (2016) 63 EHRR 1.
10 (2008) 46 EHRR 41.
11 (2009) 49 EHRR 35.
12 *Öcalan v Turkey* (App. Nos. 24069/03, 197/04, 6201/06 and 10464/07, judgement of the Second Section of the ECtHR, 18 March 2014); *Magyar v Hungary* (App. No. 73593/10, judgement of the Second Section of the ECtHR, 20 May 2014); *Trabelsi v Belgium* (App. No. 140/10, judgement of the Former Fifth Section of the ECtHR, 4 September 2014); *Harakchiev and Tolumov v Bulgaria* (App. Nos. 15018/11 and 61199/12, judgement of the Fourth Section of the ECtHR, 8 October 2014); *Bodein v France* (App. No. 40014/10, judgement of the Fifth Section of the ECtHR, 13 November 2014).
13 Grand Chamber, 17 January 2017, App. No. 57592/08.
14 Dissenting opinion of Judge Pinto De Albuquerque: "It is odd that the majority pretend that a future clarification of the law is capable of remedying its present lack of clarity and certainty and thus the violation that exists today, but it is even odder to assume that this clarification will result from the adhesion of the Secretary of State to the Court's desired policy" (paragraph 34).
15 (2017) 64 EHRR 3 (16 April 2016, App. No. 10511/10).
16 (2009) 49 EHRR 41 (11 April 2006, App. No. 19324/02).
17 ibid, paragraphs 7–13.
18 30 June 2015, App. No. 41418/04, paragraphs 121–122.
19 Case No: 77633/16; 13 June 2019.
20 (2013) 56 EHRR 12.
21 (2016) 62 EHRR SE13.
22 https://www.gov.uk/government/uploads/system/uploads/attachment_data/file/217433/provisional-ipp-figures.pdf. By contrast, the number of prisoners serving more conventional life sentences was 8,100.
23 ibid, 1,550 IPP prisoners had tariffs of 2 years or less, whereas more than half of other lifers had tariffs of between 10 and 20 years and over a thousand had tariffs of 20 years to whole life.
24 Legal Aid Sentencing and Punishment of Offenders Act 2012, Section 123.
25 *Unintended Consequences*, Thematic Report by HM Inspectorate of Prisons, November 2016, page 12 (https://www.justiceinspectorates.gov.uk/hmiprisons/wp-content/uploads/sites/4/2016/11/Unintended-consequences-Web-2016.pdf).
26 supra 19.
27 *Kaiyam, Haney and others v Secretary of State for Justice* [2014] UKSC 66.
28 *Kaiyam v United Kingdom* (2016) 62 EHRR SE13, 12 January 2016.
29 7 September 1999, App. No. 47922/99.
30 ibid, page 4.
31 26 October 2004, App. No. 968/04.

32 ibid, page 5.
33 Criminal Justice Act 1991.
34 *R. v Governor of Brockhill Prison ex parte Evans* (No.2) [2001] 2 AC 19.
35 *Smith & West v Parole Board* [2005] UKHL 1.
36 [2015] AC 176.
37 (2014) 58 EHRR 37.
38 ibid, paragraph 124.
39 Case No: 18233/16; 30 January 2018.
40 Paragraph 33.
41 13 July 2010, App. No. 7205/07.
42 supra 11.
43 Rule 4.
44 *Obediah Makoni v Commissioner of Prisons* Judgement No CCZ 8/16, 13 July 2016.

References

Ministry of Justice, Provisional figures relating to offenders serving indeterminate sentence of imprisonment for public protection (IPPs), 21 June 2011. Available at: https://www.gov.uk/government/uploads/system/uploads/attachment_data/file/217433/provisional-ipp-figures.pdf

HM Inspectorate of Prisons, *Unintended Consequences*, Thematic Report by HM Inspectorate of Prisons, November 2016. Available at: https://www.justiceinspectorates.gov.uk/hmiprisons/wp-content/uploads/sites/4/2016/11/Unintended-consequences-Web-2016.pdf

4

THE RIGHTS OF PRISONERS WITHIN THE CJEU'S CASE LAW

Leandro Mancano

Introduction

Deprivation of liberty in the context of criminal proceedings is traditionally associated to a series of individual safeguards, which can be categorised in different ways. Firstly, there are the procedural guarantees that must necessarily accompany every decision leading to detention.[1] Secondly, there are rights that come into play after internment has started. These may be substantive[2] or procedural.[3] Some concern exclusively detainees because of their status,[4] whereas others are universal rights that find specific, tailored or limited application to persons in prison.[5]

In the European Union (EU), the legal status of prisoners is still nearly exclusively governed by the law of the member states. However, as the reach of the EU's competences has expanded over the years, so have the situations in which individual rights can be affected by the Union, or by member states acting on the basis of EU law. This holds true for criminal law especially, where the body of EU law developed in substantive criminal law, and judicial and police cooperation have together enhanced the effectiveness of law enforcement. The latter result, it goes without saying, has come with strings attached. A streamlined system of, e.g., evidence gathering or surrender of suspects and convicted people across the EU has inevitably an impact on the person subject to those measures. That is even more so the case as many of the measures of cooperation between member states involve deprivation of liberty. There is no consolidated instrument that regulates the rights of prisoners. There are, nonetheless, different scenarios where EU law plays a relevant role for the treatment of persons that might be, are or were deprived of liberty. On that basis, the present chapter provides a critical overview of the EU's approach to deprivation of liberty in the context of criminal proceedings, by focusing on a series of core rights ensuing from – or impinged upon – the status of prisoners.

DOI: 10.4324/9780429317033-6

The chapter is structured as follows. Firstly, it provides an overview of the use of custodial penalties of EU substantive criminal law. Secondly, it moves on to consider rights and principles developed mostly in the context of judicial cooperation in criminal matters. These rights and principles are: the prohibition of inhumane treatments and the principle that penalties should aim to social reintegration. Thereafter, the paper moves away from EU criminal law strictly understood and analyses the impact that detention can have on citizenship rights. The conclusions reveal the complex understanding of role and impact for custodial penalties in EU law and highlight strengths and weaknesses of the Union's approach in this area.

Approach to punishment

The approach of the EU legislature to the use deprivation of liberty as a punishment emerges primarily from measures of EU substantive criminal law. In each EU instrument, member states are required to punish a certain offence with a term of imprisonment that, at its maximum, must not go below a specific threshold (so called minimum-maximum criterion).

The first reference to the use of custodial penalties in EU law can be found in the Convention on the protection of the European Communities' financial interests and its First Protocol.[6] However, the first instance of a more specific reference to detention may be seen in FD 2000/383/JHA on money counterfeiting,[7] requiring that

> Each member state shall take the necessary measure to ensure that the conduct referred to in Articles 3 to 5 is punishable by effective, proportionate and dissuasive criminal penalties, including penalties involving deprivation of liberty which can give rise to extradition. The offences of fraudulent making or altering of currency provided for [in Article 3(1)(a)] shall be punishable by terms of imprisonment, the maximum being not less than eight years.[8]

The minimum-maximum criterion was formally adopted only in the 2002 Council Conclusions on approximation of penalties,[9] where four levels of penalties were identified based on the seriousness of the conduct involved. Over the years, the EU has adopted a plethora of instruments in substantive criminal law. All these measures require the use of imprisonment. While the 2004 Commission Green Paper on the approximation of criminal sanctions[10] endorses the use of sanctions other than deprivation of liberty,[11] the pivotal role of imprisonment has never been questioned.

As for the rationale behind the ubiquitous use of custodial penalties, the overriding reason relied on by the EU legislature is the need to address state laws' differences and to contribute to the development of efficient judicial and law enforcement cooperation. The accent is heavily on general prevention.

Imprisonment aims to increase compliance with the law[12] and has a strong deterrent effect. Occasionally, general prevention is flanked by the retributive element.[13] Nonetheless, the EU legislature has not engaged extensively with the actual impact of such a deterrent effect, or with the possibility that the latter might work better on some conduct, and worse on others.[14]

Furthermore, the use of the minimum-maximum criterion as a method of approximating the levels of penalty across EU states reveals the pragmatic nature of the EU approach to deprivation of liberty in substantive criminal law: facilitating judicial cooperation between member states. Judicial cooperation in the EU can validly operate provided that the specific judicial decision, for which a member state seeks cooperation from another member state, is based on an offence punishable by the law of the former state with a custodial sentence or a detention order for a maximum period of at least 12 months.[15] The minimum-maximum criterion is the real *fil rouge* which ties substantive criminal law to judicial cooperation in criminal matters. The use of this criterion has been debated for years, and alternative approximating criteria have been put forward in the scholarship (see Satzger, 2019).[16]

As a general principle governing the adoption of measures of EU substantive criminal law, Article 67(3) TFEU envisages approximation in criminal law only *if necessary*. Article 83(1) TFEU empowers the EU to approximate the level of penalties in areas of particularly serious crime (see for commentaries, Asp, 2012, 73–78; Mitsilegas, 2018; Satzger, 2012; 72–76; Suominen, 2014),[17] whereas Article 83(2) TFEU confers competence if essential to ensuring the effective implementation of a Union policy in an area which has been subject to harmonisation measures (Herlin-Karnell, 2012, 333; 2014; Öberg, 2014).[18] Other than being effective and dissuasive, penalties must be proportionate as per Article 49 CFREU.

In the context of criminal penalties, the effectiveness requirement goes thus hand in hand with proportionality and deterrence. Such emphasis on effectiveness and dissuasiveness is consistent with the deterrence-oriented approach to (custodial) penalties in EU law sketched above (Melander, 2014): 'The efficiency-driven EU criminal policy clearly represents utilitarian philosophy [for inducing members of the community to abide by the law] but from an integration-oriented approach' (Huomo-Kettunen, 2014). To this end, the dissuasiveness of criminal penalties should result in higher effectiveness of (compliance with) EU law.

The EU's approach to penalties has consistently placed imprisonment at its core. It focuses on particularly sensitive areas of crime, and on the implementation of important EU extra-criminal policies. Deterrence is the main driver in the Union's action in this area. Even though alternatives to imprisonment have been formally endorsed by the EU legislature, it has so far amounted more to wishful thinking than anything else. Moreover, the very method of approximation of penalties is mostly geared towards facilitating law enforcement cooperation.

Rights of prisoners in EU law. The contribution of judicial cooperation in criminal matters

Judicial cooperation in criminal matters has been one of the most important areas of development in EU law over the recent decades. The principle of mutual recognition is the cornerstone of judicial cooperation within the EU, as agreed at the 1999 Tampere Council, and aims to prevent potential offenders from exploiting free movement for criminal purposes.[19] This objective is now reflected in Article 3(2) of the EU Treaty (TEU), stipulating that the 'Union shall offer its citizens an area of freedom, security and justice without internal frontiers, in which the free movement of persons is ensured in conjunction with appropriate measures with respect to [...] the prevention and combating of crime'. (For a systemic reconstruction of the concept of the fight against impunity in EU law, and in relation to mutual recognition specifically, see Mitsilegas, 2020a, 21 onwards.)

The adoption of mutual recognition as the principle governing EU judicial cooperation in criminal matters has important legal implications, especially when compared to other forms of inter-state cooperation such as extradition. The application of mutual recognition to judicial cooperation in criminal matters has meant that the cooperation has been taken away from the executive and placed entirely in the hands of the judiciary; the principle of double criminality no longer applies,[20] the prohibition to extradite a state's own nationals has disappeared; tighter time-limits for surrender have been introduced to considerably shorten the overall procedures. Each legislative instrument governs the cooperation on (i.e., recognition of) a specific judicial decision (probation measures, custodial penalties and the like). The change in substance has come with a change in the vocabulary. In this context, we speak of 'surrender' rather than 'extradition', of 'issuing' and 'executing' rather than 'requesting' and 'requested' states. The most famous of these instruments is the European Arrest Warrant Framework Decision (EAW FD).[21] As an expression of mutual recognition in criminal matters, the FD requires that an EAW issued by a judicial authority in member state 'A' and addressed to the member state 'B' against the person 'X' must be recognised by the state 'B' – with subsequent surrender of 'X' – automatically unless the specific grounds for refusal apply.

The relevance of judicial cooperation to prisoners' rights in EU law lies mostly in the way these grounds for refusal (also referred to as exceptions to execution and surrender) are laid down in the legislation, interpreted by the Court of Justice and applied at national level. To this end, two main grounds for refusal worth exploring have emerged: the risk of inhumane and degrading treatment, and the requirement that custodial penalties pursue the social reintegration of the convicted person. To give some context, mutual recognition – and the instruments of judicial cooperation based on that – rest on the principle of mutual trust.[22] Mutual trust in judicial cooperation in criminal matters amounts to the rebuttable presumption that EU member states comply with EU law and fundamental rights more specifically (see Mitsilegas, 2020b, 69).[23] The implication is that member states may not demand a higher level of national protection of fundamental rights from another member state than that provided by EU law; check whether that other member states have actually, in a specific case, observed the fundamental rights guaranteed by the EU; and save in exceptional circumstances.[24] This is reflected in the text of instruments of mutual recognition in criminal matters, which exhaustively list the mandatory and optional grounds for refusing execution. However, they include no explicit exception to surrender based on the risk that breaches of fundamental rights will occur, once the person has been transferred to the issuing state. The presumption of mutual trust is justified on the basis that the EU states' adherence to the values listed in Article 2 TEU (which include commitment to fundamental rights and the rule of law) flows directly from their status of EU members.[25]

In the context of the EAW, the Court has, however, devised a two-step test that, if met, would allow the executing authorities to rebut the presumption and thus refuse surrender of the person concerned.[26] In particular, the executing judge must refrain from executing the warrant where there is material indicating[27]: systemic deficiencies in the issuing state concerning the protection of a fundamental right directly connected to Article 2 TEU, and the risk that those deficiencies will affect the person concerned in the specific case.[28] The risk of inhumane treatment due to poor detention conditions in the issuing state is one of the areas identified by the Court as a ground for refusing execution through the two-step test. This issue is analysed in the section below. Thereafter, the focus moves on to the pursuit of social reintegration of prisoners through instruments of judicial cooperation.

Prohibition of inhumane treatments

The Court of Justice introduced a fundamental rights exception into the EAW system for the first time in *Aranyosi and Căldăraru*.[29] The Court relied on Article 1(3) FD to do so. The test consists of a two-step assessment to be carried out by the executing judge. Firstly, it must be verified that systemic deficiencies exist, which affect the right under siege in the issuing state.[30] Secondly, it must be ascertained specifically and precisely whether those deficiencies will pose a real risk to the right of the person concerned in the specific case. The executing judge must, pursuant to Article 15(2) EAW FD, request that the issuing judge provide any supplementary information that it considers necessary for assessing whether there is such a risk.[31] That request may also relate to the existence, in the issuing state, of any national or international procedures and mechanisms for monitoring detention conditions.[32] The decision on the surrender must be postponed until the supplementary information is obtained. Meanwhile, the detention of the person can be extended provided that that measure is proportionate, with regard being had to the presumption of innocence and their right to liberty.[33] If after an examination of the available information – including that provided by the issuing state – the real risk cannot be discounted, the executing judge must refrain from executing the EAW.[34]

The first aspect to be considered, in analysing the role for detention conditions in halting judicial cooperation, concerns the legal obligations of the cooperating states. On the one hand, the responsibility that detention conditions comply with fundamental rights standards lies primarily with the state where the person is detained.[35] The existence of a remedy, in the issuing state, enabling prisoners to challenge the legality of the conditions of their detention in the light of the fundamental rights cannot, on its own, suffice to rule out a real risk that the individual concerned will be subject to inhuman or degrading treatment.[36] On the other hand, the executing judge must request additional information to the issuing state in compliance with the duty of sincere cooperation under Article 4(3) TEU.[37] The number and content of questions asked must be pertinent to the specific case. In this sense, the executing judge cannot assess the conditions of all the prisons of the issuing state. That task would be excessive and would undermine the possibility of implementing the EAW procedures within the time-limits established by the FD, which in turn would create a risk of impunity of the person concerned.[38] The executing state can establish higher standards of detention conditions than those laid down and developed in EU law and the ECHR. However, the executing judge can make the surrender subject to compliance only with the latter requirements, and not with those resulting from its own national law. According to the Court of Justice, the opposite solution would undermine the uniformity of the standard of protection of fundamental rights as defined by EU law, the principles of mutual trust and the efficacy of the EAW FD.[39] That being said, the executing judge must not balance the risk of inhumane treatment against the effectiveness of judicial cooperation. Such a balancing exercise is prevented from the absolute nature of the prohibition stated in Article 4 CFREU.[40]

Secondly, the weight attached to reassurances provided by the issuing state must be addressed. If the issuing state provides reassurance that the person will not be exposed to a real risk of inhumane treatments, the executing judge must consider the legal weight to be attached to that reassurance. If coming from a (non-judicial) authority of the issuing state (such as the Ministry of Justice), the executing judge *may* rely on that in the context of the overall assessment.[41] If reassurance is given by the issuing judicial authority, the executing judicial authority must rely on that assurance and save in exceptional circumstances where there are specific indications to the contrary.[42] However, the authoritarian plans perpetrated by national governments in some EU member states involving brazen attacks to the independence of the judiciary raise further questions about the legal weight that should be attached to such reassurances.[43]

Thirdly, there is the question of what determines the risk of inhumane treatments. In order for a violation of Article 4 CFREU to occur, a minimum level of severity is required, which depends on all the circumstances of the case, such as the duration of the treatment, its physical and mental effects and, in some cases, the sex, age and state of health of the victim.[44] There is a strong presumption of a violation of that prohibition, when the personal space available to a detainee is below 3 m^2 in multi-occupancy accommodation.[45] The presumption can be rebutted only if the reductions in space are short, occasional and minor; such reductions are accompanied by sufficient freedom of movement outside the cell and adequate out-of-cell activities; the general conditions of detention at the facility are appropriate and there are no other aggravating aspects of the conditions of the person's detention.[46] In the assessment of detention conditions, the space factor must be considered jointly with other aspects, such as access to outdoor exercise, natural light or air, ventilation, room temperature, privacy in the use of the toilet, basic sanitary and hygienic requirements.[47] These additional factors must be taken into account even if the personal space in multi-occupancy prison accommodation exceeds 4 m^2 of personal space. The calculation of that personal space must include the space occupied by furniture, with the detainees still being able to move around normally within the cell.[48]

The risk of inhumane treatment might also arise in relation to detention in a facility intended to last only for the duration of the surrender procedure, before transfer to where detention will be actually spent. While the length of a detention period may be a relevant factor in assessing the gravity of the treatment,[49] an overall evaluation of all the factors involved must be carried out. A period of a few days, spent in a detention space below 3 m^2, might be considered a short period. The same may not hold true for a period of around 20 days, especially if that period may be extended in the event of undefined circumstances.[50] In general, there cannot be any automatism between the brevity of detention and the discount of the risk of inhumane treatment.

The role for detention conditions in the context of EU judicial cooperation has become increasingly prominent, with the Court of Justice acting as the driving force in this regard. Member states cannot use their (possibly) higher standards of detention conditions as a ground to refuse surrender. However, the executing judge must be satisfied that the issuing state comply with the requirements established by the ECtHR, on which the Court of Justice heavily relies. There are constraints on the extent to which the executing judge can inquiry about detention conditions in the issuing state, mostly related to the need to ensure compliance with the time-limits established by the EAW FD (or at least trying to). That, in any case, creates no obligation for the judge to surrender within those terms, or to weight that risk against the effectiveness of judicial cooperation. Rather, those constraints orient and focus the assessment of the executing judge on the relevant aspects of the risk calculation.

Rehabilitation and judicial cooperation

Enforcement of custodial penalties in the EU is largely left to the member states. This includes mechanisms to facilitate reintegration of prisoners as they serve their sentence. The EU, however, has introduced rules of mutual recognition to foster the chances of rehabilitation of the persons concerned. These instruments of judicial cooperation must be understood in the context of the EU as a polity built on free movement. As EU citizens and their family members are entitled to enter and reside in member states other than that of nationality or residence, so increases the likelihood of being investigated, tried or sentenced there. Against that background, the opportunities of being granted alternatives to detention might be lower, and the pursuit of social reintegration harder.[51]

The main measures in questions are the FDs on: the EAW; mutual recognition of probation measures; mutual recognition of custodial penalties. As mentioned above, the EAW establishes a system of swift surrender of suspects or convicted persons, but it does provide the option, for executing judicial authorities, to refuse the surrender if that might be beneficial to the person's process of rehabilitation. Two key provisions come into play: Articles 4(6) and 5(3) FD. Article 4(6) allows the national judge to refuse the execution of an EAW, where 'the requested person is staying in, or is a national or a resident of the executing Member State and that State undertakes to execute the sentence or detention order in accordance with its domestic law' (Marin, 2011).[52] Where the warrant is issued for prosecution of a national or resident of the executing state, Article 5(3) FD allows the executing judge to make the surrender conditional on the return of the person to the executing state in order to serve there the custodial sentence or detention order passed against them in the issuing state.

The operation of those exceptions rest on the interpretation of the concepts of 'resident' and 'staying', and it is thus appropriate to begin the analysis with considerations of the latter words. 'Resident' refers to situations in which the requested person has established an actual place of residence (intended as their main centre of interest). 'Staying' entails a stable period of presence in the host member state, following which the person has acquired connections with it which are of a similar degree to those resulting from residence. In order to establish whether the person subject to the EAW falls under either of these categories, the executing judge must take into consideration factors such as the length, nature and conditions of presence and the family and economic connections which that person has with the executing member state (For comments see Herlin-Karnell, 2010; Janssen, 2013, 207 onwards; Marguery, 2011, 84–91; Mitsilegas, 2012, 338 onwards). The executing state is entitled to pursue reintegration only with those persons who have demonstrated a certain degree of integration into the society of that state – for example, by requiring for other EU citizens to have lived there for a five-year period.[53] However, member states cannot make the application of Article 4(6) FD subject to the possession of a permanent residence permit.[54] The executing state must exercise its discretion consistently with the duty to respect fundamental rights laid down in the FD, including the principle of non-discrimination on grounds of nationality.[55] Furthermore, there must be a legitimate interest which would justify the enforcement of the sentence on the territory of the executing state.[56]

As with detention conditions, defining the tasks and obligations of the cooperating states is key. It is for the executing judge to ensure that the sentence pronounced against the person is actually executed. EU law precludes a national legislation that allows the executing judge to refuse surrender by merely informing the issuing state of their willingness to take over the enforcement and makes that refusal not challengeable, should the execution of the sentence subsequently prove to be impossible.[57] The executing judge retains some discretion as to whether refusing executing.[58] The executing authority must examine whether it is actually possible to enforce the custodial sentence under its domestic law. Should that be impossible, the person must be surrendered.[59] However, the executing judge may still refuse execution if the offence on which the EAW is based is punishable in that state by fine only, provided that 'that fact does not prevent the custodial sentence imposed on the person requested from actually being enforced in that Member State, which is for the referring court to ascertain'.[60]

Beyond the EAW, the FD 2008/909 on the transfer of prisoners[61] creates a mechanism of mutual recognition of judgments involving deprivation of liberty between member states. When the judgment is recognised by the executing member state, the prisoner is consequently transferred thereto. The purpose of the FD is to increase the prisoners' chances of reintegration. Article 1(a) FD 2008/909 defines a 'judgment' as a final decision of a court of the issuing state imposing a sentence on a natural person. The emphasis is on the unchallengeable nature of that judgment, to the exclusion of decisions which are subject to appeal.[62] In the preamble of the FD, it is stated that the requirement of consent of the person concerned should no longer be dominant.[63] The FD foresees the transfer of prisoners to another member state without requiring their consent when: the executing state is where the sentenced person lives; the sentenced person will be deported once he is released from the enforcement of the sentence on the basis of an expulsion or deportation consequential to the judgment. Furthermore, the prisoner is provided with no guarantees in any phases of the recognition/transfer procedure, save a generic 'opportunity' to express his/her opinion.[64] The executing judge cannot derogate from the conditions of Article 8 FD on the adaption of the sentence and adapt the duration of that sentence to make it correspond to the sentence that would have been imposed for the offence in question in the executing member state.[65]

As mentioned above, a member state can use Article 5(3) EAW FD to make the execution of the EAW conditional upon the return of the person concerned to that state in order to serve there the sentence imposed in the issuing state. In such cases, the provisions of FD 909/2008 apply to the enforcement of that sentence.[66] In that context, the objective of rehabilitation requires that 'the return of the person concerned to the executing Member State should occur as soon as possible after that sentencing decision has become final'.[67] In cases where the custodial penalty is accompanied by further penalties (like a confiscation or a fine) and the latter have not yet been enforced, the judge in the state where the sentences have been issued is not prevented for that reason from forwarding the judgment to the executing state.[68] In that regard, the issuing judge must consider whether the presence of the person in the issuing state is essential even after the sentencing decision has become final and until a final decision has been taken on any other procedural steps coming within the scope of the criminal proceedings relating to the offence underlying the EAW. In these cases, the objective of facilitating reintegration must be balanced against both the effectiveness of the criminal prosecution for the purposes of ensuring a complete and effective punishment of the offence underlying the EAW, and the safeguarding of the procedural rights of the person concerned.[69] That judge, however, cannot systematically and automatically postpone the return of the person concerned to the executing state until those further steps have been definitively closed. Furthermore, the cooperating states are encouraged to use other instruments of mutual recognition which allow for hearing a suspected or accused person remotely via digital means.[70]

The FD on probation measures[71] provides for the application of mutual recognition to judgments and probation decisions with a view to the supervision of probation measures and alternative sanctions. The aims of the FD are to enhance the prospects of the sentenced person being reintegrated into society and to improve monitoring of compliance with probation measures and alternative sanctions.[72] To this end, the FD provides that the recognition is carried out where: the sentenced person has returned or wants to return to the member state in which he/she is 'lawfully and ordinarily residing', or the individual has opted for another member state, with the latter having allowed for the execution.[73] Though the FD may be triggered also by the person concerned, EU law even in this case provides the individual with no procedural rights during the phase of recognition and transfer. Furthermore, the FD provides for a one-size-fits-all ground (where exceptional circumstances occur) for postponing the transfer and for delaying the release of the persons concerned and their process of reintegration.[74] This FD applies to the case of a custodial sentence whose execution has been suspended on the condition that the person commits no new criminal offence during the probation period, provided that the latter obligation results from that judgment imposing the custodial sentence or from a probation decision taken on the basis of that judgment.[75]

The EU law of social reintegration has become increasingly nuanced over the years. Significant developments – in the legislation and the case law – have considerably enhanced the chances of rehabilitation for prisoners across the EU. Undeniably, the FDs especially place much emphasis on the interests of the member states. The role for the prisoner in procedures of recognition and the legal safeguards attached thereto are probably the weakest points of the legal framework – epitomised by the transfer without consent provided for in FD 909/2008. The interpretation of the Court of Justice, nonetheless, has partially restrained the discretion left to member states when an EAW has been issued for enforcing a custodial penalty, thus guiding the decision of the executing and issuing authorities towards a stronger level of protection of the process of reintegration.

Impact on citizenship and social rights

The analysis of the impact of custodial penalties on EU citizenship rights offers an interesting perspective on the approach of EU law to retribution and reintegration. The Citizenship Directive[76] puts flesh on the bones of EU citizenship, primarily – though not exclusively – through the right, granted upon EU nationals and certain family members, to enter and stay permanently in the territory of an EU state other than that of nationality (Kochenov and Pirker, 2012; for an analysis of EU citizenship and the territory, see Azoulai, 2014).[77] The legal framework sets up a system of residence security which rests on two main pillars: the right to residence and the protection against expulsion.

EU citizens and their family members are granted the unconditional right to reside in the host member state for a period of up to three months. Should the stay be longer, the right is made subject to specific requirements.[78] The right to permanent residence, provided for in Article 16 Citizenship Directive, is conferred upon Union citizens after they have legally resided for a continuous period (which is not affected by temporary absences) of five years in the host state. The Directive lays down general principles concerning expulsion from the host state. Such a measure shall follow an individual assessment of the person's conduct as a genuine, present and sufficiently serious threat to one of the fundamental interests of society.[79] The Citizenship Directive contemplates three levels of protection against the expulsion of the Union's citizens from host member states: the 'basic' level, on grounds of public policy and public security; an intermediate level, on the basis of which persons who have acquired permanent residence in the host state may be expelled for *serious* grounds of public policy or public security; and enhanced protection, whereby persons that have lived in the host state for longer than ten years can be subject to expulsion only on grounds of *imperative grounds* of *public security*.[80] Any expulsion decision on grounds of public policy or public security must take into account factors, such as the length of residence the person has spent in the host state, their age, state of health, family and economic situation, social and cultural integration into the host member state, the extent of their links with their country of origin.[81]

Since EU citizenship rights are fundamentally dependant on the lapse of a certain period of legal and continuous residence, what impact has imprisonment on that time frame? Broadly, the Court considers integration as a precondition for the acquisition of the right to permanent residence and enhanced protection against expulsion. The assessment of the existence of the integrative link between the EU national and the host state is based on territorial, temporal and qualitative elements.[82] The Court of Justice finds that a prison sentence ensues from a violation, by the person concerned, of member states' criminal law, which in turn enshrines the societal values of that state.[83] Thus, a conviction denies genuine integration into that state. The intrinsic incompatibility between detention and integration means that prison time interrupts the continuity of residence,[84] which in turn precludes the access to the citizenship rights mentioned above: for someone that commits a crime and goes to prison, the integration clock stops ticking and starts again when the person is set free.[85] That is not always and automatically the case, though. The presumption of non-integration and the interruption of continuity of residence applies if imprisonment occurs during the five years preceding the acquisition of permanent residence: that right can be granted on condition of integration in the host state.[86]

However, if the EU citizen has already resided for ten years in the host state prior to receiving a custodial penalty accompanied by an expulsion decision, they may be entitled to enhanced protection against expulsion.[87] The continuous ten-year period of residence must be calculated by counting back from the date of the initial decision of expulsion.[88] If the expulsion measures are adopted after detention, the assessment must focus on whether detention has broken the integrative links.[89] Firstly, important factors to be considered in the overall assessment are (a) the nature of the offence, (b) the circumstances in which that offence was committed and (c) all the relevant factors concerning the behaviour of the person concerned during the period of imprisonment. Especially (c) can be important in helping to maintain or restore the link that might be strained by (a) and (b).[90] Furthermore, the role of reintegration – which plays in the person's and the EU's interest – must be taken into account.[91] It is worth remembering that, in any case, an expulsion measure can be adopted as long as the person represents a genuine and present threat affecting one of the fundamental interests of society or of the host member state.[92] Where an expulsion measure is adopted as a consequence of a custodial penalty but is enforced more than two years after the penalty was adopted, the member state must: review the level of threat posed by the person concerned; assess whether there has been any material change in the circumstances since the expulsion order was issued.[93] Such a review is required also in the scenario where a lengthy period has elapsed between the date of the expulsion order and that of the review of that decision by the competent court.[94]

The impact of prison time on EU citizenship rights is the area where the retributive side of custodial penalties and criminal law comes more prominently to the fore. The Citizenship Directive – and the case law of the Court of Justice as it has developed over the years – provide for strict conditions on the adoption of coercive measures towards EU citizens. However, crime and detention have emerged as game changers in the determination of the legal status of those EU citizens residing in states other than that of nationality. While the Court has adopted a more cautious approach to the relationship between prison time and expulsion when long-term residents are involved, it has also established an absolute presumption of non-integration for EU nationals that have been living in the host state for less than five years – and possible for less than ten years too, although that question has not yet reached the Court of Justice. A realistic understanding of the use of custodial penalties at national level would cast doubt on the legal soundness of the Court's approach, which builds very much on what imprisonment *should* mean – breach of offences enshrining a member state's values – as opposed to what the practice actually is.

Conclusions

The approach to custodial penalties and their impact on individual rights in EU law offers a complex picture. This is related to the expansion of EU competences in criminal law – with the subsequent emergence of a large of body of law in this area – and the increasing scenarios of interaction between states' criminal law and EU law more broadly such as citizenship. The Union's legislature relies significantly on custodial penalties as a mean to increase deterrence and compliance with EU law as well as facilitate judicial cooperation. The generalised use of imprisonment as a punishment in EU substantive criminal law has neither been accompanied by in-depth analysis of its real impact or necessity nor has been reflected upon depending on the specific area of crime involved. Judicial cooperation has certainly been the realm where rights of prisoners have developed more clearly. On the one hand, specific conditions have been set to halt surrender of suspects or convicted in case of risk of inhumane or degrading treatment in the state enforcing the custodial penalty or detention order. On the other hand, several provisions of EU law are geared towards reintegration of the person concerned. The considerable discretion left to member states – though partially nuanced by the Court of Justice – raise questions on the effective pursuit of that objective. Reintegration is also a factor that national authorities must take into account when deciding about expulsion of EU citizens from the territory of their states. The safeguards in the law are important, the absolute presumption of non-integration in case of commission of any crime resulting in imprisonment seems not particularly realistic and could have detrimental effects on EU citizens rights.

Notes

1 To an extent, these guarantees go beyond the specific context of criminal law and apply to any kind of deprivation of liberty.
2 For example, entitlement to a certain personal space in the prison cell.
3 Consider, for instance, the right to appeal a decision on a specific aspect of the detention regime.
4 The principle that penalties (notably custodial ones) must aim to the social reintegration of the person concerned is one of the most important scenarios.
5 The right to family life finds very specific applications to prisoners.
6 Art 2, Convention on the protection of the European Communities' financial interests of 26 July 1995, [1995] OJ C316/49–57; Article 5, Protocol to the Convention on the protection of the European Communities' financial interests of 27 September 1996, [1997] OJ C313/2–10.
7 Council Framework Decision 2000/383/JHA of 29 May 2000 on increasing protection by criminal penalties and other sanctions against counterfeiting in connection with the introduction of the euro, [2000] OJ L140/1, 14.6.2000.
8 Ibid, Art 6.

9 Council document of 25 April 2002 on the approach to apply approximation of penalties, 9141/2002.

10 Commission Green Paper on the approximation, mutual recognition and enforcement of criminal sanctions in the European Union, Brussels, 30.04.2004 COM(2004) 334 final.

11 Ibid, 15 onwards.

12 See in particular Directive 2008/99/EC, recital 3 and Directive 2009/52/EC, recital 21.

13 The retribution element may be used in a generic way (where the EU instrument requires punishment of more serious violations with imprisonment) or specifically providing for aggravated penalties where the offence is committed in the context of a criminal organisation, or where the crime is conducted on a large scale, affecting a significant number of persons, or it causes serious damage (see e.g. Directive 2013/40/EU, recital 13).

14 This is the case even though, in its impact assessments, the European Commission refers to the deterrent effect of criminal penalties in certain areas. See in particular Commission Staff Working Paper, accompanying the document Proposal for a Directive of the European Parliament and the Council on the protection of the financial interests of the European Union by criminal law, SWD(2012) 196; EP report on the proposal for a Directive of the European Parliament and of the Council on the protection of the euro and other currencies against counterfeiting by criminal law, and replacing Council Framework Decision 2000/383/JHA (COM(2013)0042 – C7-0033/2013 – 2013/0023(COD)), A7-0018/2014, 10.1.2014; Commission Staff Working Document Impact Assessment Accompanying the document Proposal for a Regulation of the European Parliament and of the Council on new psychoactive substances and proposal for a Directive of the European Parliament and of the Council amending Council Framework Decision 2004/757/JHA of 25 October 2004 laying down minimum provisions on the constituent elements of criminal acts and penalties in the field of illicit drug trafficking, as regards the definition of drug, Brussels 17.9.2013, SWD(2013) 319 final, 20 onwards; Commission Staff Working Paper Impact Assessment Accompanying the document Proposal for Regulation of the European Parliament and of the Council on insider dealing market manipulation (market abuse) and the Proposal for a Directive of the European Parliament and of the Council on criminal sanctions for insider dealing and market manipulation, Brussels, 20.10.2011 SEC(2011) 1217 final.

15 See, inter alia, Council Framework Decision of 13 June 2002 on the European arrest warrant and the surrender procedures between Member States (2002/584/JHA) [2002] OJ L190/1, 18.2.2002, Article 2.

16 It is also worth noting that the European Commission has tried to go beyond the minimum-maximum approach at least on two occasions, by proposing the establishment of minimum penalties in case of money counterfeiting and the protection of the EU's financial interests. In both cases, however, that attempt was halted during the ordinary legislative procedure and the two final texts of the relevant Directives only include reference to the minimum-maximum.

17 These areas include: terrorism, trafficking in human beings and sexual exploitation of women and children, illicit drug trafficking, illicit arms trafficking, money laundering, corruption, counterfeiting of means of payment, computer crime and organised crime. See for commentaries.

18 The instrument must be (1) *essential* to ensure the (2) *effective* implementation in an area (3) *already subject to harmonisation measures.*

19 Tampere European Council, 15 and 16 October 1999, Presidency Conclusion.

20 The abolition of double criminality concerns, more specifically, a list of 32 areas of serious crime as per e.g. Article 2(2) European Arrest Warrant Framework Decision. For other offences, states are still feel free to impose a verification of double criminality along the lines indicated by the CJEU in Case C-289/15, *Joszef Grundza*, EU:C:2017:4.

21 See fn no. above.
22 EAW FD, recital 10. C-303/05, *Advocaten voor de Wereld VZW v Leden van de Ministerraad*, EU:C:2007:261, para 57.
23 For a recent and broader taxonomy of the areas where the challenges of trust will emerge more prominently in the future.
24 *Opinion 2/13*, EU:C:2014:2454, paras 191–192.
25 C-216/18 PPU, *LM*, EU:C:2018:586, para 35.
26 This 'evidence' refers to the material indicating the risk of a fundamental rights breach, rather than to the evidence supporting the charge or judgment at the basis of the EAW. 'Evidence' is the term used by the Court as well, when referring to the information exchanged under Article 15 EAW FD. See C-367/16, *Dawid Piotrowski*, EU:C:2018:27, paras 60–61.
27 'Evidence' is here used in a-technical way. It refers to the material indicating the risk of fundamental rights breach, rather than the evidence supporting the charge or judgment at the basis of the EAW. 'Evidence' is the term used by the Court as well, when referring to the information exchanged under Article 15 EAW FD. See C-367/16, *Dawid Piotrowski*, EU:C:2018:27, paras 60–61.
28 C-404/15 and C-659/15 PPU, *Aranyosi and Căldăraru*, EU:C:2016:198, para 104.
29 Although the Court has not applied the *exceptional circumstances* doctrine to asylum and criminal law cooperation exactly in the same way, there are similarities and cross-references between the CJEU's case-law in the two areas. *Aranyosi and Căldăraru* is referred to in C-578/16 PPU, *C.K. and Others*, EU:C:2017:127, paras 59 and 75. There, the CJEU further clarified that the prohibition of transfer of an asylum-seeker may apply even in the absence of systemic deficiencies in the state responsible, where there is a real risk that the transfer will lead to a breach of the prohibition of inhumane treatment.
30 The assessment should be based on objective, reliable, specific and properly updated material. That information may be obtained from, inter alia, judgments of international courts, such as judgments of the European Court of Human Rights, judgments of courts of the issuing Member State, and also decisions, reports and other documents produced by bodies of the Council of Europe or under the aegis of the United Nations *Aranyosi and Căldăraru*, EU:C:2016:198, para 89.
31 *Aranyosi and Căldăraru*, EU:C:2016:198, para 97; *LM*, EU:C:2018:586, paras 76.
32 *Aranyosi and Căldăraru*, EU:C:2016:198, paras 95 and 96.
33 *Aranyosi and Căldăraru*, EU:C:2016:198, paras 98–101.
34 *Aranyosi and Căldăraru*, EU:C:2016:198, para 101.
35 Case C-220/18 PPU, ML, EU:C:2018:589, para 90.
36 ML, EU:C:2018:589, para 73.
37 ML, EU:C:2018:589, para 104.
38 ML, EU:C:2018:589, paras 84–85.
39 Case C-128/18, Dumitru-Tudor Dorobantu, EU:C:2019:857, para 79.
40 Dumitru-Tudor Dorobantu, EU:C:2019:857, para 84.
41 Case C-220/18 PPU, *ML*, EU:C:2018:589, para 117.
42 Case C-128/18, *Dumitru-Tudor Dorobantu*, paras 68–69.
43 See the Court of Justice's judgments declaring the reforms carried out by the Polish government incompatible with EU law: Joined Cases C-585/18, C-624/18 and C-625/18, *A. K., CP and DO*; Case C-192/18, *European Commission v Republic of Poland*, EU:C:2019:924; Case C-619/18, *Commission v Poland (Independence of the Supreme Court)*, EU:C:2019:531.
44 ML, EU:C:2018:589, para 91.
45 ML, EU:C:2018:589, para 92.
46 ML, EU:C:2018:589, para 93.
47 Dumitru-Tudor Dorobantu, EU:C:2019:857, paras 75–76.
48 Dumitru-Tudor Dorobantu, EU:C:2019:857, para 77.
49 ML, EU:C:2018:589, para 97.

50 ML, EU:C:2018:589, para 99.
51 See Council of the EU, 'Roadmap with a view to fostering protection of suspected and accused persons in criminal proceedings' doc 11457/09, 1 July 2009 (Roadmap); Draft Resolution 12116/09, 15 July 2009.
52 C-66/08, *Kozłowski*, EU:C:2008:437, para 54.
53 Case C-123/08, **Dominic Wolzenburg,** EU:C:2009:616, para 78.
54 Case C-123/08, **Dominic Wolzenburg**, para 53.
55 Case C-42/11, *Proceedings concerning the execution of a European arrest warrant issued against João Pedro Lopes Da Silva Jorge*, para 34.
56 C-66/08, *Kozłowski*, EU:C:2008:437, para 44.
57 C-579/15, *Daniel Adam Popławski*, EU:C:2017:503, para 24.
58 Popławski, C-579/15, EU:C:2017:503, para 21.
59 Judgment of 29 June 2017, Popławski, C-579/15, EU:C:2017:503, para 22.
60 Case C-514/17, Marin-Simion Sut, EU:C:2018:1016, para 50.
61 Council Framework Decision 2008/909/JHA of 27 November 2008 on the application of the principle of mutual recognition to judgments in criminal matters imposing custodial sentences or measures involving deprivation of liberty for the purposes of their enforcement, [2008] OJ L327/27, 5 December 2008.
62 C-582/15, van Vemde, EU:C:2017:37, paras 23, 24 and 27.
63 Framework Decision 2008/909/JHA, recital 5, Art 4.
64 Framework Decision 2008/909/JHA, Art 6.
65 Case C-314/18, *SF*, EU:C:2020:191, para 68.
66 Framework Decision 2008/909/JHA, Article 25.
67 *SF*, EU:C:2020:191, para 54.
68 *SF*, EU:C:2020:191, para 55.
69 *SF*, EU:C:2020:191, paras 56 and 59.
70 *SF*, EU:C:2020:191, paras 60–61.
71 Council Framework Decision 2008/947/JHA of 27 November 2008 on the application of the principle of mutual recognition to judgments and probation decisions with a view to the supervision of probation measures and alternative sanctions, [2008] OJ L337/102, 16 December 2008.
72 Framework Decision 2008/947/JHA, Art 1.
73 Framework Decision 2008/947/JHA, Art 5.
74 Framework Decision 2008/947/JHA, Art 12(2).
75 Case C-2/19, *A. P.*, EU:C:2020:237, para 59.
76 Directive 2004/38/EC of the European Parliament and the Council of 29 April 2004 on the right of citizens of the Union and their family members to move and reside freely within the territory of the Member States, [2004] OJ L158/77, 30.4.2004.
77 As Kochenov argues, 'Residence security is at the core of what the essential legal essence of the citizenship status is now about', which also explains why (even the mere possibility of) being deported and expelled 'play[s] an essential role in outlining with clarity the scope of those who are citizens of a polity, as opposed to merely residents'.
78 Directive 2004/38/EC, Articles 6(1) and 7(1).
79 Directive 2004/38/EC, Art 27(2).
80 Directive 2004/38/EC, Art 28.
81 C-145/09, *Tsakouridis*, EU:C:2010:708, para 26.
82 Case C-378/12, *Nnamdi Onuekwere v Secretary of State for the Home Department*, EU:C:2014:13, para 25.
83 *Onuekwere*, EU:C:2014:13, para 26.
84 *Onuekwere*, EU:C:2014:13, para 32.
85 Case C-400/12, *Secretary of State for the Home Department v MG*, EU:C:2014:9, paras 28–33.
86 *Onuekwere*, EU:C:2014:13, para 24.

87 Joined Cases C-316/16 and C-424/16, *B v Land Baden-Württemberg and Secretary of State for the Home Department v Franco Vomero*, EU:C:2018:256, para 78.
88 *G.*, C-400/12, EU:C:2014:9, paras 24.
89 *Vomero*, EU:C:2018:256, para 83.
90 *Vomero*, EU:C:2018:256, paras 73–74.
91 C-145/09, *Tsakouridis*, EU:C:2010:708, para 50.
92 C-348/09, *I*, EU:C:2012:300, para 30.
93 *I*, EU:C:2012:300, para 31. Article 33(2) Directive 2004/38.
94 *Vomero*, EU:C:2018:256, para 94.

References

Asp, P, *The Substantive Criminal Law Competence of the EU* (Skrifter utgivna av Juridiska fakulteten vid Stockholms Universitet, 2012) 73–8.

Azoulai, L, 'The (Mis)Construction of the European Individual: Two Essays on Union Citizenship Law', EUI Department of Law Research Paper, No 2014/14, 2014.

Herlin-Karnell, E, 'European Arrest Warrant Cases and the Principles of Non-Discrimination and EU Citizenship' (2010) 73(5) *The Modern Law Review* 824.

Herlin-Karnell, E, 'EU Competence in Criminal Law after Lisbon' in A Biondi, P Eeckhout and S Ripley (eds), *EU Law after Lisbon* (Oxford, Oxford University Press, 2012) 333.

Herlin-Karnell, E, 'Effectiveness and Constitutional Limits in European Criminal Law' (2014) 5(3) *New Journal of European Criminal Law* 267–73.

Huomo-Kettunen, M, 'EU Criminal Policy at a Crossroads between Effectiveness and Traditional Restraints for the Use of Criminal Law' (2014) 5(3) *New Journal of European Criminal Law* 314 onwards.

Janssen, C, *The Principle of Mutual Recognition in EU Law* (Oxford, Oxford University Press, 2013) 207 onwards.

Kochenov, D, and Pirker, B, 'Deporting the Citizens within the European Union: A Counter-Intuitive Trend in Case C-348/09, PI v Oberburgermeisterin Der Stadt Remscheid' (2012) 19(2) *Journal of European Law* 369.

Marguery, TP, 'EU Citizenship and European Arrest Warrant: The Same Rights for All?' (2011) 27(73) *Merkourios* 84–91.

Marin, L, '"A Spectre Is Haunting Europe": European Citizenship in the Area of Freedom, Security and Justice – Some Reflections on the Principles of Non Discrimination (on the Basis of Nationality), Mutual Recognition and Mutual Trust Originating from the European Arrest Warrant' (2011) 17(4) *European Public Law* 705–28.

Melander, S, 'Effectiveness in EU Criminal Law and Its Effects on the General Part of Criminal Law' (2014) 5(3) *New Journal of European Criminal Law* 274–300.

Mitsilegas, V, 'The Limits of Mutual Trust in Europe's Area of Freedom, Security and Justice' (2012) 31(1) *Yearbook of European Law* 319, 338 onwards.

Mitsilegas, V, *EU Criminal Law After Lisbon Rights, Trust and the Transformation of Justice in Europe (Hart Studies in European Criminal Law)* (Oxford: Hart Publishing, 2018).

Mitsilegas, V, 'Conceptualising Impunity in the Law of the European Union', in L Marin and S Montaldo (eds), *The Fight against Impunity in EU Law* (Oxford: Hart Publishing, 2020a) 21 onwards.

Mitsilegas, V, 'Trust' (2020b) 21 *German Law Journal* 69.

Öberg, J, 'Do We Really Need Criminal Sanctions for the Enforcement of EU Law?' (2014) 5(3) *New Journal of European Criminal Law* 370–87.

Satzger, H, *International and European Criminal Law* (Oxford, Hart Publishing, 2012) 72–6.

Satzger, H, 'The Harmonisation of Criminal Sanctions in the European Union – A New Approach' (2019) (2/19) *eucrim* 115–20, available at https://eucrim.eu/articles/harmonisation-criminal-sanctions-european-union-new-approach/

Suominen, A 'Effectiveness and Functionality of Substantive EU Criminal Law' (2014) 5(3) *New Journal of European Criminal Law* 388, 390 onwards.

PART II

EFFECTIVENESS OF HUMAN RIGHTS IN PRISON AND EUROPEAN RESPONSES TO HUMAN RIGHTS VIOLATION IN PRISON

5

IRELAND

The weak European supervision of prison policies and its explanations

Mary Rogan and Sophie van der Valk

Introduction

One of the most notable features of Irish penal policy and practice is that there has never been a full judgement of the European Court of Human Rights (ECtHR) concerning prison conditions or practices. This striking lack of supervision under the judicial machinery of the Council of Europe's framework for the protection of rights in prison suggests that direct European supervision of Irish prisons through judicial means is very weak. The use of the European Convention on Human Rights (ECHR) in domestic cases concerning prisons has also been limited, though recent years have seen a significant increase in the numbers of prison-related cases generally, including arguments based on Convention rights. There remains, however, reluctance to decide prison cases on Convention grounds, with judicial decision-making continuing to focus on the traditional grounds of rights under the Constitution of Ireland (Bunreacht na hÉireann), or principles of civil liability. The impact of the Convention on domestic legal cultures of prisoners' rights protection has also been very modest. Responses to the European Committee for the Prevention of Torture and Inhuman or Degrading Treatment or Punishment (CPT) have also been variable, though some important improvements in conditions can be attributed to its influence. International human rights standards, including European norms, have also been cited as bases for domestic law and standards for domestic prison monitoring. This chapter examines the European supervision of Ireland's prison system. It argues that while the formal regulation of prisons by means of judicial oversight using European norms has been weak, the influence of European supervision is nonetheless apparent in the Irish system. The chapter commences by describing Ireland's approach to the ECHR, its membership of the Council of Europe, as well as providing a brief description of the Irish prison system. The ways in which the Convention has been used in domestic cases

DOI: 10.4324/9780429317033-8

are then examined. We then assess Ireland's response to the European Committee for Prevention of Torture and Inhuman or Degrading Treatment or Punishment, before exploring other ways in which the European influence is visible in practice. Empirical research exploring the ways in which people in prison conceive of European human rights protections is also presented.

Ireland and the Council of Europe

Ireland became a member of the Council of Europe on 5 May 1949, being one of nine founding states. Ireland ratified the European Convention on Human Rights (hereafter 'the Convention' or 'ECHR') in 1953, and applicants have long been able to make petitions to Strasbourg when domestic avenues have been exhausted. As a dualist legal system, the Convention did not have effect in domestic law until December 2003, with the commencement of the ECHR Act 2003. This Act incorporated the Convention into Irish law, allowing Convention rights to be considered before the domestic courts. It also requires those courts, as far as possible, to interpret laws in line with ECHR obligations (European Convention of Human Rights Act 2003, S.2(1)).[1] The term 'as far as possible' means that, while the courts should consider Convention rights, they are not overriding (de Londras 2014). Bunreacht na hÉireann, the Constitution of Ireland, takes precedence where there is a conflict between it and the Convention. Under Section 5 of the 2003 Act, the High Court or Supreme Court can also make a declaration of incompatibility, which states that a particular law or statutory provision is incompatible with Convention obligations. This order is then required to be presented before each House of the Oireachtas (Parliament) 21 days after it has been made. Unlike a declaration that a law breaches the Constitution, a declaration of incompatibility does not mean that the law in question becomes invalid.

The relevant legislation or part thereof in breach of the Convention remains in force until an alternative is passed or the relevant legislation is revoked by the government, which can take a substantial period of time to happen, if at all.[2] Additionally, as noted by McKechnie J, a declaration of incompatibility **'could not give rise to the automatic release' of a prisoner due to the fact that the law is not declared invalid by the court** (*McDermott v Governor of Cloverhill Prison & Ors* [2010] IEHC 324, para. 18).

Under the ECHR Act 2003, every organ of the state, including the Irish Prison Service (IPS) which administers the prison system, is obliged to perform its functions in a manner compatible with the Convention. Under Section 42 of the Irish Human Rights and Equality Commission Act 2014, IPS is obliged to have regard to the need to 'protect the human rights of its members, staff and persons to whom it provides services'.

Ireland is also a party to the European Convention against Torture and Inhuman or Degrading Treatment or Punishment. The CPT has visited Ireland on seven occasions, most recently in September/October 2019. Ireland has agreed to the publication of each of the CPT's reports on its visits to date but does not implement the automatic publication procedure.

The Irish prison system

Ireland has a relatively small prison system, consisting of 12 prisons with 3,714 prisoners as of 30 September 2020 (IPS 2020), and a prison population rate of 74 per 100,000 (World Prison Brief 2020). As elsewhere, the Irish prison population 'is characterised by mental health issues, addictions, homelessness, poverty, unemployment, education disadvantage, chaotic family background and social marginalisation' (Joint Committee on Justice and Equality 2018, p. 10). Ireland's prison system has been the subject of domestic and international criticism for poor sanitary conditions, including the ongoing, though reducing, practice of 'slopping out' whereby people in prison do not have access to in-cell sanitation and must use a receptacle for human waste (CPT 2007, 2011, 2015; IPRT 2019; Office of the Inspector of Prisons 2009b). It has also been criticised for high levels of inter-prisoner violence, inadequate healthcare and overcrowding (CPT 2007, 2011, 2015; IPRT 2019; Office of the Inspector of Prisons 2009b). In recent years, some reform of both penal policy and practice has taken place. A strategic review of penal policy was published 2014, recommending a reduction in the use of imprisonment and improvement of the penal estate. A new prison has been built, with renovations taking place in older prisons to improve physical conditions (IPRT 2019; Penal Policy Review Group 2014).

People in prison may take cases arguing that their rights under the Constitution and/or Convention have been breached, seek judicial review of decisions taken concerning them, or take actions arguing, for example, that the prison authorities have negligently caused her/him harm. In extreme circumstances involving egregious breaches of constitutional rights arising out of prison conditions, a prisoner may be released from custody by way of the *habeas corpus* procedure, provided for in the Constitution. While access to the courts is not formally restricted for prisoners, the lack of funded legal aid for prison cases (with the exception of *habeas corpus* applications) is a major barrier to the vindication of rights (Rogan 2014). This may, in part, explain the historically low levels of prison litigation in Ireland. When domestic remedies have been exhausted, a person may apply to the ECtHR.

Outside of the judicial sphere, Ireland has an Inspector of Prisons, a monitoring body whose independence from the prison authorities is outlined in the Prisons Act 2007. This body has recently undergone considerable expansion and reform including through the establishment of a new system of standards guiding monitoring visits, discussed further below (Office of the Inspector of Prisons 2020). It is tasked with visiting prisons and writing reports on the treatment of prisoners. Visiting Committees are also attached to each prison. These bodies, established under the Prisons (Visiting Committees) Act 1925, visit prisons to hear concerns from prisoners and write reports. Neither the Inspector of Prisons nor the Visiting Committees have formal enforcement powers. At present, people in prison in Ireland cannot access either a specialised or general Ombudsman, though plans have been announced to remove the bar on prisoners taking complaints to the office of the Ombudsman (Fitzgerald 2016a,b).

Using the Convention to protect the rights of people in prison in Ireland

The ECtHR has never pronounced upon Irish prison conditions. This is remarkable given the Court has dealt with several seminal decisions concerning Ireland, including on Article 3's prohibition on torture (*O'Keeffe v Ireland* Application no. 35810/09; Ireland Press Country Profile 2020), and in light of the criticisms of Irish prison conditions across several fronts. Prison litigation is only now maturing in Ireland (Rogan 2014). This, combined with a lack of funded legal aid, deference to the prison authorities (Rogan 2012) and the fact that the majority of people in prison in Ireland are serving short sentences and are less likely to take cases which may take years to resolve, has inhibited the development of a strong prison law culture. While there are no cases at the European level to analyse, domestic decisions have referred to the Convention in several instances, though with less enthusiasm than when traditional Constitution-based arguments are involved. This situation is not confined to prison cases; as noted by de Londras, the ECHR act has had a limited impact on domestic rights litigation due to the primacy of constitutional rights in Ireland (2014). There is, however, evidence of a greater willingness to engage with ECHR case law and standards in more recent decisions, though no breaches of the Convention have yet been found.

The Irish courts have recognised as a general principle that prisoners retain all rights which are not incompatible with imprisonment. Furthermore, as the High Court has stated in the case of *Mulligan v. Governor of Portlaoise Prison* [2010] IEHC 269:

> [A]ny attenuation of rights must be proportionate; the diminution must not fall below the standards of reasonable human dignity and what is expected in a mature society. Insofar as practicable, a prison authority must vindicate the individual rights and dignity of each prisoner.
>
> *para. 14*

The Irish courts have considered a wide variety of rights in the prison setting. This chapter will focus on sanitary conditions, in particular 'slopping out', due to the fact that the issue itself is particularly egregious, and the discussion of it in the Irish courts illuminates some of the tensions and promise of using the Convention in Irish cases.

'The function of the Irish Courts is to uphold the Constitution'3: slopping out and the limited impact of European supervision

'Slopping out' or the lack of in-cell sanitation facilities has long bedevilled the Irish prison system. While improvements to the physical infrastructure of prisons have greatly reduced the number of people in prison subject to this practice,[4] the problem has not yet been eliminated despite repeated criticism and some litigation over 40 years. The Irish courts have largely played catch-up on the issue when compared to their counterparts in Strasbourg, but, like there, tolerance of the practice has declined over time.

One of the earliest cases in relation to prison conditions and slopping out was that of *State (Richardson) v Governor of Mountjoy Prison* ([1980] ILRM 82), which concerned slopping out in a woman's prison. The applicant relied exclusively on domestic rights in the Irish Constitution and the Irish Prison Rules (secondary legislation governing the running of prisons and the treatment of prisoners), which were in force at the time. Slopping out itself was not found to breach the applicant's rights but rather the way it was being done, namely the use of sinks for washing to dispose of human waste. While the High Court found that the state had breached the applicant's rights due to its failure to protect her health, it declined to make an order requiring a change in practice on the basis that the authorities were willing to amend the situation.

The issue of slopping out came before the courts again in the case of *Brennan v Governor of Portlaoise Prison* ([1998] IHEC 140). The applicant relied not only on the Irish Constitution, but also on the ECHR. As this case predated the 2003 Act which incorporated the Convention into domestic law, Budd J noted that while the Convention was not part of domestic law 'this Court can look to the European Convention as being an influential guideline with regard to matters of public policy' (para. 61). In comparing the protections offered by the Constitution and the Convention, Budd J stated: 'the Irish Constitution both by enumerated and unenumerated rights gives appropriate protection in particular to those who are deprived under law of their liberty whether by way of being mental patients or convicts duly sentenced' (para. 61). The court held that slopping out did not violate the rights of the applicant without reference to any ECtHR decisions on the subject. The court's position concerning the relative roles of the Constitution and Convention was, however, a harbinger of later judgements.

The issue of slopping out came before the courts again in 2010 in the case of *Mulligan v Portlaoise Prison* ([2010] IEHC 269). In that case, the applicant claimed the absence of in-cell sanitation, unhygienic conditions and the necessity to engage in 'slopping-out procedures' gave rise to a violation of his constitutional and ECHR rights, specifically relying on Articles 3 and 8 of the Convention. In setting out the background to the case, MacMenamin J discussed a range of international and domestic expert reports, which called into question prison accommodation and standards in Ireland, including overcrowding, the lack of in-cell sanitation and the practice of 'slopping-out'. The Court noted criticism of the practice by the CPT which went as far back as 1993. The failure to follow through on assurances of remedial work made to the CPT was also noted, along with the frustration and deep concern of the Committee at the lack of progress.

Despite these trenchant criticisms, MacMenamin J held '... the situation [in Portlaoise prison] was different from the "impoverished" or poor general regime described in some of the international jurisprudence' (para. 64). In so doing, the court engaged in an extensive review of ECtHR decisions, holding that slopping out *per se* did not violate the Convention, but must be combined with other sub-optimal practices for a breach to be found. The case was notable for being the first in which a thorough analysis of ECHR jurisprudence was undertaken in an Irish prison judgement. The case further held that it is only when there is a failure to establish a breach under the Constitution that the courts will turn to the ECHR. Additionally, MacMenamin J held that the intent of the authorities was relevant in deciding if a violation under the Constitution had occurred, in contrast to the position under the Convention when intention of the authorities is not exculpatory. Here, we see the European approach to Article 3 not penetrating Irish judicial practice concerning prisons. However, the court left open the possibility that slopping out in combination with other factors, such as doubling up of cells, could lead to a violation of Article 3.

The Supreme Court was eventually required to consider 'slopping out' in *Simpson v. Governor of Mountjoy Prison [2019] IESC 81.* Its judgement contains a very illuminating guide to how the Convention is viewed and may be used in prison law cases in Ireland. Here, the plaintiff argued that his conditions of detention breached both the Constitution and the Convention. The High Court held that the applicant's right to privacy under the Constitution had been violated by reason of the fact that he had to 'slop out' in the presence of others. An argument that the conditions breached his right to be free from inhuman and degrading treatment failed. Before considering the nature of the violation at issue on appeal, the Supreme Court pointed out that a court must consider the position under the Constitution before examining arguments under the Convention, and that resorting to the Convention will arise only if no other remedy in damages is available. Two *dicta* of MacMenamin J are particularly revealing in this respect. The court held: 'if a constitutional remedy which vindicates an infringement is available, it will seldom be necessary for a court to go further' (para. 6), and 'Member States have the primary duty to ensure that prison conditions comply with national constitutions and, where necessary, the ECHR' (para. 7). The court was critical of what it saw as the applicant's efforts to frame his claims for damages as arising under the Convention, which was impermissible. The court was also at pains to point out that it is not appropriate for a court to rely on Convention jurisprudence in the same way as Irish law. While the Strasbourg cases were important, the principles developed therein should not be applied as matters of domestic law. They cannot, in particular, be building blocks for a claim made in damages under Irish constitutional principles. The court also considered that there were important differences between the constitutional guarantee to the protection of the person and Article 3, with that Article's absolute prohibition being irreconcilable with the principles of causation and contributory negligence in civil liability or tort claims arising out of constitutional wrongs. MacMenamin J also expressed concern about the evolutive interpretation of Article 3 by the ECtHR over the years and was disinclined to replicate it in

Irish law. Nevertheless, the Supreme Court held that there had been a breach of the applicant's right to privacy and the constitutional values of dignity and autonomy through exposure to conditions which were 'distressing, humiliating, and [which] fell far below acceptable standards in an Irish Prison in the year 2013' (para. 129), and damages were appropriate.

The court decided to consider Convention decisions on Article 3 in the prison context in light of the importance of the case but did not make a finding under the Convention. The court did, however, take note of CPT criticism of slopping out and the fact that the government had not implemented the CPT's suggestions for how to remedy some of the worst features of the conditions.

The tension between constitutional protections for the person under domestic law and that of the Convention was on display in this case. In a concurring opinion, O'Donnell J held that there was no doubt the Irish Constitution prohibits conduct prohibited under Article 3, but the way in which that Article has been interpreted in ECtHR decisions cannot be synonymous with those under Irish law. O'Donnell J held:

> ... the function of the Irish Courts is to uphold the Constitution, and that duty cannot be performed if the scope of rights protected under the Constitution is to be determined by the jurisprudence of a court which is not established under the Constitution and has no obligation to uphold it. While it is to be expected that the two instruments guaranteeing rights considered fundamental would tend to cover much of the same ground, and the interpretation of one is often helpful in understanding similar provisions contained in the other, they are different instruments and there will be many areas, particularly at the margins ... where the approach, or substance, may be different.
>
> *para. 6*

It is notable that the Supreme Court in *Simpson* went to great lengths to discourage arguments suggesting that Convention principles applied to prison conditions can be automatically applied under Irish law or considered to be of precisely the same content. Moreover, the Irish courts have signalled some disquiet about what it sees as the ECtHR's expansive interpretation of Article 3 in prison cases. O'Donnell J noted, for example, that 'it strains credulity' (para. 6) to suggest that the Irish Constitution, dating from 1937, could have anticipated the insertion of an express prohibition on torture found in the Convention, describing the approach of the ECtHR to expanding the protection of rights as 'evolutive'. While we await future decisions to see how this dynamic plays out, this position does indicate that Article 3's application may be limited by the Irish courts. This approach to the Convention by the judiciary is another factor which limits the influence of the ECtHR on prison conditions in Ireland. As such, we cannot describe European supervision of prison conditions through judicial means as being strong in Ireland.

European influences on Irish prison law and practice outside of the judicial sphere

Outside of the courts, European sources, particularly reports of the CPT, have been cited as influences on change. Eliminating slopping out, and the attendant criticism from the CPT, has been given as a reason for building a new prison (Fitzgerald 2016a,b, Shatter 2013), with a Minister for Justice going so far as to say that the CPT's criticisms of slopping out 'played a significant part in almost completely eliminating that practice' (Flanagan 2019). The length of time involved in this process of improvement, however, suggests that the CPT's influence did not expedite progress in any dramatic way.

More directly, the Inspector of Prisons has cited the CPT's standards alongside the European Prison Rules (EPR) and ECtHR decisions as sources against which Irish prisons are assessed. The first set of standards produced by the Inspector of Prisons cited several ECtHR decisions, EPR and CPT standards (Office of the Inspector of Prisons 2009a), noting the important role of the Convention in advancing prisoners' rights (Office of the Inspector of Prisons 2009a). CPT reports and standards are regularly cited in reports of the Inspector of Prisons (Office of the Inspector of Prisons 2009b, 2012, 2016). The Inspectorate published a new Framework for Inspection in 2020 and referred to the EPR as 'particularly relevant' and 'authoritative' and CPT reports as 'very relevant' (p. 10) and 'recognised best practice' (p. 14) as sources to guide the analysis of the Inspectorate.

There is also evidence of Convention influence, albeit scant, on domestic legislation. Ireland introduced legislation to provide the necessary infrastructure to vote in prison shortly after the Irish Supreme Court held that there is no requirement in the Constitution to allow prisoners to cast their ballots. It stated: 'there is no obligation on the State to provide the machinery, since the right remains in suspension or abeyance during the period of the applicant's imprisonment' (*Breathnach v Ireland [2001] IESC 59, para 27*). The Minister responsible for the legislation stated that it would 'bring certainty to Ireland's position in meeting fully our obligations under the Convention' as well as referring to the ECHR decision of *Hirst v. United Kingdom (No 2) (2005) ECHR 681* (Roche 2006). While not European specifically, international human rights obligations have also been cited as an influence on changes to Irish law on the use of solitary confinement. The Prison (Amendment) Rules 2017 provide, with exceptions, for prisoners to spend a minimum period of 2 hours out of his or her cell or room with an opportunity for meaningful human contact (Prison (Amendment) Rules 2017 SI 276/2017, s.3). The accompanying policy document of IPS describes the aim of the policy as being to incorporate rules 44 and 45 of the Mandela Rules (Irish Prison Service 2017).

These two changes in the law, while significant, cannot be said to be representative of a trend in Irish prison law towards incorporating European or international human rights law directly into domestic legislation. We do not see widespread reference to European principles as the basis for legislation in the penal sphere.

European supervision of Irish prison policy – a quiet but enduring presence?

Perhaps one of the most overlooked aspects of the interaction of human rights and penal policy concerns the ways in which people in prison themselves view European protections of their rights. We have sought to redress this gap by examining how prisoners in Ireland viewed the CPT as part of the wider study mentioned above. Understanding how European supervision is experienced by those it is most directly intended to protect is important. To explore these issues, we conducted a survey (n = 508) and 44 semi-structured interviews with people in prison in Ireland. We have found that awareness amongst prisoners of the CPT is low (van der Valk, Aizpurua and Rogan forthcoming), with 25% of 508 prisoners surveyed in three medium-security prisons having heard of the CPT. Perhaps unsurprisingly given the infrequent nature of visits by the CPT, only 2% had ever met or contacted the CPT.

Interviews with people in prison revealed a similarly low level of familiarity with monitoring bodies generally, including the CPT. Across three male prisons in Ireland, 44 people in prison serving a sentence were interviewed by the second author. These participants were randomly selected and asked questions about their experiences with oversight bodies in Irish prisons, including the CPT. When the concept of the CPT and its work was described to participants, some concern was expressed about its ability to effect change. Some participants were concerned about the frequency of visits, with one participant (03), who despite having extensive experience of prison had not known of the CPT, noting '[e]*very 4 to 5 years? That's a bit long ain't it …. Anything could happen in 5 days in this place never mind 5 years*'. Others expressed concern about talking to an outside body, a feeling which related not only to the CPT, but monitoring bodies more generally. Participant 38 reflected on the prison culture of keeping your head down, stating: '*I wouldn't draw attention to anyone like that*'. But felt that '*[i]f it was confidential yeah … but I don't want them [the prison officers] to know what I have to say about this place*'. The small number of participants who were aware of the CPT, however, referred to the CPT's criticism of 'slopping out' and the use of padded cells, with one participant attributing the phasing out of slopping out to the CPT, and another noting: '*they are against all this punishment in prison, so they don't like inhumane treatment of prisoners which is all about … it's about lock ups and stuff like*'.

It was also evident that people in prison valued the concept of an outside body coming to assess conditions and treatment (van der Valk and Rogan 2020). Cliquennois and Snacken's contention that '[w]hen practiced routinely monitoring creates conditions that make extreme turns in penal policy less likely and protect human rights in prisons when populist pressures do build' (2018, p. 16) seems to be shared by many of our participants. One participant noted the importance of an impartial outside observer, saying: '*all these people that are non-biased or whatever are really the ones that can make the difference*' (Participant 22). Views on this were, however, mixed, with scepticism also evident about the likelihood of any positive change happening in prison. Participant 23 summed up this feeling well, describing the CPT as '... *just another thing that just happens for a second*', suggesting that visits were quickly forgotten about.

The relevance of the 'Europeanness' of the CPT was also explored with participants. Some participants felt that being a European body was an advantage, and that its work could be a way of sharing ideas about prison practices from different European countries and using them to improve the Irish system. However, others felt that the varying standards across prisons in Europe meant that CPT members might not think the Irish system was especially poor and could even be viewed favourably compared to other prisons; as stated by Participant 33, '*there's some jails in Europe that have it a lot of worse or have it a lot better*'; with Participant 24 saying that CPT members might think '*sure that's only a hotel, compared to theirs*'. For some, the CPT was a body with greater authority and credibility than domestic bodies because of its European nature, and that it had more chance of being listened to by the government as a result. The distance of the CPT from Irish monitoring bodies and the Irish system generally was perceived as a positive by some.

While much more research is needed on the impact of the CPT on prisoners' views of their conditions and their position as rights-holders across Europe, there is some evidence that the concept, at least, of an independent, neutral body visiting prisons in Europe is of value to people in prison, and that its European nature is something of particular merit. Notably, however, it cannot be said that people in prison in our study considered European supervision of prisons to be a strong influence on Irish prison practice or were even especially aware of it. This suggests that more work needs to be done at the national and European level to raise awareness of European-derived rights and protections amongst people in prison.

Conclusion

The lack of direct pronouncement by the ECtHR on Irish prison conditions and penal practices is a singular feature of the Irish system. While it could be read as an indication of Convention-compliant conditions, it is clear from domestic and international criticism of some Irish penal practices, this would be misleading. Rather, this lack of European supervision is attributable to the only recently emerging field of prison litigation in Ireland. With so few cases being decided domestically until the last few years, there simply have been fewer chances for cases to go to Strasbourg. In that sense, European supervision of Irish prisons is certainly weak. It is also clear, however, that domestic application of the Convention has also been more muted than might have been expected given the volume of Convention jurisprudence on prisoners' rights. This is, in part, attributable to the absence of a legal culture which litigates human rights violations in prisons on a regular basis, and a simple lack of experience amongst practitioners in making prison law arguments, especially under the Convention. However, the manner in which the judiciary has interpreted how the Convention is to be used is another factor explaining this picture. That the Convention must always be considered after claims under the Irish Constitution are dealt with, and the apparent judicial discomfort about the way in which Article 3 of the Convention in particular has been interpreted in prison cases by Strasbourg, means that the Convention is a weak source of regulation of Irish prisons in terms of judicial regulation. However, it also seems that non-judicial European sources, notably the CPT, have influenced reform, albeit at a rather slow pace. The fact that policymakers in Ireland are willing to attribute change to European sources and to do so in a positive way should nevertheless not be taken for granted. This desire to be portrayed as complying with European principles, and not to cast European action as illegitimate, at a remove, or unfairly demanding, suggests at least a certain acceptance of European supervision of the Irish system. Finally, it is by no means evident that prisoners in Ireland are feeling strong effects of European supervision of the conditions in which they live. This last point may be the most difficult to remedy, but, in order to ensure European supervision does what it is intended to, may be the most urgent.

Notes

1 S.2(1) European Convention of Human Rights Act 2003 states '*[i]n interpreting and applying any statutory provision or rule of law, a court shall,* in so far as is possible, *subject to the rules of law relating to such interpretation and application, do so in a manner compatible with the State's obligations under the Convention provisions.*'

2 See, for example, Foy v An t-Ard Chláraitheoir & Others [2007]. The declaration was handed down in October 2007 and it took until 2015 for the Gender Recognition Act 2015 to be passed to deal with the declaration of incompatibility in this case.

3 *Simpson v Governor of Mountjoy Prison* [2019] IESC 81, O'Donnell J, para. 6.

4 As of January 2020, 58 people in prison are slopping out, Irish Prison Service, Census Prison Population 2020, https://www.irishprisons.ie/wp-content/uploads/documents_pdf/January-2020-In-Cell.pdf, viewed 3 November 2020.

References

Cliquennois, G & Snacken, S, 2018, 'European and United Nations monitoring of penal and prison policies as a source of an inverted panopticon?' 70 *Crime, Law and Social Change* 1.

de Londras, F, February 2014, 'Declarations of incompatibility under the ECHR Act 2003: a workable transplant?' 35(1) *Statute Law Review* 50–65.

ECHR Press Country Profile, viewed 3 November 2020, https://www.echr.coe.int/Documents/CP_Ireland_eng.pdf.

European Committee for the Prevention of Torture and Inhuman or Degrading Treatment or Punishment (CPT), 2007, *Report to the Government of Ireland on the visit to Ireland carried out by the European Committee for the Prevention of Torture and Inhuman or Degrading Treatment or Punishment (CPT) from 2 to 13 October 2006*, Council of Europe: Strasbourg.

European Committee for the Prevention of Torture and Inhuman or Degrading Treatment or Punishment (CPT), 2011, *Report to the Government of Ireland on the visit to Ireland carried out by the European Committee for the Prevention of Torture and Inhuman or Degrading Treatment or Punishment (CPT) from 25 January to 5 February 2010*, Council of Europe: Strasbourg.

European Committee for the Prevention of Torture and Inhuman or Degrading Treatment or Punishment (CPT), 2015, *Report to the Government of Ireland on the visit to Ireland carried out by the European Committee for the Prevention of Torture and Inhuman or Degrading Treatment or Punishment (CPT) from 16 to 26 September 2014*, Council of Europe: Strasbourg.

European Convention of Human Rights Act 2003.

Fitzgerald, F, 2016a, Speech by Tánaiste and Minister for Justice and Equality, Ms. Frances Fitzgerald, T.D. on official opening of new Cork Prison, 18 July, 2016, viewed 3 November 2020, http://www.justice.ie/en/JELR/Pages/SP16000199.

Fitzgerald, F, 2016b, Tánaiste accepts recommendation to give Ombudsman a role in prison complaints, 8th June 2016, viewed 3 November 2020, http://justice.ie/en/JELR/Pages/PR16000125.

Flanagan, C, 2019, Speech by Minister for Justice and Equality, Charlie Flanagan T.D., at the Prison Officers' Association Conference, viewed 3 November 2020, http://www.justice.ie/en/JELR/Pages/SP19000129.

IPRT, 2019, Progress in the Penal System (PIPS): A framework for penal reform.

Irish Prison Service, 2017, Elimination of Solitary Confinement, viewed 3 November 2020, https://www.irishprisons.ie/wp-content/uploads/documents_pdf/Elimination-of-solitary-confinement-Policy.pdf.

Irish Prison Service, 2020, Prisoner Population on Wednesday 30th September 2020, viewed 20 November 2020, https://www.irishprisons.ie/wp-content/uploads/documents_pdf/30-September-2020.pdf.

Joint Committee on Justice and Equality Report on Penal Reform and Sentencing, 2018, *Report on Penal Reform and Sentencing*, 32/JAE/19.

Office of the Inspector of Prisons, 2009a, *Standard for the Inspection of Prisons*, Office of the Inspector of Prisons: Nenagh.

Office of the Inspector of Prisons, 2009b, *Report on an Inspection of Mountjoy Prison by the Inspector of Prisons Judge Michael Reilly August 2009*, Office of the Inspector of Prisons: Nenagh.

Office of the Inspector of Prisons, 2012, *Report on an Inspection of St. Patrick's Institution by the Inspector of Prisons Judge Michael Reilly 26th June 2012*, Office of the Inspector of Prisons: Nenagh.

Office of the Inspector of Prisons, 2016, *Review, Evaluation and Analysis of the Operation of the present Irish Prison Service Prisoner Complaints Procedure By Judge Michael Reilly Inspector of Prisons April 2016*, Office of the Inspector of Prisons: Nenagh.

Office of the Inspector of Prisons, 2020, *A Framework for the Inspection of Prisons in Ireland*, Office of the Inspector of Prisons: Nenagh.

Penal Policy Review Group, 2014, *Strategic Review of Penal Policy Final Report July 2014*, viewed 3 November 2020, http://www.justice.ie/en/JELR/Strategic%20Review%20of%20Penal%20Policy%20Accessible.pdf/Files/Strategic%20Review%20of%20Penal%20Policy%20Accessible.pdf.

Roche, D, 2006, *Seanad Éireann debate*, Thursday 30th November 2006, Vol. 185 No. 10, viewed 3 November 2020, 924-948, https://www.oireachtas.ie/en/debates/debate/seanad/2006-11-30/9/?highlight%5B0%5D=hirst.

Rogan, M, 2012, Dealing with overcrowding in prisons: contrasting judicial approaches from the USA and Ireland. 47 *Irish Jurist*.

Rogan, M, 2014, Judicial Conceptions of Prisoners' Rights in Ireland: an emerging field Academy of European Law, 'Improving Conditions Related to Detention', Council of Europe, Strasbourg, November 6-7.

Shatter, A, 2013, Speech by Alan Shatter T.D., Minister for Justice, Equality and Defence at the Dáil debate on the draft resolution under the Prisons Act 2007 approving the development of a new prison in Cork on Tuesday 18 June 2013, viewed 3 November 2020, http://www.justice.ie/en/JELR/Pages/SP13000239.

van der Valk, S, Aizpurua, E & Rogan, M, forthcoming, 'Towards a typology of prisoners' awareness of and familiarity with prison inspection and monitoring bodies.'

van der Valk, S & Rogan, M, 2020, 'Experiencing human rights protections in prisons: The case of prison monitoring in Ireland.' *European Journal of Criminology*. doi:10.1177/1477370820960024.

World Prison Brief, Country Overview, Ireland 2020, viewed 3 November 2020, https://www.prisonstudies.org/country/ireland-republic.

6

STRENGTHS AND WEAKNESSES OF THE JUDICIAL PROTECTION IN GERMANY

Christine Graebsch

Questioning the role of the ECtHR case law for prisoners' rights in Germany

Germany is regularly considered a state with acceptably high standards of prisoners' rights, including their implementation in practice. This is perceived to be mainly the result of the successful system of judicial review, as described by Morgenstern and Dünkel (2018, p. 24). The latter allows prisoners to complain against any decision, action or omission to a judicial authority and – in case of final defeat – to draw an individual constitutional complaint to the Federal Constitutional Court.

The assessment of the effectiveness of the judicial review system in Germany is not doubted due to the undisputed fact that prisoners' complaints are successful in less than 5% of cases. To the contrary, the low percentage of successful claims is even reinterpreted into an indicator for success:

> [...] probably less than 5 per cent of the complaints are successful. This does not necessarily mean that the complaints mechanisms are ineffective, but could be because prison administrations base their decisions in most cases on well-founded arguments.
>
> *Morgenstern and Dünkel 2018, p. 24 with further reference*

Even though this line of argumentation is not based on an empirical study and in contradiction to findings of earlier empirical research (Feest, Lesting and Selling 1997), it amounts to the conclusion:

> All in all, the complaints procedure mechanisms in Germany can be seen as a success, as every decision or action taken by the prison authorities can

DOI: 10.4324/9780429317033-9

> be made subject to a judicial review, which has a moderating effect in and of itself since the prison authorities must always explain their actions and decisions by legal arguments to prisoners.
>
> *Morgenstern and Dünkel 2018, p. 24*

Against this backdrop, the perception still prevails, that the German standards tend to be much higher than the European ones, even though this view might have been challenged by various decisions of the European Court on Human Rights (ECtHR) referring to excessive periods of remand detention, access to files, as concluded by Morgenstern and Dünkel (2018, p. 25).

In 2006, the FCC indicated in its important decision on youth imprisonment, the critical role of standards set out by the Council of Europe's institutions:

> [...] the provisions of the basic law are to be interpreted in a manner that is open to international law ("völkerrechtsfreundlich"). At the level of constitutional law, the text of the Convention and the case-law of the European Court of Human Rights serve as interpretation aids for the determination of the contents and scope of the fundamental rights and of rule-of-law principles enshrined in the Basic Law.[1]

In the discourse about the relation between the ECtHR's case law and national (constitutional) law in Germany, some authors referred to the case of preventive detention as an example of the compliant implementation of European human rights guarantees by the FCC. For instance, Payandeh and Sauer (2012) conclude that the FCC in overruling its own case decision of 2004 adapted its case law to the standards set out by the ECtHR. During the last years, the case of preventive detention was often cited as a successful example of a two-way dialogue between both courts (Giegerich 2014). Judgements of the ECtHR on preventive detention were also seen as a "legal irritant" to the national system of law resulting in

> a complex process which allowed the German legal system and its inner logic to remain 'intact' while integrating the human rights message of the judgement.
>
> *Nußberger 2014*

Before having a closer look at the relation between national law and the case law of the ECtHR in the case of preventive detention after the decision of the Grand Chamber in the case of Ilnseher v. Germany (Applications nos. 10211/12 and 27505/14), three decisions of the ECtHR dealing with prisoners' rights will be analysed in the context of national law. The analysis aims at assessing the impact of the ECtHR's case law on German prison law. It is inevitable to extend the analysis in two directions as compared to how it is usually done (e.g. Morgenstern and Dünkel 2018): it is by no means sufficient to simply conclude from the law in the books; a thorough analysis necessarily has to take into account the law in action as far as possible. Moreover, the extent to which the "human rights message" of ECtHR judgements is implemented into national law depends to a large degree on the depth of understanding the ECtHR itself could develop with respect to infringements of human rights within the respective national legal system. Thus, this will also be analysed by using the example of cases in which the ECtHR states a violation of the Convention in German prison law.

The analyses will take a close look at this selection of decisions and their national law context. Apart from legal documents and scientific literature, the perspective taken is inspired by the author's experience in the field of prison litigation as a practicing lawyer, by letter communication with prisoners in the context of the NGO, The Prison Archive ("Strafvollzugarchiv"[2]) that is attached to the University of Applied Sciences and Arts in Dortmund, and a legal clinic for prisoners' rights that is attached to the University of Bremen.

Prisoners' rights and the right to an effective remedy (ECtHR: Hellig v. Germany)

In the case of Hellig (Application no. 20999/05), Germany was convicted for a violation of Art. 3 of the Convention. The violation was based on Hellig's accommodation in a security cell without clothes for seven days. The ECtHR considered his seven-day placement in the security cell in itself to have been justified by the special circumstances of the case. However, the ECtHR concluded that there had been no sufficient reasons to justify such harsh treatment as the removal of the applicant's clothes for the entire duration of his placement in the cell.

Even though the necessary information was all available for the ECtHR, it did not deal with the deep structure of the case and with what it revealed about loopholes in the German system of prisoners' rights (cf. Pohlreich 2011; Graebsch 2014).

What is remarkable about this case is that Hellig from the very beginning was on solid ground when expressing his right to single accommodation in a cell. However, he was supposed to be transferred from his single cell to a cell he would have had to share with two other prisoners. Moreover, the toilet was not separated from the rest of the cell. He rightly referred against this imposition to the decision of the Higher Regional Court (Oberlandesgericht Frankfurt) responsible as an appeal chamber for the very prison (Butzbach) according to which accommodation in such a cell was considered to be degrading treatment.[3] He filed a complaint to the competent court of first instance (Landgericht Gießen). The next day after having done so but before the complaint had reached the court, the staff ordered the applicant to leave his single cell and move to the multi-occupancy cell. Hellig refused to move into the latter, and a scuffle ensued between him and staff of the prison. It resulted in minor injuries on the side of Hellig while no injuries of prison staff were reported. In the procedure at the ECtHR, the applicant submitted, he was kicked and beaten by the prison staff, while he had merely passively resisted being placed into the multi-occupancy cell. According to the Government, the applicant had kicked the prison staff. He was then forcibly taken to the security cell.

Despite filing the complaint, the day before the incident, the regional court took around 3.5 years until deciding about it. The court then confirmed that it would have been unlawful beyond doubt to accommodate the prisoner in a multi-occupancy cell with toilets that were not separated by screens or curtains from the rest of the cell. Neither the national courts nor the ECtHR did engage with the lack of an effective remedy, including interim legal protection that was obvious in the case. Instead, they justified the transferal to a security cell by arguing his behaviour had constituted a risk of violence and physical harm to other persons.

Art. 114 para 2 Federal Prison Act allows the court to suspend the execution of a measure in case otherwise realization of a right of the prisoner will be endangered. In reality, the first precondition for this kind of decision is that the prison administration promptly forwards the complaint to the court to which they are obliged according to the case law of the FCC. However, even if this had happened in the case of Hellig, the next inevitable step would have been a court decision within due time. This has obviously not been the case. As we know from practice, courts often take months for their decision even in cases in which the prisoners apply for an interim measure. Since the complaint to the court has no delaying effect, the prison meanwhile enforces the measure. The case will often be declared as settled afterwards, and a special interest in continuation has to be asserted to nevertheless receive a court's decision (Fortsetzungsfeststellungsinteresse).

Neither for an interim measure nor for the main proceedings an effective remedy to pursue acceleration of the process is available. Admittedly, German legislation passed the law on legal protection in the event of excessive court proceedings and criminal investigations in 2011[4] following the finding of a violation with respect to Art. 13 and 6 para 1 of the Convention by the Grand Chamber in Sürmeli v. Germany (application no. 75529/01). The new regulation allows for compensation after an excessive length of court proceedings. However, this did rather a disservice to the implementation of prisoners' rights. Before this amendment to the law, judicial case law had developed the instrument of a complaint of failure to act (Untätigkeitsbeschwerde) addressed to the higher level court in case the excessive length of the proceedings justified the concern that it would lead to a denial of justice.[5] Since the amendment, courts refer to the possibility of a delay notice to the court responsible for the decision (Verzögerungsrüge), and the possibility of raising a complaint of failure to act is regarded to be obsolete.[6] However, with both instruments being to protracted for the usual case of a prisoner, the former instrument at least aimed at finally receiving a decision and was decided about by a different (higher) court. As opposed to this, the notification of delay has to be addressed to the inactive court and results at best in a compensation. However, the latter may be denied if the court considers alternative ways of compensation as sufficient, such as the mere observation that the length of the proceedings had been inadequate (Art. 198 para 2 and 4 Courts Constitution Act). All in all, there is still no effective way to achieve a timely court decision. Feest and Lesting (2009) have dealt a lot with what they have called "recalcitrant prison administrations" (renitente Vollzugsbehörden) and "contempt of court" – prison administrations that did not implement a court's decision despite their obligation to do so. In 2013, the threat and eventually the order of penalty payments were introduced as a possibility that can be imposed against prison administrations (Art. 120 para 1 Federal Prison Act in conjunction with Art. 172 Administrative Courts Procedure Code). Mentioning this regulation has helped at least in some cases since. The next step certainly must be to deal with "recalcitrant courts" that play for time waiting until a case will be "settled" due to the release of the prisoner or any other development that would render a decision useless to the prisoner – what it would not have been if the court had decided without delay. While this typical problem of prisoners' rights protection is quite apparent, the ECtHR did not refer to it with respect to Art. 13 ECHR.

Access to medical care, especially substitution maintenance treatment (Wenner v. Germany)

In the case of Wenner v. Germany (application no. 62303/13), the ECtHR found a violation of Art. 3 ECHR. The decision concerned the complaint by a long-term heroin addict who had been denied drug-substitution treatment in prison. The ECtHR in principle accepted a margin of appreciation in favour of the State to choose between abstinence-oriented drug therapy and drug-substitution therapy. However, the ECtHR pointed to a several vital elements indicating that drug-substitution treatment could be regarded as the requisite treatment for the applicant. Important reasons for this observation were that he had been a manifest and long-term opioid addict; that he had been brought back from a measure of obligatory drug treatment to prison against his will because the court considered the abstinence-orientated treatment as hopeless; and his drug addiction had been treated with medically prescribed drug substitution therapy for 17 years prior to his detention.

After this judgement, substitution treatment in Bavarian prisons increased. However, a number of prison doctors continued to be reluctant. They started to grant substitution treatment to (only) a very small number of prisoners to confute the argument "that it is uncontested that no drug substitution treatment had ever been provided in practice to prisoners in Kaisheim Prison" (Wenner v. Germany, para 76). However, still many prisoners who had received substitution treatment before were forced to discontinue without an individual assessment giving reasons to do so. For a perspective of successfully implementing prisoners' rights, a critical question is whether they were able to enforce their rights by litigation. Cases represented by the author as a lawyer show difficulties.

If a prisoner complains against an omission of the prison administration instead of an action of an annulment, s/he cannot successfully go to court before three months after an application. In practice, even written applications are often lost and prison administrations regularly refuse to hand out an acknowledgement of receipt. Prisoners often lose court cases because of a missing application or because they are said for having applied for the wrong thing. For example, following the standards set by the Wenner judgement, prisoners applied for a statement of an independent judge but were rebuked because they should have applied for substitution treatment as such (first). This is even a pseudo-problem considering that by admission a medical check-up is obligatory for the prison and the doctor will be in possession of all documents about prior prison stays. Furthermore, it is especially relevant in the not uncommon situation in which substitution treatment was granted during pre-trial detention but gradually discontinued upon arrival in prison. A usual way of coping with this situation is the illegal possession of drugs for which they will be indicted and punished with another prison sentence even if they were only in possession of small amounts of a substance they had before received for substitution treatment. Applications to a court by means of prison law still take as a rule much longer than these penal procedures. They often take years, like in the case of Hellig that was mentioned above. They also often take longer than the prison term, and after release, the need to adjudicate will be no more accepted by the court except where a continuing interest for a declaratory judgement is acknowledged. Another way of dealing with the complaint by prisoners aiming at substitution treatment after the court has postponed it for a long time is to state the prisoner had managed to become clean in between and therefore does not need substitution treatment anymore. Certainly, prisoners who were not drug-tested for a long time will not object to this and offer counterproof while risking to get punished.

In general, the myth of the medical doctors' sacrosanct discretion is still prevalent. Even the Wenner judgement is cited in alleged support for it. However, as was made very clear by the ECtHR in the case of Wenner, this discretion does not cover infringements of professional medical standards. Another way that prisoners sometimes choose to enforce their right to adequate medical treatment is to bring a criminal charge against the prison doctor for, i.e., denial of assistance. However, in respective cases, the prosecution service had never investigated into the possibility that the prison doctor could have failed. Instead, they immediately pressed charges against the prisoner for aspersions, etc. Even if the prisoner is acquitted later, the burden of the accusations had been imposed on him or her. Also, the adequate medical treatment will at least not be obtained by means of the legal proceedings, indirectly at best.

The appropriate legal remedy to achieve a timely decision on an urgent matter is to apply for an interim measure (Section 114 para 2 Federal Prison Act). In a decision substitution treatment, the Bavarian Supreme Court in 2019 quashed a ruling of a district court that had granted substitution treatment to a prisoner. Following the argument of the Bavarian Supreme Court, the lower court had not sufficiently respected that it was prohibited to anticipate the result of the decision in later main proceedings (Hauptsachevorwegnahme).[7] This stipulation will de facto lead to the impossibility of receiving an interim measure for substitution treatment, even more since courts anyway tend to use this line of rejection, and since decisions about interim measures usually cannot be appealed against.

Moreover, the Bavarian Supreme Court distinguished between the continuation of substitution treatment and its initiation. Thereby, the court used an understanding of "initiation" that included a case of a formerly substituted prisoner, who had however (involuntarily) been without substitution treatment in another prison before. The court also approved the pseudo compliant practice of Bavarian prison that start with substitution treatment only shortly before release. It refers to the argument of prison being a rather safe and drug-free place; thus, substitution treatment was only needed afterwards. This is not only a circumvention of the ECtHR's guidelines in Wenner. In connection with playing for time and the procedural thresholds to receive a positive court decision, especially an interim measure, it leaves prisoners in Bavaria without a possibility to receive adequate treatment.

Access to therapy and rehabilitation for foreign nationals (Rangelov v. Germany)

In the case of Rangelov (5123/07, 22.03.2012), Germany was convicted for a violation of Art. 14 in conjunction with Art. 5 of the Convention. The case dealt with the discrimination of a Bulgarian national in preventive detention. He was denied access to social therapy as well as relaxations, namely leave under escort. Both measures are acknowledged to be critical preparatory steps and preconditions for release from preventive detention after the sentence, which is in principle unlimited. The ECtHR concluded that they had not been offered to the applicant "in view of the final expulsion order made against him, which he was and could only be subject to as a foreign national" (Rangelov v. Germany, para 95). It is crucial to understand that the ECtHR identified a discrimination with respect to the existence of an expulsion order as discrimination because of the nationality even without discussion. As obvious as this might be according to the fact that only foreign nationals can be expelled and deported, it is usually seen differently in the national context.

The legal as well as the factual situation of foreign national prisoners until today is very similar to the situation the ECtHR described for Rangelov in preventive detention as discrimination. This is not only despite this judgement that has not received broad recognition in Germany. It is also despite a decision of the FCC issued in the same year stating that the aim of rehabilitation in principle also applies to prisoners who are going to be deported from prison.[8] In fact, they are not in general excluded from relaxations of conditions like prison leave with or without being escorted. According to the law, the only criterion for these relaxations is whether a danger of absconding or misuse of offences can be substantiated.[9] However, federal states issued administrative regulations stating a final expulsion order and an intention to deport the prisoner during their custodial sentence constituting a reason to exclude the prisoner from relaxations. In one federal state, this regulation even is codified directly in its Prison Act.[10] One might wonder how these regulations could persist. The reason is that they are usually not applied explicitly. A case like the one of Rangelov in which prison and judicial authorities express the argument of possible deportation as the reason for denial of relaxations is rare. Usually, they would rather refer to an unfavourable risk assessment. In a version of kitchen sink psychology that is widespread among penal policy experts, they argue that the risk of absconding during prison leave is higher in cases involving not only the remaining part of a prison sentence but also the threat of being deported.[11] This is also said to be the logic behind these regulations.

When it comes to the experience of everyday practice in prison, foreign nationals are subjected to conditions that differ completely in nature from those for German citizens. Due to a possible deportation from prison at some unknown point in the future or simply a pending decision about expulsion or deportation, foreign national prisoners are subjected to a regime that can be called "wait-and-see treatment" (Abwartevollzug, cf. Graebsch 2017a, 2017b). There are no systematical statistic data on this issue published. Nevertheless, the answers to a minor interpellation for the federal state of Saxony revealed that in 2016 only 1.93% of the foreign national prisoners were granted prison leave as opposed to 32.30% of the German citizens; 0.35% non-citizens were allowed to work outside prison, but 5.29% of the citizens; 0.38% of the non-citizens were placed in an open prison, but 6.66% of the citizens (Sächsischer Landtag, Drs.-Nr: 6/10857, 6/10008).

Despite their legal responsibility to decide about rehabilitation measures, prison administrations perceive themselves as bound to the decisions and expressed intentions of the immigration authorities. This attitude is enforced by regulations, as mentioned above. The Recommendation CM/Rec(2012)12 of the Committee of Ministers to member States concerning foreign prisoners suggests a completely different approach to perceiving foreign national prisoners as a deprivileged group in need of special support and to counteract against possible discrimination. These recommendations are widely unknown in Germany. The European Prison Rules are often seen as unnecessary for the German context with all of its legal regulations and court decision, especially the ones by the FCC. Hopefully, No. 37 of the 2020 revised version of the EPR will help to change the perspective in German prisons towards taking positive measures to meet the distinctive needs of prisoners who are foreign nationals instead of continuing with their discrimination.

To date, arguments similar to the ones used in the national court decisions preceding the judgement in Rangelov can still be heard a lot in Germany's prison practice: it was impossible to reintegrate foreign nationals into society because it was unknown whether they would stay in the country and thus unclear how integration could work. This perception is not only against the law but also far from being conclusive. Vocational training, language courses, therapy or relaxations to put them to the test in terms of relapse prevention are in no way dependent on the place where the prisoner will later live.

Another argument that is often used to justify the neglect of foreign prisoners' needs has thankfully also been addressed by the Rangelov decision. Deportation is often seen as a benefit to foreign prisoners because they reattain their liberty afterwards. However, not all prisoners prefer freedom in their country of origin to prison in Germany. The ECtHR at least pointed out that the reference to the benefit may not be used as an argument if rehabilitation measures are denied with reference to the pending deportation, while deportation is denied at the same time with reference to the lack of progress made by the prisoner. However, this catch 22 still broadly exists in Germany. While rehabilitation in prison is denied because of the situation in migration law, the consequences in migration law are connected to rehabilitation efforts in prison. Moreover, current developments can be described as "crimmigration law". According to this analytical category criminal law and migration law increasingly merge to the detriment of the concerned individuals' legal position – in Germany (Graebsch 2019a, 2019b) no less than in other countries (Franko 2020).

(Retroactive) Preventive detention after punishment

There is a lot to say about the persistence of preventive detention after a prison term (Sicherungsverwahrung, Section 66 ff. Penal Code) and measures of correction and prevention (Maßregeln der Besserung und Sicherung) in general despite frictions occurring with regulations of the Convention. It has been a long way from M. v. Germany in 2009 (no. 19359/04) when the ECtHR declared preventive detention to be a punishment under Art. 7 para 1 of the ECHR until the Grand Chamber judgement Ilnseher v. Germany (nos. 10211/12 and 27505/14). In Ilnseher, the ECtCH accepted the new conception of (retroactive) preventive detention as presented by the German state. As said before, this is often perceived as an example of Germany's compliance with the ECtHR case law. However, as closer look reveals how Germany simply circumvented the "human rights message" (Nußberger 2014, as cited above) that was set out by the ECtHR by making use of very complicated regulations that were not well understood or disregarded in its meaning by the ECtHR. The category of "persons of unsound mind" was taken from Art. 5 para 1 (e) ECHR and implemented into the German system to find a legally solid basis for what had been planned to be implemented before: retroactive versions of preventive detention, for cases in which preventive detention had not been ordered by the sentencing court but was implemented later due to the impressions of the prisoner during his incarceration. Retroactive versions of preventive detention have officially been abolished by the fundamental decision of the FCC of 4 May 2011.[12] However, by means of a "temporary provision",[13] it will survive for a long time. Additionally, these changes of the law, which were implemented to circumvent the consequences of M. v. Germany, have changed the system of criminal sanctions and caused insurmountable frictions. Preventive detention is now justified with reference to therapeutic efforts. Conversely, the therapeutization of the criminal justice system is fostered. In this, therapy is not understood as an offer for cure but as precondition for release and relaxations during confinement. If therapy is ineffective, a responsibilization takes place that holds the prisoner accountable for lack of success. This works hand in glove with developments extending unlimited forms of detention with their being connected to a favourable prognosis that might be enforced by therapy.

These complex developments have been described elsewhere in detail.[14] In the remaining part of the chapter, the line of argumentation that was used by the FCC on how to deal with the case law of the ECtHR in the field of preventive detention will be discussed.

According to the long-standing case law of the FCC, the Convention and its interpretation in judgements of the ECtHR may enhance but not restrict the scope of fundamental rights granted by the German constitution.[15] In its decision of 4 May 2011,[16] the FCC reiterated that only the fundamental rights in the German constitution were the basis for their decision but that they were to be understood in a way that was friendly towards international public law taking the decisions of the Court into account as if they were legally relevant changes of law. This acknowledged role of the decisions of the ECtHR as an auxiliary instrument for interpretation of the Constitution would though not afford to schematically parallelize the case law of both courts, but to adopt the valuations that were expressed in the jurisprudence of the Court as far as this seemed methodically acceptable and did not contradict the standards set out by the German Constitution (para 86 ff.).[17] As an example, the FCC stated that the ECtHR understandably decided to follow its own interpretation on what constitutes "punishment" within the framework of the Convention and independent from concepts of national law. The interpretation of what was considered to be a punishment according to German constitutional law could not be determined by following the case law of the ECtHR but was to be decided about in accordance with the German constitution (alone).[18] This argument led inter alia to the maintenance of Art. 2 § 6 Criminal Code which still allows for the retroactive imposition of measures of treatment and prevention.

The FCC then refers to so-called "multipolar relations of fundamental rights" ("mehrpolige Grundrechtsverhältnisse"). It described them as relations of rights in a situation in which an asset of freedom for one holder of fundamental rights will result in a lessening of the fundamental rights of another.[19] Referring to Article 53 of the Convention, the FCC describes multipolar relations as the typical situation in which the application of the Convention and the implementation of the ECtHR's decision are excluded because it would result in violations of the German Constitution. With this construction, the FCC enables itself to weigh the consequences of observing the decisions of the Court against the expected infringements of the fundamental rights of the public or potential victims. The term and idea of these multipolar relations derive from the area of civil law. In criminal law, a multipolar relation would only be acceptable if a decision would interfere with the subjective rights of several parties which have to be harmonized but if only one of them was able to represent him- or herself in court. As opposed to this, in criminal law, it is the obligation of the state to protect the public and the government has always been party to the case. The public is not a party as such and, as a core element of criminal law, is not supposed to be one but is represented by the state. If the public or the potential victims are constructed as one of the poles to be considered in a multipolar relation, this could be applied for decisions of the ECtHR in the field of criminal law and prison law in general. Thus, in the area in which absolute rights of the offender are to be respected for the protection of his or her freedom, fundamental rights are opened up for weighing by the FCC.[20] This results in the contrary to what the FCC had set out in the beginning – that the application of the Convention could only lead to a stronger protection of fundamental rights, not to their weakening.

Resume

As a resume, the conception of prisoners' rights as anchored in the German constitution may rightly serve as a model meriting international recognition. The guarantee of individual rights in prison law and the myriad of pathbreaking judgements by the FCC[21] have been broadly documented in national as well as international publications. As opposed to this, the practical implementation of these benchmark setting regulations is less often discussed. When it is included into the analysis, things look quite different. Moreover, in the case of preventive detention, the FCC revealed its own reservations towards implementing the human rights message sent to him from Strasbourg. Even worse, the ECtHR gave way to the continuation of a kind of compliance that takes place on the surface but does not alter the deep structure of the law.

Notes

1 Bundesverfassungsgericht (BVerfG), 31.05.2006, – 2 BvR 1673/04, 2 BvR 2402/04, marginal no. 63, translation following the citation of this passage in the translation of the FCC with respect to the press release about its decision on preventive detention of 04.05.2011 which will be discussed below, https://www.bundesverfassungsgericht.de/SharedDocs/Pressemitteilungen/EN/2011/bvg11-031.html
2 www.strafvollzugsarchiv.de
3 OLG Frankfurt NStZ 1985, 572.
4 Bundesgesetzblatt I p. 2302.
5 Hanseatisches Oberlandesgericht Hamburg, 27-01-2005 – 3 Vollz (Ws) 2/05 –, juris.
6 For example, OLG München, 20-09 2012 – 4 VAs 038/12 –, juris.
7 Bayerisches Oberstes Landesgericht, 15-04-2019 – 203 StObWs 227/19 –, juris.
8 BVerfG, 10-10-2012 – 2 BvR 2025/12, juris.
9 There are different but similar laws in the 16 federal states, cf. an overview and discussion of Lesting and Burkhardt (2017).

10 Section 38 para. 5 No. 3 Prison Act Saarland.
11 For example, decision by the regional court (Landgericht) Stade 13-08-2015 – 101 AR 11/15, *Strafverteidiger* 2016, p. 249.
12 BVerfG, 04-05-2011, 2 BvR 2333/08 –, juris.
13 Art. 316 f. Einführungsgesetz zum Strafgesetzbuch.
14 For example, Graebsch (2017c; 2019a, 2019b); cf. an overview in English the dissenting opinion of Judge Pinto de Albuquerque to the Grand Chamber judgement in Ilnseher v. Germany.
15 BVerfG, 14-10-2004, 2 BvR 1481/04 para 30 ff.
16 BVerfG, 04-05-2011, 2 BvR 2333/08 –, juris.
17 BVerfG, 04-05-2011, 2 BvR 2333/08 –, juris, para. 88.
18 BVerfG, 04-05-2011, 2 BvR 2333/08 –, juris, para. 142.
19 BVerfG, 04-05-2011, 2 BvR 2333/08 –, juris, para. 93.
20 Cf. a summary of the arguments (Dax 2017, p. 97).
21 Cf. a collection of Lübbe-Wolff (2016).

References

Dax, A. (2017). *Die Neuregelung des Vollzugs der Sicherungsverwahrung. Bestandsaufnahme sowie kritische Betrachtung der bundes- und landesrechtlichen Umsetzung des Abstandsgebots*, Berlin: Duncker & Humblot.

Feest, J. and Lesting, W. (2009). "Contempt of Court. Zur Wiederkehr des Themas der renitenten Strafvollzugsbehörden." In: H.E. Müller, G.M. Sander and H. Válková (eds.), *Festschrift für Ulrich Eisenberg zum 70. Geburtstag*, München: C. H. Beck, pp. 675–690.

Feest, J., Lesting, W. and Selling, P. (1997). *Totale Institution und Rechtsschutz. Eine Untersuchung zum Rechtsschutz im Strafvollzug*, Opladen: Westdeutscher Verlag.

Franko, K. (2020). *The Crimmigrant Other. Migration and Penal Power*, London: Routledge.

Giegerich, T. (2014). "The Struggle by the German Courts and Legislature to Transpose the Strasbourg Case Law on Preventive Detention into German Law." In: M.E. Villiger, A. Seibert-Fohr (eds.), *Judgments of the European Court of Human Rights – Effects and Implementation*, London: Routledge, pp. 207–236.

Graebsch, C. (2014). "Kontrolle des Strafvollzugs durch unabhängiges Monitoring." *Forum Strafvollzug* 63(6), pp. 390–396.

Graebsch, C. (2017a). "Resozialisierungsauftrag bei Nichtdeutschen." In: H. Cornel, G. Kawamura-Reindl and B. Sonnen (eds.), *Handbuch Resozialisierung*, 4th edition, Baden-Baden: Nomos Verlag, pp. 433–448.

Graebsch, C. (2017b). "Vollzugliche Situation von Nichtdeutschen." In: J. Feest, W. Lesting and M. Lindemann (eds.), *Strafvollzugsgesetze*, 7th edition, Köln: Wolters Kluwer, p. 99.

Graebsch, C. (2017c). "Precrime und Strafvollzug. Resozialisierungsanspruch und Situation von Gefangenen bei prognoseabhängiger Entlassung."*Kritische Justiz* 2, pp. 166–175.

Graebsch, C. (2019a). "Die Gefährder des Rechtsstaats und die Europäische Menschenrechtskonvention. Von Sicherungsverwahrung und „unsound mind "zum Pre-Crime-Gewahrsam?" In: I. Goeckenjan, J. Puschke and T. Singelnstein (eds.), *Für die Sache – Kriminalwissenschaften aus unabhängiger Perspektive. Festschrift für Ulrich Eisenberg zum 80*, Geburtstag, Berlin: Duncker & Humblot, pp. 312–325.

Graebsch, C. (2019b). "Krimmigration: Die Verwobenheit strafrechtlicher mit migrationsrechtlicher Kontrolle unter besonderer Berücksichtigung des Pre-Crime-Rechts für „Gefährder." *Kriminologie-Das Online-Journal* 1(1), pp. 75–103, https://www.kriminologie.de/index.php/krimoj/article/view/9

Lesting, W. and Burkhardt, S.-U. (2017). "§ 38 LandesR – Lockerungen zur Erreichung des Vollzugsziels." In: J. Feest, W. Lesting and M. Lindemann (eds.), *Strafvollzugsgesetze*, 7th edition, Köln: Wolters Kluwer, p. 245.

Lübbe-Wolff, G. (2016). *Die Rechtsprechung des Bundesverfassungsgerichts zum Strafvollzug und Untersuchungshaftvollzug*, Baden-Baden: Nomos.

Morgenstern, C. and Dünkel, F. (2018). "Monitoring prisons in Germany. The role of the European Court of Human Rights." In: G. Cliquennois, H. de Suremain (eds.), *Monitoring Penal Policy in Europe*, London: Routledge, pp. 17–35.

Nußberger, A. (2014). "Subsidiarity in the Control of Decisions Based on Proportionality: An Analysis of the Basis ofthe Implementation of ECtHR Judgments into German Law." In: M.E. Villiger, A. Seibert-Fohr (eds.), *Judgments of the European Court of Human Rights – Effects and Implementation*, London: Routledge, pp. 165–185.

Payandeh, M. and Sauer, H. (2012). "Menschenrechtskonforme Auslegung als Verfassungsmehrwert: Konvergenzen von Grundgesetz und EMRK im Urteil des Bundesverfassungsgericht zur Sicherungsverwahrung." *Juristische Ausbildung (Jura)* 34, pp. 89–298.

Pohlreich, E. (2011). "Gewalt gegen Haftlinge und Unterbringung in besonders gesicherten Hafträumen." *Juristenzeitung* 66(21), pp. 1058–1063.

7

THE CONDUCT OF PRISON REFORMS

An assessment of the effectiveness of domestic remedies in Italy

Sofia Ciuffoletti and Paulo Pinto de Alburquerque

Introduction

As the recent doctrine has shown (see Re, 2006), the phenomenon of the "prison boom" has migrated from the United States to Europe in less than a decade. To date, prison overcrowding[1] is characterized by its endemic and structural nature in many European countries.[2] The most effective judicial response to this issue has been provided by the case law of the European Court of Human Rights (from now on, the Court – see the summary of the principles set by the ECtHR on the issue of prison overcrowding, Pinto de Albuquerque, 2019). The combat against prison overcrowding in Europe is therefore an excellent proof of the capacity of Strasbourg case law to provide responses that form a common narrative and force Member States, through substantive and procedural, positive and negative obligations, to renegotiate the policies of protection of prisoners at the national level (See, Van Zyl Smit and Snacken, 2009; Cliquennois and de Suremain, 2018; Cliquennois and Snacken, 2018).

From this analytical perspective, Italy stands out as one of the countries most affected by the phenomenon of prison overcrowding, with one peculiarity. In Italy, this phenomenon has historically been accompanied by the absence of a general judicial remedy capable of eliminating the human rights violation in progress and compensating for the damage suffered. It was only thanks to the European impulse that the inhuman dimension of detention was finally perceived from a rights-oriented perspective with the corollary of remedies designed to protect these rights in the Italian system.

In this essay, we will trace the Italian process of adaptation (and resistance) to the European case law on the protection of prisoners' rights.

DOI: 10.4324/9780429317033-10

The Strasbourg Court as the driving force for the implementation of prisoners' rights at the national level

The Italian public, political and even legal discourse about prisoners' rights as human rights has been largely Strasbourg-driven. *Sulejmanovic v. Italy*[3] is without any doubt the very first time the inhuman and degrading conditions of Italian prisons become an open topic for the public debate, thus confirming the trend that sees international courts, and the Strasbourg Court in particular, as the arena in which social conflicts arise and are solved, shaping a new grammar of rights in our contemporary societies.

If the *Sulejmanovic* judgement confirmed the inhuman and degrading prison condition in Italy, the lack of internal effective remedies was sanctioned by the subsequent *Torreggiani* pilot judgement.[4] The European Court affirms not only that the remedy deriving from Articles 35 and 69 of the penitentiary law[5] is ineffective:

> le seul recours indiqué par le gouvernement défendeur dans les présentes affaires qui était susceptible d'améliorer les conditions de détention dénoncées, à savoir la réclamation devant le juge d'application des peines en vertu des articles 35 et 69 de la loi sur l'administration pénitentiaire, est un recours qui, bien qu'accessible, n'est pas effectif en pratique, dans la mesure où il ne permet pas de mettre rapidement fin à l'incarcération dans des conditions contraires à l'article 3 de la Convention.
>
> *paragraphe 55 ci-dessus*[6]

and that no compensatory remedy exists:

> D'autre part, le Gouvernement n'a pas démontré l'existence d'un recours qui permettrait aux personnes ayant été incarcérées dans des conditions ayant porté atteinte à leur dignité d'obtenir une quelconque forme de réparation pour la violation subie.[7]

but it also declares that no common normative ideology exists, within the Italian interpretative community (For a comprehensive theoretical approach to the concept of interpretative community from a legal realistic perspective, see Santoro, 2008), on their role as protector of prisoners' rights:

> À cet égard, elle observe que la jurisprudence récente attribuant au juge de l'application des peines le pouvoir de condamner l'administration à payer une indemnisation pécuniaire est loin de constituer une pratique établie et constante des autorités nationales.[8]

This constituted a real failure in the domestic legal order, defeating the purpose of the system of human rights' protection at a national level. Notwithstanding the repetitive *stimulus* of the Constitutional Court, the surveillance judiciary was not able to produce a consistent case law aiming at the protection of prisoners' rights as human rights (For a comprehensive account of the Italian post-Torreggiani case law on detention conditions and overcrowding see Passione, 2017).

It is, therefore, remarkable that in the *Stella v. Italy*[9] case, the ECtHR offered a positive evaluation of the system of remedies put in place by the Italian government in the pilot judgement's execution procedure, noting that no evidence enabled the Court to find that said remedies did not offer "in principle" prospects of appropriate relief for the complaints submitted under Article 3 of the Convention. Yet the Court also underlined that this positive evaluation did not preclude an eventual re-assessment of the effectiveness of the remedies, "considering the ability of domestic Courts to provide a uniform case-law that is compatible with the requirements of the Convention[10]".

There is no doubt that the Italian government showed a compliant attitude, introducing for the first time a combination of preventive and compensatory remedies with Law-Decrees No. 146 of December 2013 and No. 92 of June 2014. Subsequently, the Committee of Ministers ratified, with Resolution CM/ResDH(2016)28,[11] the Italian government's action and decided to close the case, "welcoming the response given by the Italian authorities to the *Torreggiani* pilot judgment through the adoption of major reforms aimed at solving the problem of prison overcrowding and the significant results achieved to date in this area". This decision was an additional and final *placet* towards the policies enacted by the Italian government in order to comply with the pilot judgement procedure and created the rethoric *topos* of the "Italian way" as a positive paradigm for compliance with this kind of pilot judgement procedure.[12]

It seemed like the issue of prison overcrowding had been solved. Unfortunately for the Italian prisoners and former prisoners, the domestic case law in this area has shown a reluctant attitude and a restrictive approach that is undermining the real reach of the so-called Italian model (For an assessment of both compensatory and preventive remedies in light of the principle of effectiveness, see Ciuffoletti and Caputo, 2017; Caputo and Ciuffoletti, 2018).

The role of the domestic judge. Testing and comparing the civil law tradition faced with the "jurisprudential source"

Thanks to the introduction of Article 35 ter of the Italian penitentiary law and for the first time in a civil law country, the domestic legislator acknowledged and formally affirmed the value of precedents as a binding source of law. Article 35 ter of the Italian penitentiary law introduced in the Italian legal order the compensatory remedy required by the Strasbourg's decision in the *Torreggiani* case. The new Article contains a rule of interpretation for the assessment of the violation of Article 3 of the Convention, namely that it should be assessed "*as interpreted by the European Court of Human Rights* [italics added]". This rule seems capable of undermining the very basis of the "textualist faith" of the Italian judiciary. Still, it remains unclear how effective a legal provision referring to a jurisprudential source (See the concept of "jurisprudential law" in R Guastini, 2011: 325) can be in creating a shared normative ideology. In short, it remains unclear how many judges will follow the referred jurisprudential source.

Discussing the sources of law, Alf Ross wrote that, contrarily and counterintuitively in respect to our understanding of the traditional separation between common law and civil law tradition, European-continental judges are more inclined to follow the precedents than their colleagues across the channel. In his understanding, this is due to the peculiar interpretation of their role within the shared normative ideology. While on the shoulders of the Anglo-American judge lie not only the task, but also the challenge, to adapt the law to the changes in social reality, its continental homologous "leave to the legislation any attempt to reform [...]. And the results might be that, as against the official ideology, he will in fact be less inclined to depart from precedent".[13]

Adopting the perspective of the ECtHR case law on degrading and inhuman prison conditions and exploring both the dignity based and resocialization-oriented perspective, we will try to assess the new trends in the protection of prisoners' right and the Italian degree of implementation of this protective paradigm. In the light of a judgement by the Italian Corte di Cassazione, which dealt with the issue of cell space and dignity, we will offer an account of the resistance of the recent domestic case law, underlining some aspects that appear to be shaping the common normative ideology of the Italian Judiciary.

Overcrowding from a dignity and resocialization-oriented perspective

Part of the observations that follow has been expressed in a detailed essay commenting on the Italian Surveillance judiciary case law (see Ciuffoletti, 2017).

Since 2009, prison overcrowding has been on the agenda of the Court with two famous quasi-pilot judgement Polish cases,[14] immediately followed by Russian, Italian, Belgian, Bulgarian, Hungarian, Lithuanian, Croatian, Romanian cases.[15] This situation marked the transnational dimension of the phenomenon in the European continent (And worldwide, see Albrecht, 2012:45).[16] The Court has dealt with the issue by building a rich case law under Article 3 of the Convention.[17]

Prison overcrowding can be considered from a twofold perspective: it is inhuman treatment and therefore a violation of human dignity and it is one of the primary impediments to resocialization[18]. Both perspectives are highly meaningful in the Court's case law, but if traditionally the issue of overcrowding and prison conditions involved a strong use of the human dignity category, recently the issue gained relevance under the resocialization viewpoint.

Starting with *Dickson*,[19] the Court made express reference to the English term "rehabilitation" (or the French "*réinsertion*"[20]) in order to frame the possible objectives of a prison sentence. If traditionally, scholars have considered retribution, prevention (deterrence), protection of the public (incapacitation) and rehabilitation as legitimate prison objectives, more recently, "there has been a trend towards placing more emphasis on rehabilitation, as demonstrated notably by the Council of Europe's legal instruments[21]". This shift is based on a different understanding of the concept of rehabilitation.

The Court is building its own, autonomous concept which is no more grounded on the Anglo-American (negative) version of mere rehabilitation "as a mean of preventing recidivism[22]", but rather as a positive "idea of re-socialisation through the fostering of personal responsibility[23]". The Court further clarifies "the legitimate aim of a policy of progressive social reintegration of persons sentenced to imprisonment".[24] In its most recent case law on life sentences, the Court expanded the concept of social rehabilitation or resocialization, indissolubly connecting it with human dignity. Drawing from the German Federal Constitutional Court's statement that "the prison authorities have the duty to strive towards a life sentenced prisoner's rehabilitation and that rehabilitation was constitutionally required in any community that established human dignity as its centrepiece" (For an English translation of extracts of the judgement, see Kommers, 1997: 306–313.)[25], the Court established the same link between human dignity and rehabilitation, referring to:

> the Convention system, the very essence of which, as the Court has often stated, is respect for human dignity (see, inter alia, Pretty v. the United Kingdom, no. 2346/02, § 65, ECHR 2002-III; and V.C. v. Slovakia, no. 18968/07, § 105, ECHR 2011 (extracts)).[26]

Subsequently, in *Murray*, the Court specified that the deprivation of liberty can be compatible with human dignity only if it strives towards rehabilitation.[27] This perspective has contributed to the elaboration of a case law which defines rehabilitation as a positive obligation for member states. The Court underlined that there is no obligation to rehabilitate, but an obligation to give prisoners a real chance to rehabilitate themselves. This obligation is, therefore, an obligation of means, not of result[28]. Nevertheless, it is a positive obligation which implies a State effort to enable prisoners to make progress towards their rehabilitation.[29] When the possibility of progress is undermined by an impoverished prison regime, coupled with deleterious material conditions of detention[30], the State has failed its positive obligation towards rehabilitation and additional State action is required. As Snacken and van Zyl Smit put it:

> Indeed rehabilitation and social reintegration are only possible if prison regimes provide opportunities for prisoners, not only to better themselves in various ways, but also to participate in activities that limit the detrimental effects of the detention itself. This encompasses normalization of the prison regime and the full recognition and implementation of their fundamental rights.
>
> *Van Zyl Smit and Snacken 2009:83*

The scope of the positive obligation to provide the possibility of rehabilitation is further broadened when the Court affirms that the rehabilitation and reintegration penological paradigm "has become a mandatory factor that the member States need to take into account in designing their penal policies"[31]. Nonetheless, as noted in the joint concurring opinion to *Khoroshenko*, the Court failed to draw clearly and unequivocally the consequence from the *Vinter v. United Kingdom* judgement, by acknowledging the rehabilitative aim as the primary purpose of imprisonment[32]. At the same time, the opinion highlights the inconsistency of the Grand Chamber's statement on rehabilitation and reintegration as "mandatory factors" in designing penal policies and on "narrowing of the margin of appreciation left to the respondent State in the assessment of the permissible limits of the interference with private and family life in this sphere[33]", on the one hand, and the affirmation that "Contracting States enjoy a wide margin of appreciation in questions of penal policy[34]", on the other hand. In order to enhance the findings in *Vinter* and *Murray* and to give value to the concept of rehabilitation and social reintegration as defined in *Dickson*, an individualized sentence plan can be seen as the "cornerstone of a penal policy aimed at resocialising prisoners[35]". Thus, the individualized sentence plan "under which the prisoner's risk and needs in terms of health care, activities, work, exercise, education and contacts with the family and outside world should be assessed[36]" should be considered another dimension of the State obligation deriving from a rehabilitation-oriented perspective grounded on human dignity and Article 3 of the Convention.

The rehabilitation-oriented paradigm stemming from the Strasbourg case law is an architecture that rests on Article 3 and ultimately on human dignity, which lays at the very basis of the construction. From human dignity originates the autonomous concept of rehabilitation as an idea of resocialization through the fostering of personal responsibility, as well as the States' obligation to give prisoners a real chance to rehabilitate themselves. This positive obligation has three components: firstly, to take into account rehabilitation and social reintegration perspectives as mandatory factors in designing penal policies, secondly, to recognize the rehabilitative aim as the primary purpose of imprisonment, and thirdly, last but not the least, to propose an individualized sentence plan under which the prisoner's risk and needs in terms of health care, activities, work, exercise, education and contacts with the family and outside world should be assessed.

The rehabilitative paradigm needs to be tested in light of the Strasbourg case law on overcrowding and prison conditions. From the principles stated above, it seems clear that an international obligation exists for the State to consider resocialization as the primary purpose of imprisonment. Resocialization is seriously hindered by both an impoverished prison regime and detrimental material conditions of detention.

The question of the interplay between cell space and human rights should, then, be assessed and investigated upon, keeping the perspective of both human dignity and the rehabilitative paradigm in mind. The detrimental effect of overcrowding on rehabilitation and social reintegration has been variously assessed at the international level. Starting from the UNODC *Handbook on strategies to reduce overcrowding in prisons* (2010), a direct negative link has been drawn between overcrowding and social reintegration and rehabilitation (UNODC 2010, see, *inter alia*, p. 14)[37], as well as a connection between social reintegration and the reduction of reoffending, which is itself one of the main causes for the phenomenon of overcrowding (See, UNODC, 2012, p. 10)[38]. Promoting the effective social reintegration of all prisoners is then seen as a long-term strategy to reduce overcrowding.[39]

If we interpret cell space from a rehabilitation-oriented point of view, affirming the principle that "resocialization is the primary purpose of imprisonment of human beings[40]" and considering that, according to the aforementioned international documents, "prison overcrowding, with its physical, psychological and social consequences, is the first obstacle to the implementation of any resocialisation program[41]", the question of the personal living space available for prisoners stands as an essential prerequisite for resocialization.

This hermeneutic construction seems consistent with the consequences of *Vinter* and with the principle of evolutive interpretation[42]. Unfortunately, the Court relied on a different theoretical basis, when called to ensure the consistency of the "strong presumption" of violation of Article 3 whenever the minimum of 3 square of personal cell space is not guaranteed.[43] Without any reference to the issue of resocialization, the Grand Chamber in *Muršić* operates a relativization of the absolute nature of Article 3 of the Convention, by introducing the concept of cumulative effect of compensating factors[44] able to rebut the mentioned "strong presumption". As already noted[45], the use of the cumulative approach in *Muršić* is inconsistent and contradictory since it is used in two very different senses:

> on the one hand, the cumulative effect of "compensating factors" serves to attenuate the Article 3 obligations, in order to exonerate the respondent Government of any Convention liability (see paragraphs 137 and 138 of the judgment); on the other hand, the cumulative effect of "aggravating circumstances", such as poor material conditions and lack of out-of-cell activities, can be considered inhuman or degrading, even in the case of sufficient cell space.
>
> *see paragraph 140 of the judgment*[46]

The latter argument pursues the laudable goals of stressing the relative nature of the evaluation of the space factor and the necessity of its contextualization, as well as of rejecting the automatization of the assessment and its reduction to a numeric calculation of square metres. The risk of "trivialization of rights"[47] is particularly relevant within the context of an absolute right (From a philosophical perspective this discussion gains intensity starting from the debate between Gewirth and Levinson: Gewirth, 1981; Levinson, 1982; Gewirth, 1982. For an account of the absoluteness of Article 3, see N. Mavronicola, 2012: pp. 723–758.), such as Article 3.[48]

The former argument of the "cumulative effective of compensating factors" is able to "water down the absolute Article 3 standard, inviting the prison authorities to go down a slippery slope with no objective limits[49]", and providing the government with the possibility of rebutting the strong presumption of violation by showing the co-existence of compensating factors.[50]

Prison overcrowding is an essentially space-based phenomenon and the same space factor is intrinsically linked to detrimental consequences in terms of "cramped and unhygienic accommodation; constant lack of privacy; reduced out of cell activities, due to demand outstripping the staff and facilities available; overburdened healthcare services; increased tension and hence more violence between prisoners and between prisoners and staff[51]". In fact, as correctly put by the CPT, "the likelihood that a place of detention is very overcrowded but at the same time well ventilated, clean and equipped with a sufficient number of beds is extremely low[52]". These detrimental consequences follow automatically whenever the minimum standards are violated. Clearly there are no "natural" standards, only normative, interpretative and case law-made ones. The Grand Chamber in *Muršić* refused to use the CPT standards, distinguishing its role as an adjudicator and the CPT's preventive, standard-setting function[53] which aims at a supposedly higher degree of protection.[54] In our view, this distinction does not take into consideration the fact that overcrowding, as affirmed *supra*,[55] is a phenomenon that must be combated with precise judicial standards. These judicial standards should work as a minimum guarantee (*i.e.* below which the conditions of detention amount to inhuman and degrading treatment), not as a ceiling. The CPT has developed, by way of experience, minimum standards for personal living space (6 m^2 of living space for a single-occupancy cell and 4 m^2 of living space per prisoner in a multiple-occupancy cell, excluding a fully partitioned sanitary facility, with at least 2 m between the walls of the cell and at least 2.5 m between the floor and the ceiling of the cell) as well as higher, "desirable" standards.[56] These are instruments of great value and their practicality derives from the fact that CPT developed them in light of its long-lasting experience, based on the technical assessment of different situations within all the State members of the Council of Europe. These standards do not represent an abstract evaluation, rather they are rooted on a wide and deep practice and knowledge of the phenomenon of overcrowding. In sum, in cases of prison overcrowding, the minimum level of severity that an ill-treatment must attain to fall within the scope of Article 3 must be defined by the minimum standards of personal space available, in accordance with the CPT standards.

It is regrettable that the majority in *Muršić* decided to downgrade the 4 square metres minimum standard and to reduce it by a quarter and even affirmed its relativity and its rebuttable nature by virtue of the cumulative effect of compensating factors[57]. Neutral, basic conditions, such as "sufficient" freedom of movement outside the cell and "adequate" out-of-cell activities or a an "appropriate" detention facility cannot be assumed as positive compensating factors able to challenge a strong presumption of violation of Article 3. From a simple linguistic analysis, adjectives like "sufficient", "adequate" and "appropriate" are basic, objective terms, unable to operate a value commutation whenever an absolute right is concerned, all the more so when a "strong" presumption of violation of that absolute right is assumed. The factor of the short, occasional and minor periods of deprivation of personal living space is too vague a factor to rebut the strong presumption and, ultimately, waters down the absoluteness of Article 3, by allowing a dangerous time parameter which was not included in the CPT standards.[58]

Since a direct negative link can be established between prison overcrowding and resocialization, the lack of sufficient personal cell space should be considered an absolute impairment to the resocialization regime[59] and therefore as a violation of the State's positive obligation to offer prisoners a real chance of rehabilitate themselves. The question of minimum standards for personal cell space and whether the allocation of personal cell space below the minimum requirement creates a presumption or in itself leads to a violation of Article 3 should then be reconsidered in light of the resocialization paradigm under Article 3.

Muršić v. Croatia, the Italian version. On bed, space and human dignity

Unfortunately, the approach adopted by the Grand Chamber in the *Muršić v. Croatia* case pushed the Italian judiciary towards an overall relativization of the protection offered by the new compensatory remedy. It is suggestive to note that for a long time, since the knowledge of the referral to the Grand Chamber under Article 43 of the *Muršić v. Croatia* case,[60] the Italian Surveillance Judges claimed to be waiting for the solution of the "3 square meters dilemma" therefore adopting a sort of cautious and relativistic attitude[61] towards the Strasbourg case law and the findings in *Ananyev*,[62] *Sulejmanovic* and *Torreggiani*. As a result, the turning point, clearly showing the real attitude of the Italian Surveillance Judiciary, has been the Grand Chamber decision in *Muršić*. From this decision on, the Italian case law focused on a reductionist reading of *Muršić*, confirming Ross's thesis on the precedent-following attitude of the civil law judge.

The Grand Chamber's decision has been read[63] not only as a clear endorsement of a relativization of the minimum standard for multi-occupancy accommodation in prisons,[64] but also as an indication for the inclusion of the furniture in the calculation of the available surface area.[65] Until then indeed, the Italian Judiciary struggled with the identification of a clear rule for the calculation of the personal cell space and specifically of a rule on the inclusion of the space occupied by the bed. This was due to the simple reason that in many situations brought before the Surveillance Judges in Italy, the data provided by the Prison Administration contained a calculation of 3 square metres, including pieces of furniture and the beds for prisoners in multi-occupancy cell. Not including the space occupied by the beds in the calculations would have, therefore, led to the finding of a violation, making the bed the tiebreaker in many Article 35 ter applications.

In the mayhem deriving from the post-*Torreggiani* situation in Italy, many answers have been attempted at a local level and different solutions have been proposed by the domestic case law. The majority of the Surveillance Judges included the furniture and beds in the calculation and only a minority expressly excluded the space occupied by the beds.[66]

Interestingly enough, the Corte di Cassazione established the following principle: "to calculate the minimum space available in multi-occupancy cells, the surface of the cell must be understood as a space that can be used by the prisoner and is suitable for the movement, which means that the space allocated to the toilets and the area occupied by the fixed furniture, comprised the one occupied by the bed, must be deducted from the overall area".[67] The ground of the ruling took into account the then released decision of the Grand Chamber in *Muršić* and tried to blend the *ratio decidendi* and the *dicta* of the European Court, highlighting, on one hand, the fact that the Grand Chamber never employed the word "bed", and on the other hand, enhancing the "functional interpretation" of the "living space" criterion, by stressing the affirmation in *Muršić* that "What is important in this assessment is whether detainees had a possibility to move around within the cell normally".

This remarkable decision of the Italian Supreme Court reads *Muršić* in the light of *Ananyev*, integrating, at the domestic level, the steps required by the *Ananyev* test[68] and enhancing its third criterion ("the overall surface of the cell must be such as to allow the detainees to move freely between the furniture items"), that allows for the necessary individualization of the assessment. From this non-formalistic perspective, based on the principle of the effectiveness (*effet utile*) of the protection, *Sciuto* is absolutely correct. The Cassazione, in *Sciuto*, adopts a vision that contextualizes the personal cell space and the rights-oriented *ratio* behind and beyond the calculations and the cadastral assessment of the cell space. Transposed to the national context, valuing the space factor in this perspective means not so much working on abstract calculations, but getting to know the actual situation, the arrangement of the cell, the type of furniture, the existence of a separate or exposed bathroom, the type of beds, whether bunk or not, the distance between the bunk bed and the ceiling, etc. ....

Furthermore, *Ananyev*, which was cited by *Muršić*, expressly excludes bunk beds from the total area of the cell, so as to evaluate the criterion of the freedom of movement:

> Where the cell accommodated not so many detainees but was rather small in overall size, the Court noted that, deduction being made of the place occupied by bunk beds, a table, and a cubicle in which a lavatory pan was placed, the remaining floor space was hardly sufficient even to pace out the cell.[69]

This is a persuasive reading of the Strasbourg Court's case law, but it also appears to be the only one that allows the discussion about calculation, square metres, deduction or inclusion of the bed and furniture to be brought back to the legal level. The domestic case law in Italy has long been engaged on abstract calculation and consideration regarding the possibility of assessing a sufficient living space by moving tables in the bathroom, by using the beds as a base, as a space for activities of everyday life, for reading, for the expression of personality[70]. The Corte di Cassazione in *Sciuto* seemed to clear the discussion and to stabilize the case law (see also Conti, 2017).[71] Unfortunately the simultaneous release of the Grand Chamber decision in *Muršić* and its reductionist reading created a sort of cognitive dissonance[72] among the Italian Surveillance judges.[73]

Contested loyalty or the principle of subsidiarity

The question arises for Italian Surveillance judges whether to follow the Strasbourg case law or the domestic Cassazione case law on the issue of the calculation of the bed, supposing, in a reductionist reading of the Grand Chamber's judgement, that the two decisions go on opposite directions. Many Surveillance Judges are using *Muršić* in an attempt to set aside the principle expressed by the Italian Cassazione in *Sciuto*, claiming that their loyalty derives from the obligation to follow Strasbourg imposed, *expressis verbis*, by the legislator in the text of Article 35 ter.[74]

In the matter of overcrowding and inhuman and degrading prison conditions in violation of Article 3 of the Convention, it seems that the surveillance judiciary considers that the Grand Chamber's decision in *Muršić* is now consolidated European case law, and particularly its relativization of the absolute nature of Article 3 and its principle according to which: "calculation of the available surface cell area should include space occupied by furniture".

Nevertheless, if we consider the multilevel system of protection of rights in the domestic and international context, the solution to the loyalty dilemma seems exactly the opposite. The Strasbourg Court, in fact, represents the minimum standard of protection of rights that must be guaranteed by the member states of the Council of Europe, as affirmed by Article 53 of the Convention.[75] From this postulate derives the implicit, but permeating, principle of subsidiarity which informs the whole system of protection of human rights in the Council of Europe. In short, in deference to what has been called "complementary subsidiarity", the national and European guarantee systems for the protection of human rights must proceed hand in hand (see H. Petzold, 1993: 42–43), and:

> [...] the Court cannot disregard those legal and factual features which characterise the life of the society in the State which, as a Contracting Party, has to answer for the measure in dispute. In so doing it cannot assume the role of the competent national authorities, for it would thereby lose sight of the subsidiary nature of the international machinery of collective enforcement established by the Convention.[76]

From this principle, it appears that the Italian standard of protection of human rights regarding the deduction of the bed and fixed furniture from the available cell space should prevail. And this result can be justified with the principle of effectiveness (*effet utile*), which is expressed in the European case law itself and therefore with a direct reference to the case law of Strasbourg. The only condition to achieve this result is that the domestic judiciary be conscient of its active role (and not its subjection) within the system of "complementary subsidiarity".

This has been recently made clear by a subsequent judgement of the Corte di Cassazione[77] which reacts to the recalcitrant positions of the surveillance judiciary. Having acknowledged that *Muršić* "is not free from ambiguity", the Cassazione declares that, "with a choice inspired by the expansion of the prisoners' rights", its case law has conformed to the Grand Chamber's interpretation of individual minimum space available, with deference to the "specific novelty, at least from the formal point of view, constituted by the inclusion of the ECtHR's interpretation of Article 3 of the aforementioned Convention among the primary sources of law".

Hence, the Cassazione consolidated the approach, inspired by the ECtHR's case law, that expands and strengthens the protection of prisoners' rights in light of the principle of effectiveness (*effet utile*). Recently this trend has been reaffirmed by a judgement on the burden of proof in the procedure for compensatory remedy (Article 35 ter p.l.).[78] The Cassazione reiterates that, in order to safeguard the effectiveness of the remedy, the Italian judiciary needs to adopt "an interpretative technique which, due to the asymmetry of conditions between the prisoner and the administration regarding the access to information, verifies the possibility of softening the rigidity of the principle of the burden of proof, incumbent upon the plaintiff[79]". What is relevant is that the judge-rapporteur engages in a comprehensive analysis of the ECtHR's principles concerning the burden of proof in cases of violation of Article 3 in prison. From this case law emerges a trend towards reversing the burden of proof[80]:

> The point of interest – common to such decisions – is represented by the affirmation of the existence of a reasonable presumption of truthfulness of the statements made by the prisoner, in consideration of the need to balance the asymmetry deriving from the condition [of imprisonment]. The administration is the sole holder of that complex of information essential to appreciate the lawfulness of the treatment.[81]

Along with this principle, the Cassazione clearly affirms that, in situation of evidentiary uncertainty, the Surveillance Judge needs to employ *ex officio* inspection and verification powers on the actual conditions of detention.[82]

Conclusion

The "Alf Ross' paradox" seems only partly confirmed. If the domestic judge is inclined towards an acritical adherence to the European "jurisprudential source of law", such as the Grand Chamber's decision in *Muršić*, the same does not holds true when it comes to the domestic "jurisprudential source of law". Rather, it seems that the answer to the paradox can be found in the reluctance of the majority of the Surveillance Judiciary (albeit, sometimes, for cogent reasons of lack of resources) to embody and assume the human rights protective role assigned to them by the Constitutional Court and now, openly, by the legislator, which in fact calls for the pro-active protection of the rights of the persons held in the Italian prison system.

The evolving situation requires quick action from the judiciary, including the Italian Constitutional Court. The situation of the Italian prison overcrowding is again dramatic. In an open rebellion against the reassuring prospects offered by the Italian government and positively ratified by the Committee of the Ministers at the conclusion of the pilot judgement procedure in the *Torreggiani* execution procedure, prison overcrowding has started to increase again and constantly since the beginning of 2016.[83]

In this context, as said, Italy responded to the European stimulus mainly through the compensatory remedy, which can be seen in itself as a strategy of killing two birds with one stone (As brilliantly puts by Santoro, 2015: 15), *i.e.* answering to the lack of an effective remedy in prison situation and to the explosive prison overcrowding by finally implementing a fundamental right to an effective remedy, which would (in the mind of the Italian legislator) produce the virtuous effect of reducing overcrowding … Unfortunately for all the parties involved, the compensatory remedy has shown its limits (For an assessment of both compensatory and preventive remedies in light of the principle of effectiveness, see Ciuffoletti and Caputo, 2017; Caputo and Ciuffoletti, 2018).

In order to avoid the possible reopening of the Italian file, it is imperative that the common normative ideology of the Italian judiciary finally integrates what the Constitutional Court, the Corte di Cassazione and the European Court of Human Rights are requesting, *i.e.* that prisoners' rights are human rights in need of an effective judicial protection.

Notes

1 In the absence of any internationally agreed precise definition, overcrowding is generally defined with reference to the occupancy rate and the official capacity of prisons. Using this simple formula, overcrowding refers to the situation where the number of prisoners exceeds the official prison capacity. The rate of overcrowding is defined as that part of the occupancy rate above 100 per cent. However, contrary to Section 18.3 of the European Prison Rules there remain a number of member states who have not a definition of minimum space.

2 According to the CDPC, *White Paper on Prison Overcrowding* (30 June 2016), p.7: "It is important to clarify that in SPACE overcrowding is measured through an indicator of "prison density" which is obtained by calculating the ratio between the number of prisoners and the number of places available in prisons and is expressed as the number of prisoners per 100 available places. However the capacity of prisons is calculated in different ways in each country and SPACE statistic rely on the information provided by each country. Without a common standard established by the Council of Europe to calculate prison capacity in the same way across Europe, the figures included in SPACE are not strictly comparable".

3 *Sulejmanovic v. Italy*, application no. 22635/03.

4 *Torreggiani and Others v. Italy*, [GC], (Applications no. 43517/09, 46882/09, 55400/09 et al.)

5 It is eloquent that the ECtHR traditionally refers to this piece of legislation with the wording: "*loi no 354 de 1975 sur* ***l'administration pénitentiaire***" (emphasis added), (and rightly so), pointing out that this law relates more to the prison administration than to the prisoners' subjective position and rights.
6 *Torreggiani*, cit, § 97.
7 Ibidem.
8 *Torreggiani*, cit, § 97. See also §§ 20–22. It is worthy to note that the only judicial intervention granting a judicial redress was the decision of the Surveillance judge of Lecce, 9 June 2011, according to which: "it does not appear as a convincing reconstruction the fact that the Surveillance judge should limit himself/herself to ascertain the infringement of the detainee's right, assuring its protection directly, without prejudice to the possibility for the prisoner to obtain a compensation for damages suffered as a result of the established injury" and condemned the administration to pay "as a compensation for damages the total amount of 220.00 €" (See, *contra*, Surveillance Judge of Udine, 24 December 2011, Surveillance judge of Vercelli, 18 April 2012 and Corte di Cassazione, n. 4772/2013).
9 *Stella v. Italy*, application no. 49169 of 2009, 16 September 2014.
10 *Ivi*, §63. "*La Cour estime qu'elle ne dispose d'aucun élément qui lui permettrait de dire que le recours en question ne présente pas, en principe, de perspective de redressement approprié du grief tiré de la Convention. La Cour souligne toutefois que cette conclusion ne préjuge en rien, le cas échéant, d'un éventuel réexamen de la question de l'effectivité du recours en question, et notamment de la capacité des juridictions internes à établir une jurisprudence uniforme et compatible avec les exigences de la Convention (Korenjak c. Slovénie, no 463/03, § 73, 15 mai 2007, et Şefik Demir c. Turquie (déc.), no 51770/07, § 34, 16 octobre 2012), et de l'exécution effective de ses décisions. Elle conserve sa compétence de contrôle ultime pour tout grief présenté par des requérants qui, comme le veut le principe de subsidiarité, ont épuisé les voies de recours internes disponibles (Radoljub Marinković c. Serbie (déc.), no 5353/11, §§ 49-61, 29 janvier 2013).*"
11 Available at: https://search.coe.int/cm/Pages/result_details.aspx?ObjectID=09000016805c1a5b
12 Significantly, the Court has cited the Italian model of compliance in two subsequent pilot judgement procedures: *Neshkov and Others v. Bulgaria* (Application Nos. 36925/10, 21487/12, 72893/12, 73196/12, 77718/12 and 9717/13), and *Varga and Others v. Hungary* (Application Nos. 14097/12, 45135/12, 73712/12, 34001/13, 44055/13, and 64586/13).
13 A. Ross, *op.cit*, p. 90.
14 *Orchowski v. Poland*, no. 17885/04, § 154, 22 October 2009 and *Norbert Sikorski v. Poland*, no. 17599/05, § 161, 22 October 2009.
15 *Ananyev and Others v. Russia*, nos. 42525/07 and 60800/08, *Torreggiani*, cited, *Vasilescu v. Belgium*, no. 64682/12, *Neshkov and Others v. Bulgaria*, nos. 36925/10, 21487/12, 72893/12, 73196/12, 77718/12 and 9717/13, *Varga and Others v. Hungary*, nos. 14097/12,45135/12,73712/12,34001/13,44055/13and64586/13, *Varga and Others v. Hungary*, nos.14097/12,45135/12,73712/12,34001/13,44055/13and64586/13, *Muršić v. Croatia*, cited.
16 Interestingly enough, prison litigation and Courts' rulings around the world are assessed as an effective leverage for a decrease of prison population, p. 45: "Prison litigation has resulted in California being pressured into changing prison politics. In June 2007, the Delhi High Court ordered for example the Tihar authorities to release 600 prisoners charged with disturbing public peace, considered a relatively minor offence, to reduce overcrowding in the prison".
17 As assessed in the Partly dissenting opinion of Judge Paulo Pinto de Albuquerque, in *Mironovas and Others v. Lithuania*, nos. 40828/12, 29292/12, 69598/12, 40163/13, 66281/13, 70048/13 and 70065/13, §2.
18 As the UNODC Handbook on strategies to reduce prison overcrowding (2010) has indicated, prison overcrowding is "the root cause of a range of challenges and human rights violations in prison systems worldwide, threatening, at best, the social reintegration prospects, and at worst, the life of prisoners".

19 *Dickson v. United Kingdom* [GC], no. 44362/04.
20 The terminology is not neutral. The concept of 'rehabilitation' has been a source of controversy in the literature during the 80s (See, Allen, 1981, and, in general, Garland, 2001) and has been superseded by terms (and concepts) like social reintegration or resocialization, especially in the continental European penology. Some authors have understood this different terminology as embedded in a different normative ideology: the Anglo-American concept of rehabilitation as opposed to the continental (mainly German, but also Italian made) concept of resocialization or social reintegration (See the excellent, Lazarus, 2004, explaining this different approach and assessing why when the 'rehabilitative model' was facing a crisis of political legitimacy, German penologists, as well as legislators, policy makers and reformers shared a commitment to 'resocialization' as a substantive aim of imprisonment). More recently terms such as 'reintegration' have been used in order to potentiate the idea of a full legal position of the prisoner (see, Van Zyl Smit and Snacken, 2009). Finally the concept of (re)integration is used by Article 6 of the 2006 version of the European Prison Rules: "6 All detention shall be managed so as to facilitate the reintegration into free society of persons who have been deprived of their liberty". The Italian Constitution specifies that punishment shall aim to "re-educate" the person upon whom sentence is passed (see Article 27: "Punishment cannot consist in treatment contrary to human dignity and must aim at re-educating the condemned". See for references to case law of the Italian Constitutional Court, ECHR, *Vinter and others v. the United Kingdom* (§ 72). For an historical and theoretical account of the "re-educative" principle in the Italian constitutional history, see, Pugiotto, 2014.
21 *Dickson*, cited, §28.
22 Ibidem.
23 Ibidem.
24 *Boulois v. Luxembourg* [GC], no. 37575/04, § 83, with further references to *Mastromatteo v. Italy* [GC], no. 37703/97, § 72, 2002-VIII; *Maiorano and Others v. Italy*, no. 28634/06, § 108, 15 December 2009; and *Schemkamper v. France*, no. 75833/01, § 31, 18 October 2005.
25 *Lebenslange Freiheitsstrafe*, 21 June 1977, 45 BVerfGE 187 (Life Imprisonment case).
26 *Vinter v. U.K.*, [GC], nos. 66069/09, 130/10 and 3896/10, §113.
27 *Murray v. the Netherlands*, no. 10511/10, §101.
28 *Harakchiev and Tolumov v. Bulgaria*, nos. 15018/11 and 61199/12, §264.
29 *Murray*, cit, §104.
30 *Harakchiev*, cit, §266.
31 *Khoroshenko v. Russia*, [GC], no. 41418/04), § 121.
32 Ivi, Joint Concurring Opinion of Judges Pinto de Albuquerque and Turković, §§ 2–8.
33 *Khoroshenko*, cit, §§ 121 and 136.
34 Ivi, §132.
35 Ivi, Joint concurring opinion, cited, §10.
36 Ibidem. See also, *Murray*, cited, Partly Concurring Opinion of Judge Pinto de Albuquerque, §2 and *Tautkus v. Lithuania*, n. 29474/09, Dissenting Opinion of Judge Pinto de Albuquerque on the international obligation to provide an individual sentence plan.
37 "Thus, overcrowding is the root cause of a range of challenges and human rights violations in prison systems worldwide, threatening, at best, the social reintegration prospects, and at worst, the life of prisoners."
38 "Although prison overcrowding represents a complex challenge, prison populations are increasing and one of the main reasons for that increase is the large number of offenders who reoffend or breach the conditions of their probation order or conditional release. Although prison overcrowding is a complex problem, there is no doubt that it is due in part to the large number of repeat offenders who populate the prisons and for whom imprisonment has had little or no effect in terms of their desisting from crime. One key strategy in reducing the number of persons in prison is to provide effective rehabilitation programmes for prisoners and assist their social reintegration

upon release. Unfortunately, prison overcrowding itself affects the ability of prisons to offer meaningful rehabilitation programmes and tends to limit prisoners' access to existing programmes". See also, F. Lösel, "Counterblast: the prison overcrowding crisis and some constructive perspectives for crime policy", *Howard Journal of Criminal Justice*, vol. 46, No. 5 (2007), pp. 512–519.

39 See UNODC, *Introductory Handbook on the Prevention of Recidivism*, cited, part II, chapter F.

40 *Mironovas and Others v. Lithuania*, Partly dissenting opinion of Judge Paulo Pinto de Albuquerque, cited, §9.

41 Ibidem.

42 Given the growing attention to the phenomenon of overcrowding and the establishment of its connection with resocialization, as seen in the various aforementioned International instruments.

43 For an overview of the different approaches, see the Dissenting opinion of Judge Sicilianos in the Chamber judgement in *Muršić v. Croatia*, Application no. 7334/13.

44 *Muršić*, [GC], cited §§ 137 and 138.

45 P. Pinto de Albuquerque, Partly dissenting opinion, in *Muršić v. Croatia*, cited.

46 Ibidem.

47 See V. Zagrebelski, "Allargare l'area dei diritti fondamentali non obbliga a banalizzarli", in *Questione Giustizia*, 1/2015.

48 See the discussion in the Dissenting opinion of Judge Zagrebelski and Jočienė in the *Sulejmanovic* judgement: "*La tendance que cet arrêt semble mettre en lumière, à savoir que la Cour place son examen dans le cadre de ce qui est « souhaitable », devrait avoir pour effet d'accroître la protection contre les traitements prohibés par l'article 3. Or, même si cette tendance se nourrit de générosité, elle favorise en réalité une dérive dangereuse vers la relativisation de l'interdiction, puisque plus l'on abaisse le seuil « minimum de gravité», plus on est contraint de tenir compte des raisons et circonstances (ou bien de réduire à néant la satisfaction équitable).*"

49 P. Pinto de Albuquerque, Partly dissenting opinion, in *Muršić v. Croatia*, cited.

50 Ibidem.

51 CPT, *Living space per prisoner in prison establishments: CPT standards*, 15 December 2015, p. 2.

52 Ivi, p. 5.

53 *Muršić*, [GC], cited § 113.

54 This reasoning borrows from the already cited dissenting opinion in *Sulejmanovic*. The theoretical approach, though, appears to be more aptly articulated by the dissenters, who expressly refer to the difference between what is to be considered intolerable and what is to be assessed as desirable: "*L'article 3 prévoit une interdiction absolue de la torture et des traitements inhumains ou dégradants. Même le droit à la vie (article 2) n'est pas aussi absolu. Je crois que la raison de la nature absolue de l'interdiction des traitements prohibés par l'article 3 réside dans le fait que, dans la conscience et la sensibilité des Européens, de tels traitements apparaissent comme intolérables en soi, en toute occasion et dans toute situation. Or, entre ce que l'on considère dans le cadre de l'article 3 comme étant intolérable et ce que l'on peut considérer comme étant souhaitable, il y a, à mes yeux, la même différence que celle qui a cours entre le rôle de la Cour et les rôles du CPT, du Conseil de l'Europe, des organisations non gouvernementales et des Parlements nationaux.*"

55 See, note n. 3.

56 2 prisoners: at least 10 m^2 (6 m^2 + 4 m^2) of living space + sanitary annex; 3 prisoners: at least 14m^2 (6 m^2 + 8 m^2) of living space + sanitary annexe; 4 prisoners: at least 18 m^2 (6 m^2 + 12 m^2) of living space + sanitary annexe.

57 *Muršić*, [GC], cited §§ 137 and 138.

58 By ICRC standards, see the ICRC Water, Sanitation, Hygiene and Habitat in Prisons Supplementary Guidance, 2012, and, in the European context, by the revised 2006 EPR and by the Committee of Ministers and the CPT, See the Commentary to Rule 18 of the EPR, the CPT's "Living space per prisoner in prison establishments: CPT standards", adopted in December 2015, and the CM White Paper on prison overcrowding, 23 August 2016, § 37.

59 See P. Pinto de Albuquerque, Partly dissenting opinion, in *Muršić v. Croatia*, cited.
60 *Muršić*, cited On 10 June 2015, Mr Muršić requested that the case be referred to the Grand Chamber under Article 43 (referral to the Grand Chamber) and on 6 July 2015 the panel of the Grand Chamber accepted that request. The case was, then, decided on the 20th of October 2016.
61 The reductionist approach of the Italian judiciary on the compensatory remedy has been variously exposed by the literature, see, Della Bella, 2014; Malavasi, 2014; Santoro, op.cited; Giostra, 2015; Bortolato, 2014; Braccialini, op. cited; Masieri, 2015; Pugiotto, 2016a; Pugiotto, 2016b; Passione, op.cited; Della Bella, 2017, p. 318 ss.
62 *Ananyev and Others v. Russia*, n. 42525/07 and 60800/08.
63 For an example of this trends, see, *inter alia*, Surveillance judge of Pisa, decision 28 June 2017, n. 1952/2017 SIUS, and decision 22 September 2017, n. 4855/2016. Contra Surveillance judge of Venice, decision 27 June 2017, n. 2016/1961 SIUS.
64 See paragraphs 137 and 138 of the *Muršić v. Croatia*.
65 See §114: "Lastly, the Court finds it important to clarify the methodology for the calculation of the minimum personal space allocated to a detainee in multi-occupancy accommodation for its assessment under Article 3. The Court considers, drawing from the CPT's methodology on the matter, that the in-cell sanitary facility should not be counted in the overall surface area of the cell (see paragraph 51 above). On the other hand, calculation of the available surface area in the cell should include space occupied by furniture. What is important in this assessment is whether detainees had a possibility to move around within the cell normally (see, for instance, Ananyev and Others, cited above, §§ 147-148; and Vladimir Belyayev, cited above, § 34)".
66 For a comprehensive analysis of the Italian case law on this aspect, see Surveillance Judge of Venice, decision 27 June 2016, n. 2016/1961 SIUS: "Therefore we assist to a variegated case law scenario with very different kind of decisions: the ones which refers to the gross surface (trend that seemed to be ending after the *Torreggiani* case, but that has been resumed after the pronouncement of the Grand Chamber); the ones which exclude fixed furniture and beds (if bunk beds); the ones which does not exclude the beds, but excludes the wardrobes and the wall units (provided they are placed at a certain height); the ones which exclude only the beds occupied by roommates and closets, but computes the surface occupied by the claimant's bed, etc. Moreover, even the judgments of the Cassazione were wavering before the aforementioned judgment of the Grand Chamber [*i.e.*, *Muršić v. Croatia*, ed.]: some did not detract the space occupied by furniture (Cass. pen, sez.1, October 18, 2013, hearing 27 September 2013, n. 42901); others, on the contrary, detracted it (Cass. pen., section 1, No. 5728 of 5 February 2014, hearing 19 December 2013; Cass. pen., section 1, n. 5729 of 5 February 2014, hearing of 19 December 2013); others, even if in the form of an *obiter dictum*, affirmed that the space occupied by the bed cannot be included in the available space (Cass. pen., sez. 1, No. 8568 of February 26, 2015, October 29, 2014 hearing); in others the term "floor surface" is used cursorily" (Cass. pen, sez. 6, No. 23277 of 3 June 3 2016, hearing 1 June 2016; Cass. pen., sez. 6, n. 25423 of 17 June 2016, hearing of 14 June 2016; Cass. pen., sez. 6, n. 29721 of 13 July 2016, hearing of 28 July 2016).
67 Cass. pen., sez. I, 09/09/2016, *Sciuto*: "*per spazio minimo individuabile in cella collettiva va intesa la superficie della camera detentiva fruibile dal singolo detenuto ed idonea al movimento, il che comporta la necessità di detrarre dalla complessiva superficie non solo lo spazio destinato ai servizi igienici e quello occupato dagli arredi fissi, ma anche quello occupato dal letto*".
68 See *Ananyev*, cited: "It follows that, in deciding whether or not there has been a violation of Article 3 on account of the lack of personal space, the Court has to have regard to the following three elements: (a) each detainee must have an individual sleeping place in the cell; (b) each detainee must dispose of at least three square metres of floor space; and (c) the overall surface of the cell must be such as to allow the detainees to move freely between the furniture items. The absence of any of the above elements creates in itself a strong presumption that the conditions of detention amounted to degrading treatment and were in breach of Article 3".

69 *Ananyev*, cited, at §147.

70 See, *inter alia*, Surveillance judge of Florence, decision 8 September 2015, n. 2922/15 which suggested the possibility of moving temporarily the table in the toilet in order to have more space in the cell and affirmed that the bed constitutes a space available for the prisoner during the day. It is interesting to note that this decision, in line with a consolidated interpretative trend of the time, affirms that the *Sulejmanovic* and *Torreggiani* approach has been "undermined by the recent ECtHR's decision, 12 March 2015 (Mursic [sic] c/o Croazia)".

71 See, *inter alia*, Cass. pen., sez. 1, n. 13124/2016, Rv. 269514; Cass., sez. I, n. 3547/2016; Cass., sez. I, n. 2690/2016, *Soriano*; Cass., sez. I, n. 175/2017, *Gallo*; Cass., sez. I n. 147/2017, *Iannì*.

72 According to Festinger, 1957, cognitive dissonance is a mental discomfort experienced by a person who simultaneously holds two or more contradictory beliefs, ideas or values: "Suppose an individual believes something with his whole heart; suppose further that he has a commitment to this belief and he has taken irrevocable actions because of it; finally, suppose that he is presented with evidence, unequivocal and undeniable evidence, that his belief is wrong: what will happen? The individual will frequently emerge, not only unshaken, but even more convinced of the truth of his beliefs than ever before. Indeed, he may even show a new fervor for convincing and converting other people to his view."

73 The resulting hermeneutical "double standard" has been recently dealt with by a very recent decision of the "Sezioni Unite" of the Cassazione (NRG 37128/2019), which seems to consolidate the deduction of the "fixed furniture", such as "bunk beds". Since the decision has not been filed yet, we shall wait to read the ground and the reasoning of this *dictum*.

74 See, *inter alia*, Surveillance judge of Pisa, decision 28 June 2017, n. 1952/2017 SIUS, and decision 22 September 2017, n. 4855/2016. Contra Surveillance judge of Venice, decision 27 June 2017, n. 2016/1961 SIUS.

75 Article 53 ECHR: "Safeguard for existing human rights. Nothing in this Convention shall be construed as limiting or derogating from any of the human rights and fundamental freedoms which may be ensured under the laws of any High Contracting Party or under any other agreement to which it is a party".

76 Jurisconsult, *Interlaken Follow-Up. Principle of Subsidiarity*, 2010, p. 3.

77 Cass., sez I, n. 49793/2017.

78 Cass., sez. I, 23362/2018.

79 Ivi, p. 5.

80 Ivi, pp. 6–9. The judge-rapporteur, Raffaello Magi, cites, *inter alia*, *Torreggiani*, cited, §72, *Khoudoyorov v. Russia*, n. 6847/2002, §113; *Benediktov c. Russia*, n. 106/2002, §34, *Brânduşe v. Romania*, n. 6586/2003, §48, *Ananyev*, cited, §123; *Ogică c. Roumanie*, n. 24708/2003, §43; *Koureas et autres c. Grèce*, n. 30030/15, §77; *Creangă v. Romania*, n. 29226/03, §§88–89.

81 Ivi, p. 9.

82 Already in this sense, P. Pinto de Albuquerque, Partly dissenting opinion, in *Muršić v. Croatia*, cited, § 7. Significantly, this power has never been employed by the Surveillance Judiciary, except for the decision of the Surveillance judge of Bologna, 26 September 2014.

83 As overtly shown by the statistics provided by the Department of Prison Administration. See the historical series at the Ministry of Justice website, which reveals that since 2015 the prison population is constantly increasing. The last survey of March 31st 2018 reveals a number of prisoners currently held in the Italian prisons of 58.223, while the prison capacity is of 50.613. An assessment of these data can be found in Della Bella, 2017b. As affirmed by the author: "Statistics show that prison population has significantly decreased since 2010. In the last two years, though, it has started rising again. Now is the time to think about the short and long term effects of the

reforms following the judgment Torreggiani v. Italy, that has recognized a violation of ECHR Article 3. It seems to me that, regardless of the forthcoming reform of the penitentiary systems, there is no political will to implement changes that would be necessary to create sanctionary system in line with constitutional principles".

References

Cliquennois, G. and de Suremain, H. (2018). *Monitoring Penal Policy in Europe.* Abingdon: Routledge.

Cliquennois, G. and Snacken, S. (2018). European and United Nations monitoring of penal and prison policies as a source of an inverted panopticon? *Crime, Law and Social Change* 70, 1, 1–18.

8

"THE IMPACT OF THE EUROPEAN COURT OF HUMAN RIGHTS ON THE SUPERVISION OF CONDITIONS OF DETENTION BY THE FRENCH COURTS"

Isabelle Fouchard and Anne Simon

> The fact of being permanently five in a cell prevents any moment of privacy or even of calmness, not to mention the fact that it is unworthy, both physically and psychologically, to force a person to sleep on a mattress on the floor, which must be jumped over when one or other of the persons in the cell has to use the sanitary facilities during the night.
>
> CGLPL, report on the visit to the remand prison in Nice, 28 September through 6 October 2015.

The Council of Europe constitutes the forum in which the awareness of inhuman and degrading treatment caused by prison conditions arose. The successive judgements of the European Court in this field[1] have been a series of "external shocks" (see Artières and Lascoumes, 2004: 41) which have forced the national authorities to tackle this issue in order to find concrete solutions, in both political and legal terms. First of all, a dialogue was initiated between regional and national judges through the increasing integration of the requirements arising from the European Court case law into their domestic litigation. Given the limits of developments in litigation, this dialogue is now being conducted in a more direct fashion between the European Court and national legislators themselves. Legislators are indeed confronted with the need for a thorough reform of the mechanisms for regulating the prison population and the procedures intended to allow the release of prisoners whose conditions of detention would be contrary to human dignity.

As for France, all the national and international bodies responsible for supervising penal institutions have come to the alarming conclusion that imprisonment conditions have deteriorated considerably due to the combined effect of the dilapidated state of the prison facilities and prison overcrowding (see the list of relevant

DOI: 10.4324/9780429317033-11

documents referred to by the CGLPL *in* CGLPL, 2018: 4). The occupancy rates of penal institutions are well known,[2] and the average occupancy rate in remand prisons frequently exceeds 150%, resulting in physical conditions of detention which are likely to undermine the integrity of prisoners: overcrowding, insalubrity, poor air, light and privacy, proliferation of vermin – rats, cockroaches, bedbugs – and moulds and cell deterioration.[3] In recent years, this overcrowding condition has been further revealed by the Covid-19 crisis in which such situation could result in accelerated and uncontrolled transmission of the virus. Indeed, when detainees are forced to share their living area with three other persons in a ten-square-metre space, how can it be claimed that sanitary instructions and "protective measures" imposed elsewhere are respected, or that they are enforced?

Beyond the evident deterioration of the prison buildings, overcrowding raises concerns regarding human dignity and the compliance on the part of the public authorities with the prohibition of inhuman and degrading treatment. Furthermore, the Inspectorate of Prisons has recently released a thematic report on the impact of prison overcrowding on human rights (CGLPL, 2018). In this respect, the European Court, in the *Canali v. France* judgement, described the conditions of detention in the remand prison in Nancy as degrading treatment, considering "that the cumulative effect of overcrowding and poor hygiene conditions caused the applicant to feel desperate and inferior in a way that humiliated and demeaned them",[4] in breach of Article 3 of the European Convention. In addition, those conditions also amounted to violations of French law, according to which "the prison service shall guarantee all prisoners respect for their dignity and rights".[5] Also, with regard to remand prisoners who are mainly held in remand prisons, the Code of Criminal Procedure provides that "coercive measures (...) must be strictly limited to procedural requirements, commensurate with the degree of gravity of the alleged offence and must not undermine the dignity of the person".[6]

Considering the situation of distress that detainees may experience as a result of such conditions of imprisonment, the question arises as to what legal remedies are available to challenge them. Within the scope of the prohibition of inhuman and degrading treatment, a number of requirements under the European Convention on Human Rights apply. Indeed, the national legal systems of the Member States must first of all recognise the violations of rights that have occurred and provide redress, but at the same time they must also ensure that persons deprived of their liberty are able to seek preventive remedies to put an end to the conditions constituting a prohibited form of treatment.

The division of competences between the administrative and judicial orders, a specific feature of the French system, has resulted in a very uneven development of litigation in the field of imprisonment conditions that are contrary to human dignity and have led prisoners to "seek their judge" (Ferran, 2014) for a long time. Thanks to the advocacy of certain associations defending the rights of detainees (in particular International Prison Watch (IPW) French Section and A3D) and certain lawyers advocating for detainees' rights, awareness was raised of the limited means of remedies provided under French law in this area and, as a result, the ECtHR was finally able to rule on the issue. This led to a judgement against France at the beginning of 2020,[7] which brought about profound changes in litigation in this area and put pressure on the French legislators.

In the absence of this sudden leap forward taken by the European Court of Human Rights, the French authorities would have certainly continued to disregard the flaws in the judicial review mechanism available to prisoners (1) and would not have been able to take the initiative to finally bring about new prospects in this area (2).

Flaws in the judicial review of detention conditions that are unworthy of human dignity

The dualism of the French judicial system has resulted in a fragmentation of litigation relating to detention: the ordinary courts rule on pre-trial detention or criminal conviction but have long declined to address the physical conditions of detention from a rights-based perspective (1); the administrative courts, for their part, now deal with the conditions of detention following the combined impact of ECtHR case law and the appeals lodged by organisations defending the rights of detainees (2).

Restrictive review by ordinary courts

Refusal to consider the physical conditions in the enforcement of a sentence

Following the decision handed down by the Jurisdictional Court (Tribunal des conflits)[8] in the *Préfet de Guyane* case, the public service of the judiciary has partly been excluded from administrative litigation due to the separation of powers and the principle of independence of ordinary courts. However, for many years, ordinary courts have long considered that the conditions under which prison sentences are enforced do not fall within the jurisdiction of the courts but within the organisation of the public service and, consequently, within the jurisdiction of the administrative courts. This was despite the fact that the ordinary courts recognised that "the existence of poor accommodation conditions in detention facilities, caused by overcrowding in prisons of such a nature as to undermine the safeguarding of prisoners' dignity, cannot be called into question …".[9]

However, there is a clear understanding that "disputes relating to the nature and limits of a sentence imposed by an ordinary court and whose enforcement is pursued by the public prosecutor's office", as well as disputes relating to the enforcement of sentences, fall within the jurisdiction of the ordinary courts.[10] Undoubtedly, it would have been possible for the ordinary court to consider the conditions for the enforcement of the criminal punishment as being related to "the nature and limits of a sentence imposed by an ordinary court".

Furthermore, the ordinary courts are constitutionally recognised as the guardian of fundamental freedoms in accordance with Article 66 of the Constitution, which states: "No one shall be arbitrarily detained. The Judicial Authority, guardian of the freedom of the individual, shall ensure compliance with this principle in the conditions laid down by statute." The fact that the criminal sanctions imposed by the judiciary are, with full knowledge thereof, enforced under conditions detrimental to dignity and amount to inhuman and degrading treatment contrary to Article 3 of the European Convention on Human Rights, could it not have sufficed to claim that they were arbitrary?

The failure of the criminal law approach

Many lawyers and associations defending the rights of detainees, such as the International Prison Watch and A3D, have stepped up their efforts to try to bring the ordinary courts to address the physical conditions of detention. On the one hand, they have done so based on a number of penal criteria, with no success. For example, the offence of subjecting detainees to living conditions incompatible with human dignity under Article 225-14 of the Criminal Code was brought to bear in support of a complaint by a person held in the remand prison in Rouen, until the *Cour de Cassation* confirmed that this approach had failed.[11] Similarly, the charges brought against the Commissioner of Gard by detainees in the remand prison in Nîmes before the criminal court for "endangering the life of others" due to conditions of detention unworthy of human dignity did not succeed.[12] The failure to pursue this course of action is based in particular on the lack of classification of the offences alleged and on the principle that the State is not criminally responsible.

The limits of supervision during imprisonment

Furthermore, litigation initiatives have approached the issue from the standpoint of the unworthy nature of conditions of detention on the basis of applications for sentence adjustment or release (see Peltier 2020: 1075 s.). A first step was taken in 2009 when the Criminal Chamber overruled the judgement of a Sentence Enforcement Chamber which had dismissed an application for electronic surveillance of a detainee who claimed that the disability he suffered was incompatible with her/his imprisonment, without "looking into whether the actual conditions of detention would not subject her/him to distress or hardship exceeding the inevitable level of suffering inherent in detention".[13] Subsequently, in 2012, the same Criminal Chamber indirectly recognised that conditions of detention incompatible with human dignity could warrant a release, but only on the condition that "elements specific to the person concerned, sufficiently serious to endanger his physical or mental health",[14] were established. Such was not the case with that applicant, who had merely denounced the inhuman and degrading nature of the conditions of detention at the penal institution in Noumea as the basis for her/his request for release, without proving a risk of personal harm. In the same year, the Criminal Chamber confirmed its stance with regard to a person under investigation suffering from pneumopathy, who was considered unable to invoke conditions unworthy of human dignity as grounds for her/his request for release insofar as a medical expert had certified that her/his health conditions were compatible with continuation of her/his detention, as there was no proven causal link between her/his pathology and the conditions of detention, and an adequate medical follow-up provided while in detention.[15]

There is a constant body of case law, as evidenced at the end of 2019 by the Criminal Chamber of the *Cour de Cassation*, which held that "a potential violation of personal dignity resulting from the conditions of detention, although likely to entail the responsibility of the public authorities due to the poor functioning of the public service, cannot constitute a legal obstacle to the imposition and maintenance of pre-trial detention".[16] By doing so, the Criminal Chamber very clearly referred the consequences of the conditions of detention that are unworthy of human dignity to the administrative courts, before which appeals were much better dealt with.

The increasing supervision of the administrative courts

The case law of the ECtHR has led to far-reaching changes in administrative litigation concerning prisons since the 1990s, be it litigation regarding the abuse of power, state responsibility or the granting of interim measures. In all cases, the administrative courts consider, as a result of the ECtHR' decisions, that detainees continue enjoying their fundamental rights and freedoms subject solely to the limits set by the restrictions inherent in their detention.[17]

Broadening the scope of litigation on abuse of power

For many years, the French administrative courts have considered the decisions of the prison administration as "measures of internal order". From the 1990s onwards, the case law of the Council of State has changed significantly, particularly as a result of the ECtHR's case law on the right to an effective remedy recognised by Article 13 of the Convention.[18] Following the *Marie* judgement of 17 February 1995,[19] the Council of State established a criterion for determining which measures are subject to review: the courts had to take into account their nature and seriousness, particularly with regard to their practical impact on the detainee's situation. Subsequently, in 2007, the Council of State further broadened the scope of the litigation on abuse of power through reasoning by category of decisions,[20] which led the Council to automatically declare as admissible the appeals lodged against a growing number of types of decisions such as those relating to thorough body searches,[21] solitary confinement[22] or disciplinary sanctions.[23]

In accordance with Article 22 of the Prison Act of 24 November 2009, the Council of State ruled that "in view of the fact that detainees are entirely dependent on the prison administration, the determination of whether the conditions of detention are prejudicial to the dignity of the prisoner depends in particular on their vulnerability, which shall be assessed having regard to their age, health conditions, disabilities and personality, and also on the nature and duration of any breaches established and the reasons likely to justify such breaches having regard to the need to maintain security and good order in penal institutions and the prevention of recidivism".[24]

Broadening the scope of litigation on responsibility

The principle of unaccountability of the prison administration was abandoned at the beginning of the twentieth century in favour of a principle of responsibility in cases of "manifest and particularly serious misconduct".[25] This highly protective regime of the prison administration gradually became more lenient, giving way to the regime based on gross negligence, which, until the beginning of the 2000s, remained the basic regime concerning State responsibility for acts committed by the prison administration. However, it was the *Chabba* judgement rendered by the Council of State in 2003[26] in a case concerning the suicide of a prisoner, following a series of acts of gross negligence on the part of the prison administration, that brought about the abandonment of the gross negligence standard in prison matters in favour of the simple negligence approach, even if this change took place neither immediately nor in a linear fashion. Subsequently, the Council of State extended this shift to cases in which the State may be held responsible for the death of a prisoner caused by another prisoner.[27] Following the judgement against France in the *Lienhardt*[28] and *Yengo*[29] cases, the principles relating to the responsibility of the State for misconduct resulting from a failure to ensure conditions of detention compatible with human dignity have been further clarified. A finding of negligence leads the courts to order the French State to pay compensation for the harm sustained as a result of detention in conditions that are unworthy of human dignity. This is a compensation remedy available to persons who were held in conditions of detention incompatible with Article 3 of the Convention.[30] It is thus an *ex-post facto* remedy.

The development of emergency litigation

Unlike the first two types of administrative litigation, the proceedings for urgent applications provided for in the Code of Administrative Justice[31] have the advantage of providing a rapid jurisdictional response to the litigants, with the judge for urgent applications having to issue a decision within 48 hours. Thus, in theory, these remedies offer the possibility for detainees who are subjected to conditions of detention that are unworthy of human dignity to request the rapid termination of serious and manifestly unlawful infringements of their fundamental freedoms. These procedures, which are likely to offer a preventive remedy within the meaning of ECtHR case law, have therefore become increasingly important in prison litigation since 2010. This is especially the case of the proceedings for release from disciplinary sanctions ("*référé-liberté*")[32] which is a procedure whereby "in the event of an emergency situation and that a public person, or a private entity entrusted with the management of a public service, seriously and manifestly violates a fundamental freedom", the urgent applications judge may order "all measures necessary to safeguard the fundamental freedom". On this basis, the Council of State ruled that "[t]he Administration must take, within ten days (…) all appropriate measures likely to put an end as quickly as possible" to the violations of the dignity of detainees at the prison in Marseille due to, among other things, the proliferation of vermin.[33] Similar applications, based on the violation of prisoners' dignity due to overcrowding coupled with the dilapidated state of the premises, have been filed by the IPW French Section concerning the Ducos,[34] Nîmes[35] and Fresnes prisons, with limited success. Accordingly, the Council of State noted that the conditions of detention in the remand prison in Fresnes "are of such a nature as to undermine the privacy of detainees and to subject them to inhuman and degrading treatment"[36] but dismissed the request for the implementation of an emergency plan within the establishment in order to address the overcrowding or dilapidated state of the premises. Indeed, the Council of State considered firstly that the manifestly illegal nature of the violation is determined "by taking into account the resources available to the competent administrative authority and the measures (…) already taken" and, secondly, that it is not up to the urgent applications judge to take structural measures: "the intervention of the urgent applications judge in the conditions of particular urgency provided for in the aforementioned Article L. 521-2 is subject to the finding that the disputed situation allows the necessary safeguard measures to be taken in a useful manner and within a very short period of time".[37]

The lack of preventive remedy was sanctioned by the ECtHR

The limits of the interim relief proceedings, particularly those pointed out by the IWP French Section, which has been very active in this area (Ferran, 2019), were finally confirmed in 2020 by the ECtHR in the case of *JMB v. France*.[38] The Court stressed the limited scope of the powers of the urgent applications judge to issue interim relief orders, since that judge can only issue provisional measures and cannot order structural measures or major works to put an end to the consequences of prison overcrowding or measures aimed at reorganising the public service of justice. The Court also emphasised that, even when these relief measures are carried out, they do not always prove effective in redressing the violation of rights resulting from the overcrowding and dilapidated state of French penal institutions. It further enjoined the urgent applications judge to take general measures designed, on the one hand, to remedy the situation of prison overcrowding, in particular by "overhauling the method of calculating the capacity of penal institutions and improving compliance with such capacity" and, on the other hand, to establish "a preventive remedy enabling detainees, in an effective manner, coupled with compensation, to redress the situation of which they are victims and to ensure that an alleged violation does not continue."[39]

In a judgement of 19 October 2020, the Council of State, in response to this ECtHR judgement relied upon by the IPW French Section as evidence of a change in the Council of State's position, confirmed the limits of the powers of the urgent applications judge and considered that "it is only up to the legislator to draw the consequences of the ECtHR's judgment with regard to the absence of preventive measures to put an end to conditions unworthy of human dignity resulting from structural shortcomings".[40] The fact that the *Cour de Cassation* had in the meantime reversed its case law is undoubtedly related to this.

The prospects of judicial review

The judgement against France acted as a triggering factor. The ordinary courts seem to have fully grasped the consequences to be drawn from the unconventionality of the French system and in particular its shortcomings in terms of preventative remedies. The stance that the ordinary courts should not have to deal with the actual conditions in the institutions where prison sentences are enforced can no longer be upheld (1), and the legislator must now come up with new remedies whose implementation will make it possible to put an end to such inhuman and degrading treatment (2).

The impact of the J.M.B. v. France judgement on domestic case law

An important shift in the case law of the Criminal Chamber of the *Cour de Cassation* took place in July 2020.[41] The Chamber now refused to admit the lack of jurisdiction of the ordinary courts to deal with conditions of detention that were unworthy of human dignity,[42] while at the same time it accepted to review the constitutionality of the Code of Criminal Procedure, on the basis of which the lack of judicial intervention had been established. Indeed, a new interpretation of the provisions of the Code of Criminal Procedure seemed to be insufficient to guarantee the rights of the persons imprisoned.

The shift in the Criminal Chamber case law

Considering the evolution of the standards of observance of the dignity of detainees, the fact that an ordinary court, which guarantees individual liberties, can limit itself to merely supervising the principle of deprivation of liberty without regard to the conditions of its implementation, became hardly understandable. Beyond the illegality of such a position, the ordinary courts were depriving themselves of a decisive role in the litigation concerning the deprivation of liberty. However, this position was overturned in a judgement in which the Criminal Chamber accepted that "the ordinary courts have an obligation to guarantee a person held in conditions unworthy of human dignity a preventive and effective remedy enabling them to put an end to the continued violation of Article 3 of the Convention".[43] The liberty and custody judge may now grant requests for release provided that the alleged inhuman or degrading treatment is proven. The Court of Appeal of Noumea also immediately implemented this new approach by ordering the release with house arrest under electronic surveillance of an imprisoned person after finding that her/his conditions of detention amounted to a degrading treatment within the meaning of Article 3 of the European Convention.[44] Was this shift in approach sufficient to bring the French system into line with the requirements of the Convention? As a matter of law, the reversal was undoubtedly sufficient. However, it did not address the new issues arising from its widespread application and in particular the question of how to deal with the large volume of litigation arising from this new approach. This is probably the reason why the Criminal Chamber took advantage of this shift in case law to raise a priority question of constitutionality concerning not its own case law interpretation of the provisions of the Code of Criminal Procedure, but the texts themselves, though the major shift by the Plenary Session of the *Cour de Cassation* regarding the conventionality of the conditions for the exercise of the rights of defence in police custodial interrogation had undoubtedly also been prompted by its concomitance with an application filed with the Constitutional Council, which had already compelled the legislator to consider a more far-reaching reform.[45]

The unconstitutionality of Article 144-1 of the Code of Criminal Procedure

The Constitutional Council, having been called upon to intervene in the context of this shift in case law by way of a priority question on constitutionality, declared that Article 144-1 of the Code of Criminal Procedure was unconstitutional.[46] Moreover, it confirmed that the serious nature of the question raised should not be ruled out in view of the changes in case law embodied in the judgements of 8 July 2020.[47] According to the Constitutional Council, those provisions of the code on the basis of which the withdrawing position of the ordinary courts had been justified should be subject to review. However, it noted that the possibilities of releasing a person held in pre-trial detention are limited by the scenarios set out in Article 144-1, which only provides for cases in which detention may exceed "a reasonable length of time in respect of the seriousness of the charges brought against the person under judicial examination and of the complexity of the investigations necessary for the discovery of the truth" or in which the "detention is no longer justified by one of the causes listed in Article 144 of the same code, all of which are related to the requirements of safeguarding public order or the search for the perpetrators of offences". Moreover, Article 147-1 of the same code is only applicable to persons suffering from a particularly deteriorated health condition. Therefore, the conclusion to be drawn from these provisions of the Code of Criminal Procedure is that "no application brought before an ordinary court will enable the individual to ensure that the violations of her/his dignity resulting from the conditions of her/his pre-trial detention are brought to an end".[48]

The control of constitutionality is carried out with respect to several principles that are of constitutional status and that allow the Council to depart from the traditionally conventional basis of the prohibition of inhuman and degrading treatment. Thus, the prohibition is expressly linked to an established principle: that of "safeguarding the dignity of the human person against all forms of enslavement and degradation".[49] Reference is also made to the presumption of innocence in Article 9 of the Declaration of the Rights of Man and of the Citizen of 1789[50] and the guarantee of rights under Article 16, according to which "the right of the persons concerned to seek an effective remedy before a court of law shall not be substantially impaired". The Constitutional Council infers from this "that it falls within the remit of the judicial authorities as well as the administrative authorities to ensure that the deprivation of liberty of persons held in pre-trial detention is, at all times, implemented with respect for the dignity of the person", and that it "falls within the remit of the legislator to provide persons held in pre-trial detention with the possibility of bringing complaints before a court concerning conditions of detention that are contrary to the dignity of the human person, with a view to putting an end to such conditions".[51] Consequently, Article 144-1 failed to comply with constitutional requirements. Therefore, it is now up to the legislator to establish these new remedies.

New procedures to be devised

With the shift in the Criminal Chamber's case law, the decision of the Constitutional Council makes the legislators face up to their responsibilities. They must broaden the powers of ordinary courts to enable them to put an end to pre-trial detentions carried out in conditions that are unworthy of human dignity, also giving rise to reflections on the relevance of more far-reaching reforms.

Strengthened powers of ordinary courts

Observance of the separation of powers prohibits ordinary courts from granting injunctions against the prison administration, but they may release remand prisoners. From now on, ordinary courts, "as the custodians of individual liberty, (...) are responsible for ensuring that pre-trial detention is, at all times, enforced in conditions that preserve the dignity of persons and that the deprivation of liberty is carried out without inhuman and degrading treatment".[52] This natural jurisdiction is also the basis for the jurisdiction of the liberty and custody judge to review hospitalisation without consent[53] or police custodial interrogation beyond a specific period of time.[54] Moreover, this is a guarantee of the right to a court in matters of deprivation of liberty expressly provided for in Article 5 of the European Convention. Paradoxically, ordinary courts had not considered themselves authorised to grant requests for release on the grounds that inhuman and degrading treatment was prohibited. Yet from a legal standpoint, such a solution was justified. Inasmuch as international conventions enjoy higher authority than domestic legislation, the restrictive conditions laid down in Article 144-1 of the Code of Criminal Procedure could have been disregarded on the ground that their application entailed a violation of Article 3 of the European Convention. In contrast, from a political point of view, even if justified, such a decision would have given rise a number of issues relating to its application. Indeed, the condition of our penal institutions is such that the liberty and custody judges probably feared a sudden influx of applications, whereas the Chief Inspector of Prisons had provided, through his visit reports, valuable probative material. The repeal of Article 144-1 of the Code of Criminal Procedure has been delayed until 1 March 2021.[55] Legislators are therefore called upon to provide ordinary courts with legal tools enabling them to put an end to any inhuman and degrading treatment they may find.

Possible legal reforms

What legal reform would allow the courts to use conditions of detention that are unworthy of human dignity as grounds for release? The model of Article 147-1 appears repeatedly in the ruling of the Constitutional Council. Indeed, this text resulting from the Act of 15 August 2014[56] has enabled persons held in pre-trial detention to argue that their health conditions were incompatible with their conditions of imprisonment. Can this procedure be extended to cover all prisoners? A text based on a similar structure could be considered. Such a text would provide that "in all matters and throughout all stages of the procedure, the release of a person held in pre-trial detention may be ordered, either *ex officio* or at the request of the person concerned, where it is proven that the conditions in which he or she is imprisoned are contrary to human dignity".[57] Nonetheless, the general nature of such a text would undoubtedly have the effect feared by a court refusing to directly apply the requirements set out in Article 3 of the European Convention in litigation concerning release: a massive increase in the applications resulting from the overcrowded and dilapidated condition of our penal institutions. Furthermore, it is likely that the shift in the Criminal Chamber's case law was only possible because it was concurrent with the submission of a Priority Question on Constitutionality, which could only serve to send a reminder to the legislator, who is now forced to undertake an in-depth reform of the system of remedies available to persons in prison and also to design a more structural mechanism to regulate the prison population.

The expected structural reforms

Legislators are expected to provide a comprehensive response. Moreover, the *J.M.B. and Others v. France*[58] judgement handed down by the European Court has been described as a "quasi-pilot" judgement because, although it was not adopted under the procedure set out in Article 61 of the Rules of Court of the European Court, it does nonetheless address a systemic problem that will only be resolved by complex legislative measures. As a reminder, the ordinary court that will be required to put an end to any inhuman and degrading treatment is also "responsible for the overcrowding, mainly as a result of pre-trial detention and immediate court appearances".[59] Therefore, in order to limit the number of releases that would take place in fits and starts, with no hierarchical order of criteria in terms of the seriousness of the offences or the length of time remaining to be served in imprisonment, depending solely on the state of dilapidation of a particular facility, objective criteria are needed, allowing for systematic releases in certain situations that are specific to the prisoner and above certain occupancy thresholds. The issue must be approached in a cross-cutting manner and not restricted to pre-trial detention. Indeed, the question raised by the Criminal Chamber in July 2020 in this area will necessarily have implications for the situation of convicted persons who, very often, spend many months in remand prisons. In this regard, in the *Gülay Cetin v. Turkey* judgement, the European Court had held, through a joint application of Articles 3 and 14 of the European Convention on Human Rights, which respectively ban inhuman and degrading treatment and any form of discrimination in the "enjoyment of rights and freedoms", that it was not admissible that "one category of detainees may, without adequate justification, be treated less favourably than another".[60] Therefore, the solution provided for the benefit of remand prisoners should be considered justifying a new approach to the consideration of requests for sentence adjustments by the courts of enforcement. Considering the importance of the prohibition of inhuman and degrading treatment and its absolute nature, these courts should grant the requested adjustments if their refusal would lead to the continuation of imprisonment in conditions that are contrary to human dignity.

Furthermore, a strengthened power of ordinary courts would quickly be overtaken by failure to establish a mechanism to regulate occupancy rates in penal institutions. Such a mechanism would even appear to be essential in order to coordinate the requirement of an effective remedy available to the accused and the current condition of the criminal justice system. Such mechanisms are hardly unrealistic, as shown by the drastic decrease in the prison population at the time of the Covid-19 epidemic in the spring of 2020. The Order of 25 March 2020 provided in particular for the large-scale release of any person sentenced to less than five years' imprisonment with less than two months left to serve. [61] It also provided for the possibility of granting further reductions in sentences of up to two months to persons with good behaviour in detention. Within a few weeks of the entry into force of the scheme, the prison population was at a historically low level. Moreover, a number of studies have considered the introduction of mechanisms to regulate the prison population[62] or a *numerus clausus*, [63] without the legislator ever bringing these ideas to fruition. The Constitutional Council's ruling will clearly bring this issue to the forefront, and it must be completed before 1 March next year.[64] This is no doubt the price to pay for completing the process of aligning the French legal system with the requirements set by the European Court regarding the prohibition of inhuman and degrading treatment.

Notes

1 See in particular ECtHR [GC], 26 October 2000, *Kudla v. Poland*, App. No. 30210/96; ECtHR [GC], 15 July 2002, *Kalachnikov v. Russie*, App. No. 47095/99; ECtHR, 25 April 2013, *Canali v. France*, App. No. 40119/09; ECtHR, 8 January 2013, *Torreggiani and Others v. Italy*, App. No. 43517/09 and other cases; ECtHR, 16 September 2014, *Stella and Others v. Italy*, App. No. 49169/09 and more recently ECtHR, 30 January 2020, *J.M.B. and Others v. France*, App. n° 9671/15 et 31 others persons and ECtHR, *Barbotin v. France*, 19 November 2020, App. No. 25338/16.
2 http://www.justice.gouv.fr/art_pix/Mesure_incarceration_octobre_2020.pdf
3 CGLPL, 2018; see also CS, 19 Oct. 2020, No. 439372, D. 2020 p.2121, commentary by M.-C. de Montecler.
4 ECtHR, 25 April 2013, *Canali c. France*, App. n° 40119/09, §53 (unofficial translation).
5 Art. 22 Act No. 2009-1436 24 November 2009 concerning the prison service (unofficial translation).
6 Preliminary Art. III CCP. See, also Art. 716 CCP *in fine* (unofficial translation).
7 ECtHR, *J.M.B. and Others v. France*, App. n°9671/15 and other 31 persons, 30 January 2020.
8 Tribunal des conflits, 27 November 1952, *Préfet de Guyane*, Rec. p. 642; JCP G 1953, II, 7598, commentary by Vedel.
9 Criminal Chamber of the *Cour de Cassation* (Crim.Ch, C. Cass.), 20 January 2009, No. 08-82.807, Bull. crim. n°18.
10 Council of State, Sect., 4 November 1994, App. No. 157435, *Korber*, Rec. p. 489; JCP 1995, II, 22422, commentary by Lemaire. (Unofficial translation).
11 Crim.Ch, C. Cass., 20 January 2009, No. 08-82.807, Bull. crim. n° 18.
12 Tribunal correctionnel of Nîmes, 26 September 2017, No. 17/1965.
13 Crim.Ch, C. Cass., 25 November 2009, No. 09-82.971, Bull. crim. n° 197 (unofficial translation).
14 Crim.Ch, C. Cass., 29 February. 2012, No. 11-88.441, Bull.crim. n° 58 (unofficial translation).
15 Crim.Ch, C. Cass., 3 October 2012, No. 12-85.054, Bull.crim. n° 209.
16 Crim.Ch, C. Cass., 18 September 2019, n°19-83.950, pending publication, § 14. D. actu. 10 October 2019, commentary by W. Azoulay; AJ pénal 2019. 560, commentary by J. Frinchaboy; RSC 2019. 808, commentary by Y. Mayaud.
17 In particular, the prompting was given by ECtHR [GC], 26 October 2000, *Kudla v. Poland*, App. No. 30210/96; see also ECtHR, ref. 27 May 2005, *IPW, French Section*, No. 280866, Rec.
18 See in particular ECtHR, 27 April 1988, *Boyle and Rice v. the United Kingdom*, App. No. 9659/82 and 9658/82.
19 Council of State (hereinafter "CS"), Assembly on the Unification of Conflicting Case Law, 17 February 1995, *M. Pascal M.*, no. 97754, Rec. In this case, the Council of State declared itself competent to hear an eight-day conditional sentence to a punishment cell.
20 CS, *Boussouar*, *Payet* et *Planchenault*, 14 December 2007, no. 290730, no. 306432 and n° 290420.
21 CS, 12 March 2003, *Garde des Sceaux c. M. F.*, no. 237437, Rec. (body search decided as part of a disciplinary procedure); CS, 14 November 2008, *M. Philippe Mahmoud E. S.*, n° 315622, Rec. (body search during an external movement by order of a court).
22 CS, 17 December 2008, *IPW, French Section*, no. 293786, Rec.
23 CS, 21 May 2014, *Garde des sceaux, Minister of Justice v. Mme G.*, no. 359672, Rec.

24 CS, 6 December 2013, *M. T.*, no. 363290, Rec.
25 CS, 4 January 1918, *Mineur Zulémaro, Rec. CE*, p. 9 ; *D. 1920*, p. 1, commentary by Appleton; CS, 4 January 1918, *Duchesne, Rec. CS*, p. 10.
26 CS, 23 May 2003, *Chabba*, No. 244663, Lebon 240; *AJDA* 2004, p. 157 s., commentary by N. Albert; *Dr. Adm.* 2003, p. 44 s., commentary by M. Lombard; *JCP* A 2003, II, 1751, commentary by J. Moreau.
27 CS, 17 December 2008, *Epoux Zaouiya*, n° 292088. The legislator finally established a strict liability regime in case of "death of a detained person caused by violence committed within a penal institution by another detained person" (art. 44 of the 2009 Penitentiary Act) (unofficial translation).
28 ECtHR, *Lienhardt v. France*, No. 12139/10, 13 September 2011.
29 ECtHR, *Yengo v. France*, No. 50494/12, 21 May 2015.
30 In an ECtHR judgement, 19 November 2020, *Barbotin v. France*, No. 25338/16, the French State was held responsible for not providing an effective remedy with regard to the conditions of detention that were unworthy of human dignity, on account of the inadequacy of the compensation awarded.
31 Art. L521-1 à L521-4 and Art. R531-1 to R533-3 of the Code of Administrative Justice.
32 Art. L. 521-2 of the code of administrative justice. The appropriate interim measures ("*référé mesures-utiles*" and the interim measures for provision ("*référé-provision*") also play a useful role in the field of prison litigation.
33 CS (interim proceedings), 22 December 2012, IWP, *French Section*, No.364584, 364620, 364621, 364647, Rec.
34 Administrative Court (hereinafter "AC") of Fort-de-France (interim proceedings.), 17 October 2014, No.14000673.
35 CS (interim proceedings), 30 July 2015, *IWP, French Section et Nîmes Bar Association*, No. 392043, Rec.
36 CS (interim proceedings), 28 July 2017, *Section française de l'OIP*, n° 410677, Rec.
37 *Ibid.*
38 ECtHR, *J.M.B. and Others v. France*, App. No. 9671/15 et 31 other persons, 30 January 2020.
39 ECtHR, *J.M.B. and Others v. France*, App. No. 9671/15 et 31 other persons, 30 January 2020, § 316 (unofficial translation).
40 CS, 19 October 2020, No. 439372.
41 Crim.Ch, C. Cass., 8 July 2020, No. 20-81.739 and 20-82.472, (dismissal of appeal c/ CA Rennes, 13 February 2020), M. Soulard, Pres., M. Guéry, rapp., Mme Zientara-Logeay, Advocate General; SCP Spinozi and Sureau, Adv., AJ Pénal 2020 p.404, commentary by J. Frinchaboy; AJDA 2020 p.1383 commentary by J.-M. pastor; Gaz. Pal. 29 Sept. 2020, No. 387u3, p. 12 commentary by J.-P. Céré. Confirmed by: Crim. Ch, C. Cass., 25 November 2020, No. F 20-84.886 FS-P+B+I.
42 Falxa, 2020. The author refers to a "resounding judgment" and to the "milestone" that this decision has reached.
43 Crim.Ch, C. Cass., 8 July 2020, No. 20-81.739, cited above § 21.
44 Court of Appeals of Nouméa (Investigating Chamber), 8 Oct. 2020; https://www.lefigaro.fr/flash-actu/un-detenu-de-la-prison-de-noumea-remis-en-liberte-pour-conditions-de-detention-indignes-20201012.
45 *Cour de Cassation*, Plenary Session, 15 April 2011, No. 10-30.316, No. 10-17.049, No. 10-30.242 and No. 10-30.313: JurisData No. 2011-006078 ; Dr. pén. 2011, commentary. 72, A. Maron. The timeline was not exactly the same because in the case of police custodial interrogation, its unconstitutionality had been declared prior to the reversal of the case law. Nevertheless, it is conceivable that the Criminal Chamber would admit the reversal knowing that the Constitutional Council would soon have to make a decision, which would necessarily have to draw the consequences of such a reversal.
46 Judgement No. 2020-858/859 QPC of 2 October 2020; *Gaz. Pal.* 29 Sept. 2020, No. 387u3, p. 12 commentary by J.-P. Céré.

47 *Ibid*, Recital 11. According to the Constitutional Council, there should not be confusion between the cases of review of a case law interpretation that would itself be unconstitutional and the cases in which the legal provisions themselves are to be reviewed, even if the interpretation that has been made of them subsequently brings their application into conformity with the Constitution.
48 Judgement No. 2020-858/859 (Priority Question on Constitutionality) of 2 October 2020, recital 16.
49 The principle of dignity has been considered a constitutional principle since Judgement No. 94-343/344 DC of 27 July 1994 (bioethics laws).
50 The question conveyed concerned pre-trial detainees, but the scope of the decision may not be limited to them because of the absolute nature of the prohibition of inhuman and degrading treatment.
51 Judgement No. 2020-858/859 (Priority Question on Constitutionality) of 2 October 2020, Recital 14.
52 *Crim.Ch, C. Cass.*, 8 July 2020, No. 20-81.739, § 22. (Unofficial translation).
53 See in particular Art. L3211-12 Public Health Code.
54 Art. 706-88 al. 2 CCP.
55 Judgement No. 2020-858/859 (Priority Question on Constitutionality) of 2 October 2020, Recital 19.
56 Act No. 2014-896 of 15 August 2014 on sentencing according to individual requirements and strengthening the effectiveness of criminal sanctions.
57 The structure of the text is that of article 147-1 CCP.
58 ECtHR, 30 January 2020, *J.M.B. and Other v. France*, No. 9671/15.
59 E. Noël, « Tout bien pesé... », commentary on *Crim.Ch, C. Cass.*, 8 July 2020, No. 20-81.739, *AJ pénal* 2020, p. 377.
60 ECtHR, 5 March 2013, *Gülay Cetin v. Turkey*, App. No. 44084/10, § 132 (unofficial translation).
61 Art. 28 of Order No. 2020-303 of 25 March 2020 adapting the rules of criminal procedure pursuant to Act No. 2020-290 of 23 March 2020 as a matter of urgency to deal with the Covid-19 epidemic.
62 See the *CGLPL*'s above-mentioned report, Recommendation No. 10. Following the very effective measures taken in the Covid-19 epidemic, discussions are reportedly under way concerning the adoption of such a mechanism. See in particular the open letter of the Magistrates' Union to the Minister of Justice, "Numerus clausus, oui c'est possible, et c'est le moment", 30 April 2020.
63 See in particular *Report No. 2941 aimed at establishing a mechanism to prevent prison overcrowding, 12 November 2010.*
64 A circular on criminal policy dated 1 October 2020 mentions in particular the forthcoming publication of a circular on prison regulation (NOR: JUSD2025423C).

References

Artières, P. and Lascoumes, P. (ed.), *Gouverner, enfermer: la prison, un modèle indépassable?*, Paris, Presses de Sciences Po, 2004, p. 41.

CGLPL, *Les droits fondamentaux à l'épreuve de la surpopulation carcérale*, Paris, Dalloz, 2018, p. 4.

Falxa, J., « Indignité des conditions de détention et office du juge judiciaire: place aux droits fondamentaux », D. 2020, p. 1774.

Ferran, N., « La personne détenue encore à la recherche de son juge en France », *Déviance et Société*, vol. 38, n° 4, 2014, pp. 469–489.

Ferran, N., « Le revers du droit à un recours effectif », *in* I. Fouchard, and A. Simon (ed.), *Les revers des droits de l'homme en prison*, Paris, Mare and Martin, 2019, pp. 163–174.

Noël, E., « Tout bien pesé... », commentary on *Crim.Ch, C. Cass.*, 8 July 2020, No. 20–81.739, *AJ pénal* 2020, p. 377.

Peltier, V., « Prise en compte des conditions de détention contraires à l'article 3 de la Convention EDH pour décider de la remise en liberté d'un détenu provisoire », *La Semaine juridique*, sept. 2020, p. 1075 s.

Cases ECtHR

ECtHR, 30 January 2020, *J.M.B. and Others v. France*, App. n° 9671/15 et 31 others persons.

ECtHR, 30 January 2020, *J.M.B. and Others v. France*, App. n° 9671/15 and other 31 persons.

ECtHR, 19 November 2020, *Barbotin v. France*, App. No. 25338/16.

ECtHR, 21 May 2015, *Yengo v. France*, No. 50494/12.

ECtHR, 16 September 2014, *Stella and Others v. Italy*, App. No. 49169/09.

ECtHR, 25 April 2013, *Canali v. France*, App. No. 40119/09.

ECtHR, 8 January 2013, *Torreggiani and Others v. Italy*, App. No. 43517/09 and other cases.

ECtHR, 5 March 2013, *Gülay Cetin v. Turkey*, App. No. 44084/10.

ECtHR, 13 September 2011, *Lienhardt v. France*, No. 12139/10.

ECtHR, 27 May 2005, *IPW, French Section*, No. 280866, Rec.

ECtHR, 15 July 2002, *Kalachnikov v. Russie*, App. No. 47095/99.

ECtHR, 26 October 2000, *Kudla v. Poland*, App. No. 30210/96.

ECtHR, 27 April 1988, *Boyle and Rice v. The United Kingdom*, App. No. 9659/82 and 9658/82.

9

EUROPEAN MONITORING OF BELGIAN PRISON POLICY

Gaëtan Cliquennois and Olivia Nederlandt

Introduction

When addressing human rights, the sociological analysis of prisons pays exclusive attention to legal practices and the implementation of law, with little attention to the oversight exerted by international and European bodies, their regulations and their impact on national prison law and jurisprudence (Cliquennois and Snacken, 2018; Daems and Robert, 2017; O'Connell and Rogan, 2022; Snacken, 2011; van Zyl Smit and Snacken, 2009). The bulk of the research into prison sociology has thus concentrated on highlighting the paradoxes between the authoritarian and arbitrary structure of prisons and the principles of law, the effects of judicialisation on prison life and the prison population boom. Sociology scholars have also stated that litigation undertaken by prisoners and prisoner advocacy groups has refocused prison relations on the question of the exercise of rights (Crouch and Marquart, 1997; Jacobs, 1997) and the legitimacy of violence against inmates, particularly in terms of discipline, confinement and transfers (Belbot, 1997). They have also stressed the persistent ineffectiveness of law in prisons, perceived as both the result of the weakness of prison law (although it has been progressively – and quite considerably – reinforced) and of the anti-democratic nature of prisons, which are seen as patently incompatible with human rights. It has also been stressed that the legal complaints lodged by advocacy groups with a view to improving detention conditions (Jacobs, 1997) or promoting the exercise of human rights have had the adverse and unexpected effect of legitimising and encouraging a more extensive use of incarceration (Gottschalk, 2006; Schoenfeld, 2010) whilst not making a strong impact on prison conditions and provoking a backlash from the prison authorities in the form of so-called disciplinary governance (Cliquennois and Herzog-Evans, 2018).

Despite its interest, this sociological approach to prisons often neglects the monitoring of prisons and correctional facilities by international and regional

DOI: 10.4324/9780429317033-12

organisations (mainly the Council of Europe, hereafter 'CoE'), the content of the regulations they pass and the judgements they render. In particular, the judicial oversight exercised by the ECtHR has significantly increased over time, in particular due to the evolution of its structure and jurisdiction and its increased co-operation with the other organs of the CoE, including the Committee of Ministers, the Parliamentary Assembly and the Committee for the Prevention of Torture and Inhuman or Degrading Treatment or Punishment (hereafter the 'CPT') (Evans 2002; van Zyl Smit and Snacken, 2009).

This chapter will examine the influence of the legal supervision[1] and monitoring exercised by the Council of Europe and their bodies on the national prison services in Belgium. In order to examine the concrete impact of this legal supervision, we shall conduct a socio-legal analysis of the CoE Recommendations and CPT Reports, European Prison Rules and ECtHR rulings and their impact on domestic legislation and jurisprudence. The reactions of national governments to these European interventions remain relatively under-examined to date and deserve more scrutiny.[2] We currently know little about the nature of the reactions of the national governments concerned, the forces that determine them and their respective influence on the effectiveness of criticism and subsequent censure. Regarding the development of such European control over penal and prison policy, we question whether or not it has contributed to the shaping of prison policy and the creation of a monitoring system based on human rights, which has forced national prison administrations to develop political, legal and organisational responses.

To answer this question, we shall focus on Belgium as it has been the subject of pilot and quasi-pilot judgements and has resisted some of these judgements.[3] Therefore, this chapter intends to examine the influence of the legal supervision exercised by the Council of Europe and the ECtHR on the Belgian prison services. In order to study the concrete impact of this legal control, we shall rely on an innovative socio-legal analysis of the Council of Europe's Recommendations, Prison Rules and ECtHR rulings, action plans (submitted by Belgium to comply with pilot and quasi-pilot judgements) and the recent political plans adopted by the Belgian government and the Minister of Justice and shall examine their impacts on Belgian legislation and case-law. In doing this, we shall study the main prison-related issues covered by the ECtHR rulings and CPT recommendations, i.e. its demands on Belgium with regard to the creation of a minimum guaranteed service during prison strikes (i), to vulnerable prisoners exposed to the lack of healthcare and poor prison conditions, and especially mentally ill offenders (ii) and the non-existent or insufficient domestic legal remedies available to prisoners (iii).

Minimum guaranteed service during prison strikes

Since 2005, the CPT has several times called Belgium to create a minimum guaranteed service during prison strikes, pointing the bad effects of its absence on prison conditions.[4] However, the political commitment to set up a guaranteed service in prisons, repeated on several occasions by the Belgian Minister of Justice, did not materialise.[5]

In 2016, a strike of prison agents will last for two months. The CPT came during that time to visit Belgium and asked once again in the report following its visit Belgium to establish the guaranteed minimum service.[6] With no reaction of the Belgian government, on 13 July 2017, the CPT denounced the failure of the Belgian State to fulfil its commitments by issuing a public statement on Belgium – a highly exceptional procedure – which insisted on the persistent failure of the Belgian State to establish a minimum service to guarantee respect for the rights of detainees during prison strike.

Also in reaction to the long prison strike during the Spring of 2016, four lawyers turned to the ECtHR and filed around 50 applications. The first application submitted was that of Mr Clasens, for which the Court handed down a judgement on 28 May 2019 (*Clasens v. Belgium*, req. 26564/16). In this decision, the ECtHR held that the conditions of detention suffered by detainees in times of strike constitute degrading treatment within the meaning of ECHR Article 3. The ECtHR also found that despite the intervention of the interim relief judge, detainees have been deprived of an effective remedy. A second judgement was delivered by the ECtHR on the other applications: *Detry and al. v. Belgium*, of 4 June 2020 (req. 26565/16 and al.), confirming the findings of the *Clasens*'s Decision.

Under the pressure not only of these decisions and the CPT's recommendations – but also of national institutions and NGOs (Nederlandt and Descamps, 2020), Belgium complied with its CoE obligations by eventually passing the Act of 23 March 2019 that implements a guaranteed minimum service in the event of a strike by prison staff (the Act came into force on 1 July 2019). The prison officers' unions have challenged this Act in front of the Constitutional Court, but the Court dismissed their action (15 July 2021 Decision). Today, in practice, prison officers' unions use very short strikes in order to circumvent the Act.

Lack of healthcare in custody and poor conditions of detention

Other issues pointed out by the ECtHR (notably on the basis of CPT reports[7]) in its case-law are the lack of access to healthcare in custody in particular for mentally ill offenders, and the very poor prison conditions, mostly due to prison overcrowding. Such issues are commented on by the ECtHR with reference to ECHR Article 3 that prohibits in absolute terms torture or inhuman or degrading treatment or punishment, even in the most difficult circumstances.

Lack of healthcare

The lack of sufficient healthcare and medical staff in prisons and their psychiatric wings, and the lack of independence of these healthcare services from the prison authorities in terms of functioning and medical confidentiality, have been regularly denounced by the CPT regarding Belgium since at least 1993.[8] The CPT refers to the European Prison Rules ('EPR') of 2006 (revised in 2020),[9] which follow the CoE Recommendation 98(7) on healthcare in prison.[10] Recommendation 98(7), and Rule 40.1 and 40.2 of the EPR, precisely requires member states to establish prison medical services that are independent from the prison authorities, and which work in close collaboration with external medical and hospital facilities operating under the authority of the national Ministry of Health.

In Belgium, this principle was translated into the 2005 Prisons Act, under pressure from the CPT. While this Act grants prisoners the right to receive quality healthcare that meets the common standards set up by the Belgian health system in close collaboration with external health providers (Article 88). The Act also obliges the prison authorities to transfer prisoners whose state of health requires a medical examination that cannot be carried out in prison (Article 93) to an external hospital. But the medical provisions of the 005 Prisons Act are not yet come into force. In addition, the Belgian Ministry of Justice issued Circular 1800 on 7 June 2007 (not published), to implement its obligation under the EPR to set up prison psychiatric services closely connected to the external psychiatric services provided to the general population as part of the general, national, mental health network. Circular 1800 also delineates the division of tasks and responsibilities between the various types of prison healthcare workers and sets up an Ethics Committee to ensure the independence of newly recruited qualified prison healthcare workers (such as psychiatrists, co-ordinating psychologists, occupational therapists) from prison officers and managers.

Nevertheless, the CPT has stressed that this reform was largely insufficient and that prison healthcare should be placed under the authority of the federal public service of Health.[11] In reaction, the Belgium government has mandated a national expertise board to study the question of health in prison. In the conclusion of its report of 18 October 2017,[12] this board makes the same recommendation to put healthcare in prison within the competence of the federal public service of Health. The last government's agreement has announced its willingness to follow this recommendation as this evolution was foreseen, in consideration of the provisions of the 2005 Prisons Act organising healthcare in prison that are still not entered into force due to their expected change. In our opinion, this reason is insufficient: Acts are often changed and this uncertain situation entails a lack of protection of prisoners' rights.

Lastly, during the Covid pandemic, Belgium adopted regulations to release some prisoners, following the declaration of the CPT of 20 March 2020. However, it should be considered that Belgium has taken insufficient measures to protect the right of health of detainees, especially the detainees vulnerable to the Covid-illness (Nederlandt, 2021).

The problematic situation of mentally ill offenders in prison

In Belgium, offenders suffering from mental disorders at the moment of the decision on their guiltiness are not given a sentence, but an open-ended security measure called 'internement' if they meet certain conditions (including having committed an offence against the physical integrity of persons) provided in the 2014 *Internement Act* (entered into force in October 2016). This Act provides that special multidisciplinary courts have to decide how this internement measure will be implemented. They can decide that 'internees' will be held in specific places that they will be in the community with conditions to respect, or they can release them definitively when the conditions therefore are met. The places were internees can be held are limitatively enumerated in the *Internement Act*: places managed by the federal public service of Justice (the social defence sections within prisons[13] and the social defence establishment of Paifve), high-security forensic psychiatric centres managed both by the federal public service of Justice and the federal public service of Health (two exist so far, in Antwerp and Ghent), or in specialised psychiatric institutions that accept internees (which are only two, in Mons and Tournai). While the law prohibits[14] the detention of internees in psychiatric wings within prisons,[15] in practice, internees are still held in theses annexes while waiting for a place in one of these specific places provided for by the Act (Cartuyvels and Cliquennois, 2015).

The CPT, along with the CoE Commissioner for Human Rights, has already noted very significant issues related to the conditions of detention within these psychiatric wings: problems with the transfer of mentally ill prisoners to disciplinary blocks[16]; the complete lack of consultation of medical and psychiatric staff on mental ill offenders' admissions and discharges[17]; the continued shortage of prison healthcare staff,[18] the lack of activities (and especially during prison strikes) that result in nearly full time in cell[19] and human rights violations, the focus on security matters to the detrimental of healthcare (Cartuyvels, Champetier and Wyvekens, 2011; Cartuyvels and Cliquennois, 2015). In light of these breaches, the CPT has called for a complete revision of this system.[20]

In a number of recent rulings, the ECtHR has also condemned this system and reinforced the pressure on the Belgian government to radically reform it and to offer adequate facilities to mentally ill prisoners. The ECtHR has accused the Belgian prison authorities of failing to provide sufficient onsite medical supervision or to offer an alternative to prison for the mentally ill offenders.[21] For instance, in *Claes v. Belgium* (2013), the ECtHR held that Mr Claes's continued detention in a prison's psychiatric wing without adequate care constituted 'degrading treatment' in the breach of Article 3 and of Article 5.1 of the Convention.[22] The ECtHR also raised the more general question of the supervision of mentally ill offenders in need of treatment[23] when it denounced the inadequacy of prison psychiatric units for mentally ill prisoners, the shortages of medical and psychiatric staff in prisons, the lack of healthcare in prisons, prison overcrowding and the shortage of prison psychiatric facilities.[24] In a 2016 pilot judgement, namely the *W.D. case*,[25] the Court found that the breach of Article 3 and Article 5§1 of the ECHR was caused by a structural deficiency which is unique to the Belgian psychiatric detention system.[26] Under Article 46 (which pertains to the binding force and execution of European rulings) of the Convention, the Court, which endorsed the critics recently expressed by the CPT and the UN human rights Committee,[27] held that the State was requested to reform its psychiatric system in such a way as to comply with the Convention.[28] The Strasbourg Court has demanded the Belgian State takes action within two years to reduce the number of mentally ill offenders who are incarcerated in prison psychiatric wings without being given adequate medical treatment.[29] Recently, the ECtHR has again condemned Belgium (*Rooman v. Belgium*, 31 January 2019, req. 18052/11, and *Venken et al. v. Belgium*, 6 April 2021, req. 46130/14 et al.) in insisting on the same recurrent issues also noticed by the CPT[30] (on 1 December 2019, 537 mentally ill offenders with internee status were still being detained in prisons in inappropriate conditions[31]) and the inappropriateness of compulsory confinement to provide psychiatric and psychological treatment.[32]

In response to the ECtHR rulings and the CPT recommandations, the Belgian government launched a twofold reform with the adoption of the *Internement Act* and the Masterplan that plan to build new prisons and psychiatric institutions. In our opinion, these both reforms are insufficient to guarantee human rights protection to mental ill offenders who are still incarcerated for some of them.

On the one hand, the replacement of the 1964 Offenders and Recidivists Act by the *Internment Act* of 5 May 2014 (which came into force in October 2016) has certainly positive effects, as the *Internement Act* determines in which places an *internee* can be detained, organises a periodical judicial review of the deprivation of liberty, limits the conditions under which a released *internee* can be recalled in a closed institution and strengthens the procedural rights of internee.[33] On the other hand, the *Internment Act* limits the possibilities of internment, which results in more mentally ill offenders sentenced to prison, with little perspective of treatment.

The *Masterplan 'Detention and Internment in human conditions'* adopted in November 2016 in the context of execution of the above-cited leading judgements, aims, as far as possible, to gradually remove mentally ill offenders from the psychiatric wings within prisons (but not from the social defence sections within these prisons) and to provide them with appropriate care, by creating 860 new places by the year 2022.[34] But instead of looking for solutions in psychiatric health services and hospitals, the approach is security-oriented, as it is focused on the building of high-security forensic psychiatry centres, managed by both the federal public services of Justice and Health. Two centres have already been built (one opened in Ghent in 2015 with a capacity of 264 places, and another one in Antwerp in 2017, with a capacity of 182 places[35]). The Masterplan provides also for the creation of 620 other places, allocated as follows: 250 in a new forensic psychiatric centre in Wavre (Wallonia), 250 in a new forensic psychiatric centre in Paifve (which would replace the existing facility) and 120 in a new 'long-stay' high-security facility in Alost (Flanders). So far, these centres are not built yet. However, the Belgian Government created new defence social sections and even intends to turn old psychiatric wings into defence social sections by only renaming them (in Brussels and Namur) in order to artificially comply with the Belgian law. Therefore, the willingness of putting mentally ill offenders in appropriate facilities does not really exist up to now and even when such facilities will be built, they will be focused on security concerns rather than on healthcare.

Overall, academic analyses of the implementation of the CPT recommendations and the ECtHR judgements in several Belgian prisons and social welfare facilities, as well as the last report on the defence social establishment of Paifve of the Central Supervision Board of Prisons,[36] have shown that they are poorly being enforced, that prison mental health services remain almost entirely dependent on prison authorities (notably for medication delivery), and that ways have been found by prison officers to circumvent the division of tasks and responsibilities within psychiatric units in prisons (Cartuyvels and Cliquennois, 2015; Colette-Basecqz and Nederlandt, 2018).

Poor conditions of detention

The CoE and the Strasbourg Court have both required national states which are experiencing massive prison overcrowding to reform their penal policies through the development of alternative responses to incarceration.[37] In this regard, several states among which Belgium[38] have been condemned by the European Court due to their prison overcrowding and their very poor and inhumane conditions of detention. According to the Strasbourg Court, these States have committed large-scale systemic and structural violations of Article 3 of the European Convention.

In particular, the ECtHR unanimously held in its judgement in *Bamouhammad v. Belgium*[39] that there had been a breach of Article 3 of the Convention. This case concerned the poor conditions of detention of Mr Bamouhammad and the resulting decline of his mental health and the development of a so-called Ganser syndrome (or 'prison psychosis'). The ECHR held that Mr Bamouhammad's frequent transfers (43) between prisons and his repeated subjection to special security measures, together with the prison authorities' delay in providing him with therapy and the refusal to consider an alternative to custody, despite the decline in his state of health, had subjected him to distress of an intensity exceeding the inevitable level of suffering inherent to detention. The ECHR noted the reports by mental health professionals who, having direct knowledge of Mr Bamouhammad's detention, had repeatedly taken the view – since 2011 – that his imprisonment, which had been virtually continuous since 1984, no longer satisfied its legitimate objectives, and who had advocated alternative arrangements. The ECtHR stated that it had taken into account Mr Bamouhammad's frequent transfers, his solitary confinement under special security measures for a period of seven years and the decline in his mental health when assessing whether or not the threshold of seriousness under Article 3 of the Convention had been crossed. The ECHR noted that the need to monitor Mr Bamouhammad's psychological condition had been emphasised by all the medical reports, while his endless transfers had prevented such supervision. The level of seriousness required for treatment to be regarded as 'degrading', within the meaning of Article 3, had thus been exceeded.

Belgium has been also recently held in breach of Article 3 of the Convention by the ECHR in its quasi-pilot judgement in *Vasilescu v. Belgium*[40] for subjecting Mr Vasilescu to inhuman and degrading treatment and deplorable conditions during his imprisonment. This inmate claimed that prison overcrowding meant he had to sleep on a mattress on the floor of a shared cell in Merksplas prison which had no flush toilet or running water. He also claimed he had been denied medical treatment for his back condition and that he had been subjected to discrimination related to cell allocation and the possibility of parole. The ECtHR stressed that the problem of prison overcrowding exacerbated existing problems due to outdated and insanitary prison buildings, and that major structural reform was required. In this, it agreed with the CPT, which had concluded, on more than one occasion, that overcrowding was the cause of inhuman and degrading conditions in Belgian prisons, because it affected all the services and activities within the prisons and made it difficult to achieve minimum requirements in terms of hygienic and healthy conditions.[41] The fall in the quality of life for the prisoners affected by overcrowding was often enough to constitute a breach of Article 3. The ECtHR recommended that the Belgian government undertake the reforms necessary to guarantee conditions in its prisons compatible with Article 3 and also to ensure that prisoners were given access to effective legal remedies for their complaints about the conditions in which they were detained.

In response, the current Belgian government in its government agreement (30 September 2020) and the Minister of Justice in its political nota for justice (4 November 2020) vowed to tackle the issue of prison overcrowding, mostly by increasing prison capacity (again, as this capacity was already increased by the opening in 2013–2014 of three new prisons at Beveren, Leuze-en-Hainaut and Marche-en-Famenne which can house a total of 936 prisoners). According to the Belgian government, these new prisons meet current standards for detention: (i) the minimum space in an individual cell exceeds 4 m^2, (ii) cells are equipped with running water and flush toilets and (iii) partitions separate the toilets in shared cells from the rest of the cell. Other new prisons are due to open soon: Haren in 2022 (1,190 places), Dendermonde (444 places) and Antwerp (444 places). This extension of the prison estate can be questioned as building more prisons has never helped to reduce carceral inflation, as the CPT pointed out in its last report on Belgium.[42] Besides, from 1 December 2021, all prison sentences up to three years will be enforced into prison, while they are currently mainly executed under electronic surveillance (unless they accumulate to more than three years), which will lead to an increase of the carceral population.

In the last decades, measures have been taken to promote alternatives to imprisonment, including an expansion of the use of electronic tags for offenders serving sentences outside prison and improvements in the monitoring of sentencing and probation, which could lead to a decrease in re-offending and thus re-imprisonment. However, this potential decrease cannot be evaluated today, given the lack of available statistics and the difficulties to connect the different justices and prison databases. Of particular interest to the CPT is the Law of 28 January 2016,[43] which legalised the use of electronic tags for those on remand awaiting trial (previously they could only be used on convicted offenders). This has led to a significant increase in the number of tagged individuals (from 1,012 on 1 September 2010 to 1,151 on 1 September 2015[44]). Nevertheless, in practice, the creation of new alternative sentences has produced a net-widening effect (Aebi, Delgrande and Marguet, 2015; Phelps, 2013)[45] with the development of community measures running parallel to weakly changed prison rates rather than replacing prison sentences. Similarly, post-sentencing release measures are now competing with one another, with a similar net-widening effect: electronic monitoring has become, by far, the most prevalent release technique, thereby marginalising less constraining techniques such as parole.

The Belgian government has also accelerated the procedure for deporting foreign nationals convicted of offences in Belgium, which has led to the number of deportees doubling in less than a year.[46] The number of deportees has also increased following the Ministry of Justice's Circular 1817, which authorised the prison authorities to deport foreign nationals serving sentences of three years or less up to four months before their scheduled release dates (Breuls, De Ridder and Bellemans, 2017).

As a result, the Belgian government's statistics showed a 25% decrease in prison overcrowding by June 2013 and a further 8% fall by September 2015. Government statistics also show a fall in the overall prison population from 11,854 on 15 April 2014 to 11,074 on 2 February 2016. The Belgian government has announced its ambition to reduce the overall prison population to below 10,000, while continuing to increase capacity (which is no more than 8,820 prisoners) in order to reduce prison overcrowding that represents 124%.[47] However, the announced increase of the prison capacity which very often leads to the prison population growth is in contradiction with the objective of reducing the prison population. The prison population fluctuates now around the 10,500 inmates.[48] While the pandemic led to an historic quick decrease in this population: more than 10% decrease in a bit more than one month (10,906 – 12 March 2020, to 9,561 – 1 May 2020, lowest occupancy rate recorded during this period), no real lessons were learnt, and as soon as in June 2020, the population was back to its average occupancy rate (Nederlandt, 2021).

In this regard, the CPT has recently and repetitively denounced the very bad conditions of detention in its reports by pointing out persistent prison overcrowding, the lack of activities, insufficient prisoners' contact with their families and insufficient health and therapeutic care, and hygiene conditions in the Belgian prisons visited by its delegation.[49]

Eventually, the Belgian government and minister of Justice have the willingness to start an important reform of the penal matter: a new penal code and a new criminal procedure code are in preparation. These reforms are aimed at, among other things, reducing the use of the prison sentence and the pre-trial detention. But such reforms will take time and, so far, remain at the project stage.

Inexistent or insufficient domestic legal remedies available to prisoners

The development of effective domestic remedies is also required by the European Court[50] in order to ensure respect for human rights and in particular Article 3 of the Convention, although a margin of appreciation is granted to national states to choose and implement them. In this regard, several issues are similarly raised by the Strasbourg Court for Belgium.

The ECtHR has criticised Belgium for failing to give its courts the powers required for them to conduct effective judicial reviews of sentencing and prison conditions. In its judgement of *Van Meroye v. Belgium* (9 January 2014, req. no 330/09), the ECtHR noted the position taken by the President of the Court of Turnhout that 'the power of control exerted by a judge to whom an application has been made by a prisoner for interim measures over his current conditions of detention is completely marginal and the judge could only intervene when support and healthcare were totally absent'. The ECtHR criticised the Belgian prison authorities for transferring prisoners who had launched court proceedings about their conditions of imprisonment to other prisons outside the court's jurisdiction to prevent the court from conducting an effective judicial review. It held that 'the search for an appropriate place of detention cannot be reduced to a *prima facie* review without any consideration of the reality of the situation' and it had found no examples of any effective judicial reviews being completed. This led the ECtHR to conclude that 'under such conditions, we see no means available to the applicant to obtain efficient interim measures and reparation from the judge, and that the applicant's application was therefore ineffective'.[51]

In this respect, in the Vasilescu, the *Bamouhammad* and the *Clasens v. Belgium* cases[52] evoked above, the ECtHR held unanimously that there had been a breach of Articles 13 of the Convention. The ECtHR noted that the repeated prison transfers, to which the applicant had deliberately been submitted by the prison authorities, meant that the protection available from the interim measures judge had not proved effective, because the transfers out of the court's jurisdiction meant the proceedings became without object. The ECtHR concluded that Mr Bamouhammad had not been given the opportunity to obtain an effective remedy to his complaints under Article 3. There had thus also been a breach of Article 13. The absence of effective and efficient (in due time) domestic remedies leading to the violation of Article 5§4 in conjunction with Article 13 was also more recently denounced and condemned by the ECHR in the *W.D.* case.[53] Recently, the ECtHR has not condemned Belgium for the violation of Article 13 combined with Article 3 ECHR since it considers that the internee had the possibility to seize the interim judge in order to be transferred in a forensic centre. The Strasbourg Court had in particular taken into account the positive evolution of the jurisprudence of the interim judge and the increased number of places in the forensic centres (*Venken v. Belgium*, 6 April 2021, req 46130/14, §213–215) – a decision which is critical given the high difficulties in practice for vulnerable persons deprived of liberty and of competent lawyers to seize the interim judge.

The ECtHR noted the introduction under Belgian law of a specific right of prisoners to lodge complaints with the Complaints Board attached to the Supervisory Board of each prison. This complaint procedure is effective from 1 October 2020, and organised within the scope of the monitoring prison bodies: the federal 'Conseil central de surveillance pénitentiaire' (Central Supervisory Board) and the local (attached to one of two prisons) 'commissions de surveillance' (Local Supervisory Board). This closed relation between the monitoring bodies and the judicial complaint bodies has been criticised by some academics and NGOs, as threatening the independence and impartiality of both organs (Nederlandt and Teper, 2021). So far, it is too soon to evaluate whether such bodies will be considered 'effective remedies' by the ECtHR.

The Belgian *Conseil d'Etat* ('Council of State', the highest administrative court) had an important case-law on prisons but limited to disciplinary sanctions and, in certain circumstances, to security regime (Eechaudt, 2014). Since the entering into force of the complaints board, its intervention in these matters is now the remit of the civil supreme court.

The complaints in front of the civil courts (in order to obtain reparation for damages) remain very few, as the procedures are too long for detainees and as criminal lawyers are not experts on the civil law procedure, with two remarkable exceptions. A decision of 4 October 2013 was made by the civil tribunal of Brussels that ruled that the Belgian state was responsible for the non-entry into force of the complaint procedure and should therefore pay a damage to the detainee who lodged the complaint (no appeal has been made). More recently, the French-Speaking Bar Association seized three civil tribunals concerning prison overcrowding in three prisons (respectively located in Brussels-Liège-Mons). The Civil Tribunal of Brussels held that the Belgian State was responsible for such an issue and ordered it to reduce the number of prisoners to the maximum authorised capacity, on pain of penalty payment (Decision of 9 January 2019 – the procedure is now in appeal); while the Civil Tribunal of Liège and Mons have first designated an expert to assess the situation (the procedure is ongoing).

Besides, a small group of French-speaking lawyers, for the majority linked with the Belgian section of the 'Observatoire International des Prisons', are actively suing the Belgian State in front of the interim judge. They have notably obtained significant decisions in which interim judges have forced the Belgian State to grant to so-called radicalised detainees the same rights as the detainees in security regime, to transfer a detainee to its hearing refused by the Belgian State, to guarantee a minimum service during prison strikes (Nederlandt, 2021).

Nonetheless, more generally, prison litigation relies on few and poor activist lawyers, as Belgian human rights groups have low financial and human resources. This lack of resources hinders prison litigation as it has been observed that this factor is a condition for the effectiveness of complaints by activist groups (Epp, 1998). The Belgian branch of the *Observatoire International des Prisons (OIP)*,[54] the Belgian branch[55] of the GENEPI[56] or the collectivity fighting against prison (*LA CLAC*)[57] are, for instance, too underfunded to have permanent paid employees. While the 'prison committee' of the French-speaking section of the Belgian Human Rights League[58] is similarly and mainly composed of experts working on a voluntary basis, they are more active in litigation as they are, with lawyers specialised in criminal letters, initiating a lot of procedures in front of the Constitutional Court with some judicial results that tend to improve the protection of detainees' rights (Nederlandt, 2021). While the Dutch-speaking section of the Human Rights League[59] has more resources and includes six permanent members, its activities nevertheless appear to be limited in its capacity of prison litigant.

Interestingly, we should stress that national judicial bodies start to take into account the prison litigation and monitoring efforts made by NGOs and monitoring prison bodies. Some reports of the Belgian branch of the OIP, alongside with the reports of the prison monitoring bodies, were indeed taken into account in the above evoked civil tribunal decisions (Nederlandt, 2021).

Nevertheless, few judicial opportunities remain for prisoners to challenge the decisions made by the Belgian prison authorities, given the complexity of the Belgian prison law. In this regard, it remains hard for prisoners *to know* what rights they are entitled. Prisoners also face the lack of effective domestic legal remedies and legal aid available, the unequal power relationship and in particular the fear of retaliation from prison authorities in case of complaint lodged by them: prisoners who complaint face the risk of being transferred to another prison, far from their family, and loosing the advantages they have gained in prison (such as a job), or of receiving a negative assessment by the prison governor regarding their prison leave or parole (Cliquennois and de Suremain, 2018; Nederlandt, 2019).

Conclusion

In the course of their work, the CoE bodies have raised issues concerning the Belgian prison system to cover the provision of physical and psychiatric healthcare and opportunities for prisoners to obtain domestic legal remedies for their complaints. Such European-level oversight is increasingly tight, particularly regarding the care of mentally ill prisoners.

At the same time, we have also emphasised that the ECHR judgements against Belgium have had various, but overall rather limited effects in issues such as: failing to provide adequate healthcare and adequate living conditions for prisoners; poor prison conditions and insufficient prisoner psychiatric care. The ECtHR decisions have also contributed to the enactment of new policies which endeavour – albeit by unfortunately reducing access to fair trials and respect for prisoners' agency – to release more and more offenders early (Snacken, Beyens and Beernaert 2010) with the end goal of reducing overcrowding, the root cause of such problems.

However, Belgium has only partially complied with the ECHR's jurisprudence. Prison authorities are not as dominant (because of powerful prison unions and such European monitoring) in prisons, including into their psychiatric wing and their social defence annexes. Processes have replaced content, limiting the impact of community sentences and measures as sound solutions to prison overcrowding.

In addition, the prison litigation activities have only had a limited impact on the issues at stake. In order to make a significant dent into prison overcrowding and to improve prison conditions along with prisoners' rights, systemic and institutional changes are now required as opposed to purely mechanical 'bath-tub' measures such as the development of front door and back door community sentences and measures, which unfortunately tend to have a net-widening impact. However, the next reform of penal law and criminal procedure might be interesting opportunities in the future as only a global change in penal matters could solve the persistent issue of prison overcrowding.

In this regard, it is doubtful that, without such changes, litigation will suffice to have both significant and a long-term impact on prisoners' living conditions and on prison overcrowding.

Firstly, credible and efficient probation measures require institutions and practitioners to truly have a re-entry compass, and for institutions to be embedded in the community and collaborative network. Additionally, prison services should be subjected to a significantly higher level of scrutiny and control by independent academic, court, media and civil society in terms of performance, regulation and ethics. Such a control is made harder since the prison administration does no longer publish its annual report since 2017, nor its statistics on prison population. Additionally, even though a recommendation made by the CoE encouraged the CoE Member States to make statistics on conditional release[60], criminologists already underlined that criminal and prison statistics are lacking. As Kristel Beyens put it: 'There is a lack of reliable data, there is a lack of recent data, there is a lack of integrated data, there is a lack in transparency as to the production of the data, there is a lack of context to the data, and the sparse data that exist are only gradually made available or can only be acquired after personally asking the producer. Conclusion: the unsuspecting outsider looking for reliable statistics about the execution of sentences will end up disillusioned and empty-handed' (Beyens, 2006; see also Daems, Maes and Robert, 2013).

In addition, by operating largely in silo, prison services have been allowed – one might even say enabled – to maintain various forms of resistance to the implementation of reforms and have found new ways of disciplining prisoners and regaining some of the discretionary powers they have lost due to the regulation by legal norms and successful litigation. Nevertheless, while effective legal remedies cannot in themselves totally solve structural and penal issues, they can delay and contain the impact of long-term negative trends, as vividly shown by the European legal framework (Snacken and Dumortier, 2012) that has to be taken into account in the analysis of domestic prison policies.

Notes

1 The legal supervision refers to the monitoring of national prison policies provided for by the CoE bodies and the European Court of Human Rights on the basis of the European Convention on Human Rights.

2 Cliquennois, G. and Suremain, H. (2018) *Monitoring Penal Policies in Europe*. Abingdon: Routledge; Van Zyl Smit, D. (2010) 'Regulation of prison conditions', *Crime and Justice*, 39(1), pp. 503–563.

3 ECtHR, 6 December 2016, *W.D. c. Belgique*, no 73548/13; ECtHR, 25 November 2014, *Vasilescu v. Belgium*, n° 64682/12; ECtHR, 17 November 2015, *Bamouhammad v. Belgium*, no. 47687/13.

4 CPT report on its visit to Belgium from 18 to 27 April 2005, Strasbourg, 20 April 2006, p. 50, § 117, p. 64, § 160 et p. 76; CPT report on its visit to Belgium 28 September to 7 October 2009, Strasbourg, 23 July 2010, p. 12, § 7, pp. 36–37, §§ 81–82, p. 40, § 87 et p. 94; CPT report on its visit to Belgium from 23 to 27 April 2012, Strasbourg, 13 December 2012, p. 8, § 7, pp. 30–33, §§ 78–86, et p. 44; CPT report on its visit to Belgium from 24 September to 4 October 2013, Strasbourg, 31 March 2016, p. 6, p. 11, § 5, pp. 25–27, §§ 41–51; CPT report on its visit to Belgium from 7 to 9 May 2016, Strasbourg, 18 November 2016, p. 14, § 25.

5 A new federal government takes office in Belgium at the end of 2014 and commits to legislating for a guaranteed service in prisons. Shortly afterwards, from 7 to 19 December 2014, a strike took place in a Walloon prison. In the Spring of 2016, a two month and harsh strike took place in all French-speaking prisons. On these both occasions, a few French-speaking lawyers, experts on prison matters, decided to lodge a complaint with the interim relief judge as a matter of urgency. The judge found a violation of ECHR Article 3 and ordered the Belgian State to organise and implement a minimum service in prison. Such decisions, which were confirmed by appeal courts, did not improve the conditions of detention suffered by the detainees since the beginning of the strike as a minimum service was still not provided.

6 CPT report on its visit to Belgium from 7 to 9 May 2016, Strasbourg, 18 November 2016, p. 14, § 25.

7 CPT report on its visit to Belgium from 24 September to 4 October 2013, Strasbourg, 31 March 2016, pp. 35–38.

8 *Ibid.* and CPT report on its visit to Belgium from 24 September to 4 October 2013, Strasbourg, 31 March 2016, pp. 35–38; CPT report on its visit to Belgium from 23 to 27 April 2012, Strasbourg, 13 December 2012, pp. 15–18 and pp. 25–26; CPT report on its visit to Belgium from 28 September to 7 October 2009, Strasbourg, 23 July 2010, pp. 52–55; CPT report on its visit to Belgium from 17 to 27 April 2005, Strasbourg, 20 April 2006, p. 40, and pp. 43–45; CPT report on its visit to Belgium from 31 August to 12 September 1997, Strasbourg, 18 June 1998, pp. 54–61; CPT report on its visit to Belgium from 14 to 23 November 1993, Strasbourg, 14 October 1994, pp. 56–67.
See also the recommendations made by the National Centre for Healthcare Assessment (Centre fédéral d'Expertise des Soins de santé), « Soins de santé dans les prisons belges : situation actuelle et scénarios pour le futur », 18 octobre 2017, p. 35, available at https://kce.fgov.be/sites/default/files/atoms/files/KCE_293Bs_Soins_de_sante_prisons_belge_Synthese.pdf).

9 Recommendation (2006)2 of the Committee of Ministers to Member States on the EPR Adopted by the Committee of Ministers on 11 January 2006 at the 952nd meeting of the Ministers' Deputies.

10 Recommendation 98(7) of the Committee of Ministers concerning the ethical and organisational aspects of healthcare in prison.

11 CPT report on its visit to Belgium from 24 September to 3 October 2013, Strasbourg, 31 March 2016, p. 35. See also the recommendations made by the Central Committee of prison monitoring (Conseil central de surveillance pénitentiaire), Annual Report 2019, p. 108, available at https://ccsp.belgium.be/

12 See https://kce.fgov.be/sites/default/files/atoms/files/KCE_293Bs_Soins_de_sante_prisons_belge_Synthese.pdf.
13 They are four sections so far, within the prisons of Merksplas, Turnhout, Antwerp and Bruges.
14 With a few exceptions where internees may be held in these wings but for a very short period of time.
15 Both the social defence section and the psychiatric wing are located within a prison. The difference is that inside the social defence section, only internees can be held, while in psychiatric wings, regular detainees (among which suicidal prisoners) are held alongside internees.
16 CPT report on its visit to Belgium from 14 to 23 November 1993, Strasbourg, 14 October 1994, pp. 62–66.
17 *Ibid.*
18 Council of Europe's Commissioner for Human Rights-Visit to Belgium, 15–19 December 2008 (ref. CommDH (2009)) p.14.
19 See Observatoire International des Prisons, *Notice 2013 de l'état du système carcéral belge*, p. 166, p. 168–169; Observatoire International des Prisons, *Notice 2016 – Pour le droit à la dignité des personnes détenues*, pp. 199–200, p. 205; CPT Report on its visit to Belgium from 14 to 23 November 1993, Strasbourg, 14 October 1994, CPT/Inf(94)15, pp. 63–64; CPT Report on its visit to Belgium from 31 August to 12 September 1997, Strasbourg, 18 juin 1998, CPT/Inf(98)11, p. 59 and pp. 79–80; CPT Report from 25 November to 7 December 2001, Strasbourg, 17 October 2002, CPT/Inf(2002)25, p. 30 (pour l'annexe de Lantin); CPT Report on its visit to Belgium from 18 to 27 April 2005, Strasbourg, 20 April 2006, CPT/Inf(2006)15, pp. 42–43; CPT Report on its visit to Belgium from 28 September to 7 October 2009, Strasbourg, 23 July 2010, CPT/Inf(2010)24, p. 57, pp. 60–61; CPT Report on its visit to Belgium from 23 to 27 April 2012, Strasbourg, 13 December 2012, CPT/Inf(2012)36, pp. 17–18; CPT Report on its visit to Belgium from 24 September to 4 October 2013, Strasbourg, 31 mars 2016, CPT/Inf(2016)13, p. 40.
20 CPT report on its visit to Belgium from 27 March to 6 April 2017, Strasbourg, 8 March 2018, §§ 107–111; CPT report on its visit to Belgium from 24 September to 3 October 2013, Strasbourg, 31 March 2016, p. 43.
21 ECtHR, 10 January 2013, *Claes v. Belgium*; ECtHR, 6 December 2011, *De Donder and De Clippel v. Belgium*; ECHR, 10 January 2013, *Duffort v. Belgium*; ECtHR, 10 April 2013, *Sweenen v. Belgium*; ECtHR, 9 January 2014, *Saadouni v. Belgium*; ECtHR, 9 January 2014, *Gelaude v. Belgium*; ECtHR, 9 January 2014, *Lankaster v. Belgium*; ECtHR, 9 January 2014, *Van Meroye v. Belgium*; ECtHR, 9 January 2014, *Plaisier v. Belgium*; ECtHR, 9 January 2014, *Oukili v. Belgium* ; ECtHR, 9 January 2014, *Moreels v. Belgium*; ECtHR, 9 January 2014, *Caryn v. Belgium.*
22 ECtHR, 10 January 2013, *Claes v. Belgium*, n° 43418/09, §98.
23 ECtHR, 9 January 2014, *Saadouni v. Belgium*, §56 and 61.
24 ECtHR, 10 January 2013, *Claes v. Belgium*, n° 43418/09, §98.
25 ECtHR, 6 December 2016, W.D. c. Belgique, no 73548/13.
26 *Ibid.*, §164–165.
27 CPT report on its visit to Belgium from 24 September to 3 October 2013, Strasbourg, 31 March 2016, pp. 39–43.
28 *Ibid.*, §112 and 169.
29 *Ibid.* §170.
30 CPT, report following its visit to Belgium from du 27 March to 6 April 2017, 8 March 2018 (CPT/Inf (2018) 8), §114.
31 In April 2016, Belgium had 4,230 mentally ill offenders with internee status, of whom 807 were detained in prison. According to a communication from the Government of 19 March 2020 to the Committee of Ministers, in the context of the follow-up to the group of judgements *L.B. v. Belgium* and *W.D. v. Belgium*, on 1 December 2019, the number of internees incarcerated in prison was 537.

32 ECtHR, *Rooman v. Belgium*, 31 January 2019, n° 18052/11; *Venken et al. v. Belgium*, 6 April 2021, n° 46130/14.
33 Internment Act of 5 May 2014 (n° 2014009316), published in the *Moniteur Belge* (official journal), 9 July 2014.
34 https://www.regiedesbatiments.be/fr/projects/detention-et-internement-dans-des-conditions-humaines.
35 ECtHR, 31 January 2019, *Rooman v. Belgium*, n° 18052/11, §108.
36 Of March 2020, available at https://ccsp.belgium.be/publications-page/
37 CoE, White paper on prison overcrowding, PC-CP (2015) 6 rév 7; ECtHR, *Torreggiani and others v. Italy*, 8 January 2013, No 43517/09.
38 ECtHR, *Vasilescu v. Belgium*, 25 November 2014, n° 64682/12.
39 ECtHR, 17 November 2015, *Bamouhammad v. Belgium*, no. 47687/13.
40 ECHR, 25 November 2014, *Vasilescu v. Belgium*, n° 64682/12.
41 CPT report on its visit to Belgium from 24 September to 3 October 2013, Strasbourg, 31 March 2016, pp. 31-34; CPT report on its visit to Belgium from 23 to 27 April 2012, Strasbourg, 13 December 2012.
42 CPT report on its visit to Belgium from 27 March to 6 April 2017, Strasbourg, 8 March 2018, §64; more than 20 years ago, the Committee of Ministers wrote in its Recommendation R(99)22 concerning prison overcrowding and prison population inflation : « The extension of the prison estate should rather be an exceptional measure, as it is generally unlikely to offer a lasting solution to the problem of overcrowding ».
43 *Ibid.*
44 For the French-speaking part of the country only: 3,135 in 2019, available at https://statistiques.cfwb.be/maisons-de-justice/centre-de-surveillance-electronique/nombre-de-nouvelles-activations-par-le-centre-de-surveillance-electronique-et-duree-effective-de-la-mesure/.
45 In Belgium, these last years, the number of prisoners remains stable around 10,500 detainees (see the annual reports made by the Prison Direction) while the number of offenders being granted probation has significantly increased (see the annual reports made by the Houses of Justice).
46 *Ibid.*, p. 5.
47 *Ibid.*, p. 6
48 The annual reports of the prison administration (published online between 2007 and 2017) indicate those numbers regarding the average prison population: 9,873 in 2007, 9,891 in 2008, 10,238 in 2009, 10,536 in 2010, 10,973 in 2011, 11,330 in 2012, 11,644 in 2013, 11,578 in 2014, 11,040 in 2015, 10,619 in 2016, 10,471 in 2017.
49 CPT report on its visit to Belgium from 7 to 9 May, Strasbourg, 18 November 2016, pp. 7–9.
50 ECtHR, *Torreggiani and others v. Italy*, 8 January 2013, nos. 43517/09, 46882/09, 55400/09, 57875/09, 61535/09, 35315/10 et 37818/10, § 50; *Vasilescu v. Belgium*, 25 November 2014, no. 64682/12, § 75; *Bamouhammad v. Belgium*, 17 November 2015, no. 47687/13, §§ 165–166.
51 ECtHR 9 January 2014, *Van Meroye v. Belgium*, § 104–109.
52 In its Vasilescu judgement (ECtHRn 25 November 2014, D. H., *Vasilescu v. Belgium*, n° 64682/12), the ECtHR ruled that either the interim judge proceeding, the complaint under Article 1382 of the Civil Code, or even the complaint brought before the Supervisory Board do not constitute effective remedies that allow prisoners to get their prison conditions improved. See also ECtHR, 16 August 2017, *Sylla and Nollomont v. Belgium*, n° 37768/13 et 36467/14, §§ 19 à 21; ECtHR., *Clasens v. Belgium*, 28 August 2019, n° 26564/16, §§ 43 à 47; ECtHR, 17 November 2015, *Bamouhammad v. Belgium*, no 47687/13.
53 ECtHR, 6 December 2016, *W.D. v. Belgium*, no 73548/13.
54 http://www.oipbelgique.be/

55 The French GENEPI was recently dissolved (August 2021).
56 https://genepibelgique.wixsite.com/genepi
57 https://laclac.org/
58 http://www.liguedh.be/
59 http://www.mensenrechten.be/
60 The Committee of Ministers of the Council of Europe recommends the production of statistics on conditional release (recommendation on conditional release (CM/Rec(2003)22), points 43 to 45).

References

Aebi, M., Delgrande, N. and Marguet, Y. (2015) Have community sanctions and measures widened the net of the European criminal justice systems? *Punishment & Society*, 17(5), pp. 575–597.

Belbot, B. (1997) 'Prisoner Classification Litigation', in Marquart, J. W. and Sorensen, J. R. (eds.), *Correctional Contexts, Contemporary and Classical Readings*. Los Angeles: Roxbury Publishing, pp. 272–280.

Beyens, K. (2006) 'Het nakomertje in de Belgische criminografie', in Devroe, E., Beyens, K. et Enus, E. (eds.) *Zwart op wit? Duiding van cijfers over onveiligehed en strafrechtsbedeling in België. Handboek criminografische basisinformatie*. Bruxelles: VUB Press, pp. 297–298.

Breuls, L., De Ridder, S. and Bellemans, S. (2017) Détenus sans droit de séjour. Réinsérer ou rapatrier à tout prix? *Justice et Sécurité/Justitie en Veiligheid*, 10, 1–16.

Cartuyvels, Y. Champetier, B. and Wyvekens, A. (2011) *La défense sociale et les internés en Belgique*. Bruxelles: Presses de Facultés universitaires Saint-Louis.

Cartuyvels, Y. and Cliquennois, G. (2015) The Punishment of Mentally Ill Offenders in Belgium: Care as Legitimacy for Control. *Penal Field*, 12, available at https://journals.openedition.org/champpenal/9307.

Cliquennois, G. and de Suremain, H. (2018) *Monitoring Penal Policy in Europe*. Abingdon: Routledge.

Cliquennois, G. and Herzog-Evans, M. (2018) European monitoring of Belgian and French penal and prison policies. *Crime, Law and Social Change*, 70(1), pp. 113–134

Cliquennois, G. and Snacken, S. (2018) European and United Nations monitoring of penal and prison policies as a source of an inverted panopticon? *Crime, Law and Social Change*, 70(1), pp. 1–18

Colette-Basecqz, N. and Nederlandt, O. (2018), 'L'arrêt pilote W.D. c. Belgique sonne-t-il le glas de la détention des internés dans les annexes psychiatriques des prisons?', obs. sous Cour eur. dr. h., arrêt W.D. c. Belgique, 6 septembre 2016, *Revue trimestrielle des droits de l'homme*, 113, pp. 213–239.

Crouch, B. and Marquart, J. (1997) 'Resolving the Paradox of Reform: Litigation, Prisoner Violence, and Perceptions of Risk', in Marquart, J. W. and Sorensen, J. R. (eds.), *Correctional Contexts, Contemporary and Classical Readings*. Los Angeles: Roxbury Publishing, pp. 258–271.

Daems, T., Maes, E. and Robert, L. (2013) Crime, criminal justice and criminology in Belgium. *European Journal of Criminology*, 10(2), pp. 237–254.

Daems, T. and Robert, L. (2017) *Europe in Prisons: Assessing the Impact of European Institutions on National Prison Systems*. Camden: Palgrave Mc Millan.

Eechaudt, V. (2014) *Penitentiair Tuchtrecht*. Brugge: Die Keure.

Epp, C. R. (1998) *The Rights Revolution: Lawyers, Activists, and Supreme Courts in Comparative Perspective*. Chicago: University of Chicago Press.

Evans, M. (2002) *Combating Torture in Europe*. Strasbourg: Council of Europe Press.

Gottschalk, M. (2006) *The Prison and the Gallows: The Politics of Mass Incarceration in America*. New York: Cambridge University Press.

Jacobs, J. B. (1997) 'The Prisoners' Rights Movement and Its Impact', in Marquart, J. W. and Sorensen, J. R. (eds.), *Correctional Contexts. Contemporary and Classical Readings*. Los Angeles: Roxbury Publishing, pp. 231–247.

Nederlandt, O. (2019) 'La légalité en matière pénitentiaire: une illusion?', in Detroux, L., El Berhoumi, M. and Lombaert, B. (dir.), *La légalité: un principe de la démocratie belge en péril?* Bruxelles: Larcier, pp. 141–177.

Nederlandt, O. (2021) 'Droits des personnes incarcérées durant la pandémie: quand la crise ordinaire se double d'une crise sanitaire'. e-legal – Revue de droit et de criminologie de l'Université libre de Bruxelles, available online at http://e-legal.ulb.be/special-covid19/dossier-special-covid19/droits-des-personnes-incarcerees-durant-la-pandemie-quand-la-crise-ordinaire-se-double-d-une-crise-sanitaire.

Nederlandt, O. and Descamps L. (2020) Considérations relatives au service minimum garanti dans les prisons belges en temps de grève des agents pénitentiaires (obs. sous Cour eur. dr. h., arrêt Clasens c. Belgique, 28 mai 2019). *Revue trimestrielle des droits de l'Homme*, 2(122), pp. 187–213.

Nederlandt, O. and Teper, L. (2021) Le droit pénitentiaire va-t-il enfin prendre son envol? in Bosly, H. and De Valkeneer, C. (eds.), *Actualités en droit de l'exécution des peines et de l'internement*. Bruxelles: Larcier, pp. 69–173.

O'Connell, C. and Rogan, M. (2022) Monitoring prisons in Europe: Understanding perspectives of people in prison and prison staff. *Law and Social Inquiry*, 47(4), pp. 1–31, online.

Phelps, M. S., (2013) The paradox of probation: Community supervision in the age of mass incarceration. *Law & Policy*, 35(1–2), pp. 51–80.

Schoenfeld, H. (2010) Mass incarceration and the paradox of prison conditions litigation'. *Law and Society Review*, 44(3–4), pp. 731–768.

Snacken, S. and Dumortier, S. (eds.) (2012) *Resisting Punitiveness in Europe? Welfare, Human Rights and Democracy*. Abingdon: Routledge.

Snacken, S. (2011) *Prisons en Europe, pour une pénologie critique et humaniste*. Bruxelles: Larcier.

Snacken, S., Beyens, K. & Beernaert, M. A. (2010), 'Belgium', in Padfield, N., van Zyl Smit, D. and Dünkel, F. (eds.) *Release from prison. European policy and practice*, Cullompton, Devon: Willan Publishing, pp. 70–103.

van Zyl Smit, D. and Snacken, S. (2009) *Principles of European Prison Law and Policy: Penology and Human Rights*. Oxford: Oxford University Press.

PART III

THE IMPACTS OF THE EUROPEAN LAW ON PRISON REFORMS

10

REFORM VS. RESISTANCE IN THE ROMANIAN PENITENTIARY SYSTEM

Prison staff perceptions and attitudes regarding their role in reaching the legal goal of detention

Cristina Dâmboeanu, Valentina Pricopie and Alina Thiemann

Introduction

The academic literature on prison staff perceptions reveals a strong interest in evaluating indicators developed within organizational sociology, such as job satisfaction and motivation, stress and working conditions, career and social status, among others (Lambert et al., 2002; Lambert and Paoline III, 2008; Lambert et al., 2008). Rather than focusing on the nature of work in the penitentiary system, this study centres instead on prison staff perceptions of the legal, professional and relational frameworks that shape the respect and the practice of human rights in prison. The work of prison staff involves negotiation among legal stipulations, traditional occupational values and moral principles that define the social relations within the prison (both among employees and between prison staff and prisoners). This further affects how daily working routines are performed, as well as how prison staff perceive their responsibilities and tasks within the larger context of prison in society.

More precisely, the current study, which is based on a survey with prison staff in Romania, aims to understand how prison staff members perceive their role in fulfilling the goal of imprisonment. Built on prior studies dealing with staff members' ideology and beliefs about the aim(s) of imprisonment, it advances the knowledge in the field in at least three ways. First, it starts from the premise that occupational culture has a strong impact on how prison staff members perceive their professional role, understand prisoners' rights and how they embrace or resist to penal reforms. Second, the study investigates prison staff' perception about the aims of imprisonment in relation to the practice of human rights in prison, an aspect which was largely neglected in previous research.

DOI: 10.4324/9780429317033-14

Third, unlike most of the prior studies conducted in the United States and Western Europe, this study focuses on Romanian case, thus providing important insights in understanding prison practice in a changing context. Among different aspects that characterize the penal system in Romania, two particular events need to be mentioned: first, the penal system was demilitarized only in 2004 when prison employees became public functionaries with special status within the National Administration of Penitentiary. Second, the penal legislation has changed in 2013 to align to European recommendations in the field. In between, a transitory element is the first reform of the Romanian prison law that took place in 2006 during the negotiation of the most problematic chapter with the European Union – Justice and Internal Affairs. In this context, the year 2007 when Romania became member of the EU remains the reference point in addressing the issue of the Romanian penitentiary system reform, given its role of turning point in the social reconsideration of prison and prison system in contemporary Romania. The penal reform in Romania has been a sinuous process, still undergoing, putting pressure on the prison employees who need to adjust to the new legal environment and recently adopted penal policies. These aspects have further a crucial role in the way how prison staff reposition themselves within a changing context, especially considering that the recent changes have been challenging the existing (punitive) penal culture in Romania. This military tradition is therefore shaping a particular understanding of imprisonment which, in the case of Romania, is now challenged by a law that promotes human rights of prisoners and their social reintegration.

The following sections of the chapter include: (1) a short discussion of the Romanian legal context to clarify the current legal goal of imprisonment; (2) a review of the main theories in the field which delineates our theoretical approach; (3) a section explaining the methodology employed in our research; (4) a discussion of the results of the survey conducted with prison staff in Romania; and (5) a concluding section.

Legal understanding of imprisonment in Romania

Until recently, the penal reform in post-communist Romania was almost inexistent: for instance, the communist Criminal Code (1968) and the Law regarding execution of sentences (1969) have been in force long time after the collapse of the former communist regime in December 1989. A new prison law (Law 275/2006) was hastily adopted in 2006, shortly before Romania joined the European Union. A new Criminal Code was adopted in 2009 (but entered into force in 2014), being followed by the adoption of a revised version of the prison law (Law 254/2013), currently in force, in line with the norms and principles of the European Prison Rules (EPR). However, the Rules for the implementation of Law 254/2013 (the Government Resolution no. 157/2016) were only enforced in April 2016, few months before our study was conducted in Romanian prisons. Considering that the process of internalizing changes takes time (see Dâmboeanu

& Pricopie, 2017), a slow penal reform would therefore translate into a delayed reformation of professional prison practices, an aspect to which our study pays particular attention, especially given that the current prison law promotes social reintegration of former offenders and prisoners' human rights, in contrast to the former communist law, designed from the perspective of an extremely punitive culture and basically denying any rights to people deprived of their liberty.

The main principles on which Law 254/2013 is based are respect for human dignity (art. 4); prohibition of torture, inhuman or degrading treatment or punishment (art. 5); and prohibition of discrimination (art. 6). Yet, the Law 254/2013 defines the goal of imprisonment as "prevention of new crimes" (art. 3.1) through "the formation of a right attitude to the rule of law, to the social rules of living together, and to work, aimed at social reintegration of prisoners" (art. 3.2). This goal of social integration is also reinforced in the Rules for the implementation of the Law 254/2013, which also mention "the support given to prisoners toward their social reintegration" (art. 4). However, by first mentioning crime prevention and, second, changes in offenders' behaviour, the Romanian law puts a stronger emphasis on societal safety, thus echoing the general perception of crime and imprisonment, inherited from the communist times, rather than on prisoners' rights and their status as citizens of the same society like their free counterparts. Even the formulation of the social reintegration goal is questionable as it seems to objectify prisoners, by trying to impose "a right attitude" on them. In this way, prisoners' own needs and interests are denied at discursive level, in contrast to the EPR which strongly recommend the active participation of prisoners in the formulation of the individual sentence plan (Rule 103.3) designed to foster their personal development and further their reintegration in society. Different than the Romanian law, the EPR insist from the very first articles on the need to respect prisoners' rights (see Rules 1 and 2), through the normalization of imprisonment as much as possible (Rule 5) with the goal to facilitate "social reintegration of people deprived of their liberty in the free society" (Rule 6). By directly referring to prisoners' rights as human rights, the EPR stresses the need for society at large to understand that people who committed crimes and were sentenced to prison maintain their status of citizens and therefore benefit from most of the same rights that their free fellow citizens enjoy. Neither Law 254/2013 nor the Rules of implementation refer directly to human rights, but only to human dignity.

Prison staff perceptions of the goal(s) of imprisonment. Theoretical perspectives and empirical findings

The interrogations about the purpose, the role and the functions of imprisonment have been longstanding addressed in the criminological literature (see, for example, Garland, 1991). Four competing groups of theories usually outline the answers to these inquiries: specific deterrence theories, selective incapacitation theories, rehabilitation theories, retribution and just desert theories.

Depending on the social and political contexts, the pre-eminence of these theories has varied significantly. In the United States, for example, since mid-1970s, there has been a noticeable mutation in the penal culture from rehabilitation to punitive prison policies ("the punitive turn", see for further discussion Garland, 1991; Hallsworth, 2002). On the contrary, in Europe, the changes in the penal discourse that took place over the last five decades were in the opposite direction.

As such, the conceptualization of imprisonment and its aim have gradually passed from an indispensable punitive measure aimed to protection of society (Council of Europe, Committee of Ministers, 1973; see Resolution (73)5), to a necessary sanction in order to make offenders responsible and aware of the importance of respecting the law (see Council of Europe, Committee of Ministers, 1987; Recommendation (87)3) for in the end, to be seen as a measure of last resort employed with the purpose to reintegrate prisoners into society (Council of Europe, Committee of Ministers, 2006; Recommendation (2006)2). The role of prison officer has consequently evolved in order to add the rehabilitation tasks to those deriving from the traditional, custodial ones.

Extensive literature examines staff members' ideology and beliefs about the aim(s) of imprisonment and their commitment to various professional roles (e.g., custodial, rehabilitation, support) (Shamir and Drory, 1982; Jurik, 1985; Whitehead and Lindquist, 1989; Farkas, 1999; Tewksbury and Mustaine, 2008). These studies usually reported mixed findings. For instance, in an early study conducted by Cullen et al. (1989) among a sample of 155 line officers, rehabilitation was placed last in the hierarchy of the "main reason for putting the offender in prison" (Cullen et al., 1989, p. 37). Deterrence was on top, followed by retribution and incapacitation. Still, despite officers' strong custodial attitudes, a certain degree of support for rehabilitation was also revealed when specific items were asked. For instance, 70% admitted that "rehabilitating a criminal is just as important as making a criminal pay for his or her crime" and 54% agreed that they "would support expanding the rehabilitation programs with criminals that are now being undertaken in our prisons".

In another study conducted four years later among prison wardens (N = 375), Cullen et al. (1993) found that incapacitation was ranked as the most important aim of imprisonment. Rehabilitation placed second, along with deterrence; retribution was last in the top of their preferences. Kifer et al. (2003) came to a similar hierarchy in a study conducted among both jail and prison staff (N = 467): incapacitation was seen as the main goal of imprisonment followed by deterrence and rehabilitation, which are favoured by rather similar proportions of staff members. More recently, Tewksbury and Mustaine (2008) found in turn a high degree of agreement among prison staff (N = 554) that rehabilitation is/should be the main purpose of prison. Instead, deterrence was placed last. Interesting differences came out by the category of job. While prison staff working as administrators as well as staff delivering programs rather endorsed rehabilitation as the aim of imprisonment, security and support, staff expressed their preference for retribution as the main goal of imprisonment. The way prison staff perceive the goals of imprisonment influence the manner in which they see their job and professional duties (Cook & Lane, 2014, p. 77). For instance, a preference for incapacitation and deterrence emphasize staff members' custodial role, while the support for rehabilitation endorse the treatment role focused on support, counselling and resocialization of the offenders (Jurik, 1985).

In Romania, a study conducted in 2007 (Ministerul Justiției, Administrația Națională a Penitenciarelor, 2007), shortly after the first modern prison law was introduced, found that less than half of prison staff (42%) considered that the main role of prison is the social reintegration of offenders. Less than one fourth (23%) believed in the custodial function of prisons, while almost one fifth (18%) opted for both roles. Moreover, the study reported high levels of scepticism among prison staff regarding prisoners' chances of reintegration in the community along with the tendency to attribute the blame for this not to the penitentiary system itself, but to the society (e.g., stigmatization, offenders' lack of motivation for change, poor opportunities for finding a job, lack of post-prison programs). According to the authors of this study, these findings suggest "a generalized lack of trust in the ability of prison to fulfil its social role legally assumed" (p. 23).

Prior studies on prison staff culture

While research on the goals of imprisonment is quite extensive, only few studies focus on occupational culture in prison (see Nylander et al., 2011). Among these, the study of Farkas and Manning (1997) is referential. The authors define occupational culture as "the values, beliefs, material objects and taken-for-granted knowledge associated with a full-time occupational role" (Farkas and Manning, 1997, p. 57) and draw its main characteristics from the particularities of correctional work: "it is people work, it often involves conflict, it is risky and uncertain, and it requires both tact (when to conceal and when to reveal information) and secrecy" (p. 61). Yet, instead of talking about a unique culture among all prison staff, Farkas and Manning (1997) discern between the subculture of prison officers and those of top and middle management. An early study conducted by Duffee (1974) reported similar conclusion: the subculture of prison officers is divergent from that of prison management in terms of prioritization of a certain type of correctional policy. Officers chose prison policy based on reform and restraint, while managers preferred policies of rehabilitation and reintegration. Employing further correlations between organizational profile and social climate, as well as between social climate and prison policy, the author rejects "the common-sense conclusion that a democratic and open management would produce an officer group who were open with inmates". He asserts instead that while "officers like democratic superiors", they "feel very uncomfortable if they behave, or are asked to behave, in a democratic manner with their own subordinates, the inmates" (p. 166).

Along with the position the staff held in prison, the literature highlights the heterogeneity of prison staff working styles, arguing that the dominant group creates the occupational culture (Gordon, p. 189–190). The author identified in this regard 4-type working personalities, each holding particular views about the aims of imprisonment and supporting in various degrees the human rights approach in prison. "The careerist" promotes prisoners' rehabilitation, has a humanitarian ethos and agrees the need for prisoners to have legal and human rights (p. 215). "The humanitarian" also has a strong commitment toward prisoners' rehabilitation, although it is accompanied by scepticism. They do not share a sense of social distance with prisoners and adhere to the discourse of normalization and human rights in prisons. "The disciplinarian" has a "zero-sum mentality underscoring a strong sense of hostility to prisoners' rights from most prison officers" (p. 232). "The mortgage payer" shares a sense of moral indifference toward prisoners' rights (p. 238). Yet more recent ethnographic studies portrait prison staff as not connected with the institutional aims, considering that the penal goals are not achievable due to overcrowding and poor resources (Crewe, 2009, p. 76).

Methods

The chapter presents the results of a survey conducted in the period between August and October 2016 with 289 prison staff members from 15 Romanian prisons[1] of a total number of 35 prisons at national level (except from pre-trial detention centres, educational centres and prison hospitals). The prisons selection was based on two main objective criteria: the geographical representation at national level, and the balanced representation of all prison regimes. The survey was conducted with the prior approval of the National Administration of Penitentiaries (NAP) in a sensitive context, marked by significant prisoners' protests which were very present on the Romanian public agenda via the support of the media. The sample consisted of 289 staff members working in various prison sectors. In each prison, the deputy directors of education and psychosocial assistance sector were assigned to support the field researchers. This further meant that either they or the researchers assisted by them informed staff members about the aim and objectives of the study. A questionnaire was handed to all those interested to participate. The questionnaire was structured in nine parts, those of interested for the current study referring to prison staff perceptions of the aim of imprisonment and staff general evaluations of prisoners' rights.

Out of the total of 289 respondents, almost half (49.5%) were prison guards working in various sectors (e.g., prison regime, visits); roughly one third (30.0%) represented the top and middle management (prison directors, deputy directors, heads of education sector, heads of security and prison regime sector etc.); while one fifth (20.5%) were specialists/non-custodial staff (psychologists, educators, social workers, priests, doctors).

TABLE 10.1 Sociodemographic characteristics of staff members who participated to the survey

	N	*Mean*	*Min*	*Max*
Males	288	0.75	0	1
Age ≥ 35	287	0.68	0	1
University degree	287	0.78	0	1
Prison agents	273	0.49	0	1
Top and middle management	273	0.30	0	1
Specialists	273	0.21	0	1
Job experience: ≥15 years	286	0.39	0	1
Higher security regime	280	0.61	0	1

Fourteen respondents have refused to mention what position they hold in the prison, while two mentioned other positions; all 16 were excluded from the analysis. Regarding their sociodemographic profile, three fourths of the respondents were male, and over two thirds (69%) were aged 35 years or more. More than three forth (77%) had a university degree. Over 60% worked at higher security prison regimes and nearly 40% had 15 years or more of job experience in the prison system.

Measures

Prison staff orientation toward reintegration was measured by several variables. The first one measured staff' beliefs about the goals of imprisonment via single-choice questions, asking respondents to indicate what they consider the main purpose of imprisonment (for a similar approach, see Cullen et al., 1989). The response options were equivalent to the four aims of imprisonment discussed in the literature section: to incapacitate the offenders, to deter their future criminal behaviour, to punish the offenders or to rehabilitate the offenders and reintegrate them into society. The second variable refers to staff members' perceptions over their professional role, by asking them to choose what they consider their main job responsibilities: to guard and supervise the offenders (the custodial orientation); to help offenders solve their problems they confront in prison (the practical-support orientation); and to help offenders desist from crime (the rehabilitation and reintegration orientation). Another variable included here is prison staff perceptions of the efficiency of rehabilitation. As such, respondents were asked whether they believe that in prison, the offenders become better persons, remain unchanged or, on the contrary, aggravate their criminal behaviour. Not least, a set of six specific items derived from prior literature (Cullen et al., 1989; Shannon and Page, 2014) were included, measuring prison staff support for rehabilitation vs. punitiveness.

Prison staff members' perception of their professional priorities was, first, measured by asking respondents to rate the extent to which they consider priority in their everyday responsibilities of working with prisoners the following six options: to maintain order in prison, to protect prisoners and ensure their personal safety, to develop a good relationship with prisoners, to help prisoners solve their problems, to respect prisoners' rights. The response options were distributed on a five-point Likert scale ranging from 4 = to a very great extent to 0 = not at all. Second, prison staff' perceptions over the moral performance of the professional practice were tested by asking the participants to express their agreement to five statements phrased as: "Staff members treat prisoners with humanity"; "Staff members have been trained to learn how to fairly treat the prisoners" etc. The response options were distributed on a three-point Likert scale.

Prison staff members' perception of human rights approach was measured, on the one hand, by asking respondents to indicate to what extent they agree with two specific statements formulated as follows: "In Romania, prisoners have more rights than obligations" and "The Romanian society is more concerned about prisoners' rights than of the rights of the prison staff". The response options were as well distributed on a five-point Likert scale ranging from 4 = to a very great extent to 0 = not at all. On the other hand, respondents were asked to give a score from 1 to 10, where 1 is the minimum score and 10 the maximum, to the practice of 18 specific rights of prisoners stipulated in the prison law.

Results

Prison staff orientation toward social reintegration

Over 80% of respondents assert that the main goal of imprisonment is to reform and reintegrate the offenders back in the society. The perception is perfectly congruent with the official discourse set by the Romanian prison law (254/2013 – art. 3(2)), according to which the aim of imprisonment is to prepare prisoners for reintegration into the community via inculcating them the "right" attitude toward the law, the society and work. Yet, this high prioritization of rehabilitation goal is somehow surprising compared the prior findings, which already showed, reported rather mixed results.

Despite this overwhelming perception of the goal of imprisonment, only half of respondents consider that the role of prison staff is reformative: to help offenders go straight and to desist from crime. One third consider that their role is custodial and less than 10% consider that their role is rather domestic – to support prisoners to solve their everyday problems they face in prison. Interestingly, although respondents endorse their rehabilitation role, more than 60% consider that in Romanian prisons, prisoners either become worst either remain unchanged; only one third assert that prisoners become better persons in detention.

The perception regarding the reformative goal of imprisonment is also validated by the non-punitive attitude expressed by almost 60% of the respondents who consider that the deprivation of liberty is already a sufficient punishment for a person who broke the law. In addition, 55% reject the idea that more severe conditions of imprisonment represent an efficient way to prevent recidivism. A slightly higher percentage (62%) of employees disagree with the statement that it is already too late for offenders to be socially reintegrated once they were admitted in prison and more than two thirds of respondents (71%) agree that "offenders are people like us who made some mistakes in their life". Moreover, the majority of the participants in the study (86%) reject the idea that prisoners do not deserve to benefit from programs of social reintegration. However, the attitude regarding the prisoners' capacity and willingness to change their behaviour is not so favourable: only 37% reject the idea that social reintegration does not function because prisoners do not want to change.

Nevertheless, the study reveals aspects of a punitive attitude. Thus, about a quarter of the respondents (26%) reject the idea that imprisonment is already a sufficient form of punishment and a similar percentage of employees assert

TABLE 10.2 Prison staff attitudes on punitiveness

	Agree	*Uncertain*	*Disagree*
In Romania, prisoners have more rights than obligations	64.0	23.0	13.0
The society is more interested in prisoners' rights than in the rights of prison employees	79.6	14.7	5.6
Imprisonment is by itself a sufficient sanction for any person who breaks the law	56.8	18.1	25.1
Imprisonment is a too soft sanction for some prisoners	45.5	27.6	26.9
Only by harshening prison conditions, recidivism can be prevented	26.0	19.3	54.7
It is too late for prisoners to be re-socialized by the time they enter to prison	15.7	22.6	61.7
Most prisoners are in fact regular people who made some mistakes	70.8	18.4	10.8
Prisoners do not deserve to benefit from rehabilitation and reintegration programs	3.5	10.2	86.3
Resocialization does not work because prisoners do not want to change their behaviour	29.9	32.7	37.4
Resocialization does not work because the society is not willing to reintegrate ex-offenders	45.1	28.9	26.1

that recidivism can only be prevented through more severe conditions of imprisonment. Moreover, almost half of them (46%) consider that imprisonment is sometimes a too mild punishment for some offenders. Almost two thirds of the respondents either consider or are convinced that social reintegration does not work because prisoners do not want to change their behaviour.

Prison staff members' perception of their professional priorities

The evaluation of professional priorities in the daily work with prisoners included not only legal and moral dimensions of professional practice, but also variables which illustrate the punitive tradition inherited from the communist regime. These dimensions that are closely intertwined are explained below.

TABLE 10.3 Prison staff members' perception of their professional priorities

	Great/very great extent	*Small/very small extent*	*Not at all*	*DK*
Maintain the order in the penitentiary	94.1	4.5	0.3	1.0
Ensure prisoners' protection and security	89.3	8.0	1.0	1.7
Develop good relations with prisoners	80.6	13.8	2.1	3.5
Solve prisoners' daily problems	86.5	10.4	1.4	1.7
Respect prisoners' rights	95.8	2.4	0.0	1.7

Legal dimension: *Respecting prisoners' rights* represents a priority (almost absolute) for the employees included in our study, according to the current legal stipulations. As shown in the graph below, this priority is the most important one for the prison staff: 95.8% of the respondents identified it as such to a *great* and *very great extent*.

Punitive tradition dimension: *Maintaining order/discipline in prison*, a variable which operationalizes the legal stipulations regarding the safety of detention and, at the same time, illustrates the punitive tradition in prison, represents to a *great* and *very great extent* a priority for 94.1% of the respondents. A second item, "*Guaranteeing prisoners' protection and safety*", combines a legal dimension (safety of prisoners) with a moral and humane dimension (protection of prisoners). The nuanced difference shapes a sensitive difference in perception: the percentage of prison staff who favoured such a professional priority decreased with 5% compared with the previous item; 89.3% consider this aspect being a priority. Considering these results, we can therefore note that a punitive attitude somehow prevails regarding the right to safety and personal integrity. Moral dimension: *Mutual respect, the power of example and rational evaluation of the worthiness of one's actions* are aspects which illustrate the moral dimension of prison practice. As a significant part of the professional culture, prison staff – prisoners relations are shaped by a strong moral dimension which becomes more or less visible in practice, depending on both legal provisions and professional tradition. In this context, other two items were considered: "*Solving the daily problems of prisoners*" and, respectively, "*Developing good relations with the prisoners*". Both of them are mentioned as priorities to a *great* and *very great extent* by more than 80% of the participants in the study. Yet, the percentages are lower than those corresponding to the items concerning the legal and the punitive tradition dimensions that shape the prison practice. Thus, 11.8% of the respondents consider to a *low* or *very low extent* that solving daily problems of prisoners does not represent a priority in their work, while the good relation with the prisoners is not a priority for almost 16% of the prison staff members who took part in the study.

TABLE 10.4 Prison staff members' perception of the moral performance of their professional practice

	Agree	*Uncertain*	*Disagree*	*DK*
The staff of this penitentiary treats the prisoners with humanity	94.1	4.8	0.7	0.4
The staff of this penitentiary is very aware of prisoners' rights	93.4	4.8	1.0	0.8
The staff of this penitentiary was trained in order to know how to treat prisoners in a correct manner	90.7	6.9	1.4	1.0
The staff of this penitentiary treats all the prisoners with the same respect, irrespective of the crime they committed, their criminal history, sexual orientation or social status	86.9	10.1	2.1	0.9
The staff of this penitentiary is respected by the prisoners	48.4	34.9	14.9	1.8

Within the context of support offered to prisoners by prison staff in solving problems, a specific item was included in the study, namely helping people deprived of their liberty to solve family problems, which also illustrates the right to a social life that plays an important role for social reintegration of prisoners. The rate of positive answers regarding staff perception whether their colleagues are supporting prisoners to solve their family problems is very high: 84.1% of respondents totally agreed with this aspect, while only 2.1% totally disagreed, 8% chose a neutral position, and 5.9% opted for the non-response choice of the question. An important factor needs to be taken in consideration in this particular case, namely the low (and insufficient) number of social workers and psychologists working with the prison population. According to the official data, the specialized staff offering educational and socio-psychological support generally counts for less than 20 persons per prison, representing between 4% and 7% of the total number of prison employees. This situation is highly problematic if we consider that the main actors in supporting the process of social reintegration of prisoners are usually educators, psychologists and social workers, as already discussed in a previous section of this chapter.

Taking into consideration the above three-dimensional model, the following table shows the items related to inherent professional responsibilities (at the level of the legal dimension) that test "the moral performance" (Liebling, 2004) of the professional practice of prison staff in relation to prisoners. Moral performance is operationalized through four specific items: respect, humanity, correctitude and non-discrimination. We can therefore identify in this context, in a binary opposition, the overwhelming perception of the prison staff that they treat prisoners in a humane way (94.1% respondents mentioning to a great extent humanity as part of their daily work with prisoners to a great extent), but also the low extent of the perception that prisoners treat the prison staff members with respect (only 48.4% agree with this item, a result which is also accentuated by the neutral positioning of more than one third of the respondents). It is nevertheless important to note that humanity – the item which is the most related to the moral dimension – ranks at the top of the hierarchy of the perception levels as regards the moral items that count for the employees.

As regards the respect of the prison staff for prisoners, coupled with the non-discrimination principle, the item "*The prison staff treats all prisoners with the same respect, no matter of the crime they committed, their criminal record, sexual orientation or social status*" is perceived positively by 86.9% of the respondents. However, the rate of those who adopt a neutral position, avoiding to signal any differences based on discriminating criteria in the relation with prisoners is quite high (10.1%). This significant indicator raises questions regarding the possibility that there are discriminatory practices in some prisons. Two others items were included to test the professional practice in its moral dimension: on the one hand, *correctitude* of the prison staff in relation to prisoners, considering in this context the specialized *training* that employees benefit from, and, on the other hand, the *very good knowledge of prisoners' rights by the employees.* In other words, the two items test two theoretical transversal variables of our study – in-depth knowledge and rights circulation (according to Frezzo, 2015, p. 55). A proportion of 93.4% of the participants in the study state that prison staff who works in the same prison like them knows very well prisoners' rights, while 90.7% state that the prison staff was trained as regards the norms of interacting with prisoners so that they know how to behave correctly in relation with people deprived of their liberty.

Prison staff members' perception of human rights approach in Romanian prisons

In agreement with both the stipulations of the current national law and the European recommendations, the general opinion of the Romanian prison staff is that human dignity and human rights are respected to a high degree in the Romanian prisons. While this general perception is not surprising, what deserves attention in this context is that the sensitive issue[2] of human rights leads to a slightly more favourable perception regarding the respect of prisoners' rights (97.6% in favour) than the respect for human dignity (95.2% in favour),[3] even if the positive values are maximal.

We should also note that almost two thirds of respondents (64%) agreed that in Romania, prisoners have more rights than obligations, and over 80% feel that the public is more interested in prisoners' rights than in prison staff' safety and work conditions. Besides, over 90% believe that after 2007, the living conditions in prisons have significantly improved, but only 50% agreed that there was a similar improvement of working conditions for prison staff. Almost one quarter hold that the working environment remained unchanged, and one fifth – that it has deteriorated.

The general perception of the prison staff regarding the different rights in prison was also evaluated through a set of 18 rights included in the national legislation, giving the respondents to possibility to grade them on a scale from 1 to 10. The results are presented in Table 10.5.

While the averages for each included right exceed 9 points in each case, in the context in which 70% of the respondents gave the maximum points (10) to all rights included in the set, except "*The right to online communication*",[4] with high variations (from 1 to 9) in the case of almost one third of the participants in the study. Nevertheless, 61.9% gave this right a maximum of 10 points. Another right which was rated exceptionally low by some respondents is "*The right to nutrition, clothing, bedding and minimal necessary conditions of accommodation*", in spite of the fact that more than 82% of the employees gave the maximum points to this right. Other exceptions include the low ratings in few instances of "*The right to judicial assistance*" (2 points), "*The right to medical assistance, treatment and care*" (3 points), "*The right to work*" (3 points), and "*The right to education*" (3 points). However, all these rights also received maximum points from 70% to 80% of the respondents (the right of education being evaluated positively by even more participants in the study, more precisely, between 80% and 90%). All the other rights included in our set were evaluated with minimum 5 points or more, with six of the rights being evaluated with minimum 7

TABLE 10.5 Grades awarded by the prison staff members for the way the 18 legal rights of prisoners are respected within the prisons

	N	*Min*	*Max*	*Mean*	*Std dev*
Right to information	285	7	10	9.68	0.670
Right to access the personal file	284	5	10	9.70	0.701
Right to judicial assistance	278	2	10	9.70	0.820
Right to petition and right to correspondence	287	7	10	9.91	0.353
Right to phone conversations	286	5	10	9.88	0.463
Right to online communication	267	1	10	9.14	1.852
Right to daily walk	287	5	10	9.86	0.577
Right to receive visits	287	5	10	9.92	0.397
Right to be informed about special family situations	281	6	10	9.77	0.596
Right to intimate family visits	287	5	10	9.85	0.499
Right to receive, buy and have products	286	7	10	9.89	0.412
Right to medical assistance, treatment and care	285	3	10	9.51	1.050
Right to get married	287	7	10	9.91	0.394
Right to vote	282	7	10	9.93	0.334
Right to rest	285	7	10	9.92	0.399
Right to work	285	3	10	9.44	1.225
Right to education	284	3	10	9.74	0.748
Right to nutrition, decent clothes, bedding and minimum conditions of accommodation	286	1	10	9.45	1.128

points. More than 90% of the respondents gave maximum points to half of the 18 rights included in our set, namely "*The right to phone conversations*", "*The right to receive, buy and have products*", "*The right to daily walk*", "*The right to vote*", "*The right to petition and the right to correspondence*", "*The right to get married*", "*The right to rest*", "*The right to receive visits*".

We should mention here that, in spite of the high averages for all of the 18 rights included in our set, we consider that a simple occurrence of a right violation means that the right is not respected.

Legal vs. moral dimensions of prison staff perception of their role

Three items included in the survey directly refer to the role of prison staff in fostering the personal development of the prisoners so that they would become autonomous and self-reliable persons as part of the social reintegration process, a national priority assumed by public actors in the penal field. These are "*Prison staff members help prisoners to discover their abilities*", "*Prisoners are encouraged to develop plans for their future*" and "*Prisoners are helped to reintegrate in their community*". Around three quarters agree with them. Yet, about one fourth of participants do not take a clear stance, preferring either a neutral position, either the non-response choice.

Besides the reference to the legal responsibility of the prison staff to stimulate personal and professional development of prisoners toward their social reintegration, the above-mentioned statements have also a moral dimension. This is the case because the prisoners represent a vulnerable category of citizens, whose capacity of choosing their own path of development being severely restricted due to the inner nature of imprisonment, and therefore they need support to find their place in the free society. Under these circumstances, the prison staff members are the first moral agents who can offer this needed support. The moral dimension is even more clearly illustrated by other two statements included in the survey: "*Here (in the prison) the prisoners are learning what is right/correct*" and, respectively, "*Prison staff represents a model for the prisoners*". By including these items in the survey, the employees are invited to reflect on their own behaviour and the educational role of prison. A majority of respondents (74.4%) agree with the first statement and about two thirds (68.5%) with the second.

Discussion and conclusions

For almost 50 years, in all the CEE countries that formed the communist bloc, prisoners were considered external actors of the society first at political and administrative level, and then at the level of social practice. After the confusing and unclear social experience of political prisons and prisoners, the "other" prisoners, incarcerated for "legal" offences under the communist regimes, also became outsiders, while the military system of prison administrations did its job far away from the public sight. Then, stigmatisation, shame, physical and psychological suffering, as well as the "non-social" status of prisoners, were some of the reasons why silence prevailed over the professional community of the communist prison administrations systems. So was the case in Romania where administrative and social reforms were rapidly initiated after the fall of the iron curtain (1989), but they reached relatively late the penitentiary system. As such, the system was only demilitarized in 2004, while the first reform of the Romanian prison law took place in 2006 in the context of the EU adhesion process. Later on, a more European prison law was adopted in 2013 (L254), while its rules of implementation (R157) entered into force in April 2016, both in force in the present. As shown above, they define and clarify the aims of imprisonment and prisoners' rights, but they avoid to directly addressing human rights in the prison context, even if some universal values and principles such as human dignity and non-discrimination abound in the legal texts. Also, even if rather aligned with the European Prison Rules, the Romanian prison law still maintains a priority conception of the prison goal as society protector. This becomes challenging in scientifically interrogating current prison staff perception of their role in reaching the legal goal of detention. While it is not surprising that prison staff refer to their work, in general, and to their role in implementing the prison law, in particular in positive terms, their perceptions and attitudes contradict, on the one hand, prisoners' perceptions regarding their rights in prison, which reveals a more negative image of prison practice (see Dâmboeanu & Pricopie, 2017) and, on the other hand, the negative reports on life in prison, conducted by NGOs and the national preventive mechanism (see Dâmboeanu et al., 2017 for a comparative analysis of APADOR Helsinki Committee Reports vs. CPT Reports on prison conditions in Romanian).

In the light of their organizational culture and well-established professional identity deepen the existing gaps (Tew et al., 2015) that separate prisoners and prison employees at the level of perception. In recent years, the professional tradition centred on maintaining security has acquired a new dimension of rehabilitation and resocialization of prisoners, where the general perception of employees is based on the collective conviction that they are the main agents of protecting society against offenders. Of course, the new international and European orientation on the purpose of prison punishment – the social reintegration of the persons who committed crimes – is also a priority in the Romanian legislation and a professional task for the employees. Thus, the perception study also shows an attitudinal alignment of the Romanian penitentiary system's employees with the European rules and recommendations, by emphasizing the reformative goal of imprisonment. Nevertheless, reminiscences of the punitive tradition could be observed, while more than a quarter of the respondents considered, on the one hand, that imprisonment is not a sufficient form of punishment, and, on the other hand, that recidivism can only be prevented through more severe conditions of imprisonment. In addition, this is happening because of prisoners' lack of will for change, if we consider that two thirds of our respondents assessed that social reintegration does not work because prisoners do not want to change their behaviour. In the same time, when addressing the professional priorities of prison staff, an overwhelming majority of the respondents (about 95%) underlines the legal dimension (respecting prisoners' rights) and the security dimension (maintaining order and discipline in prison), while the moral dimension remains important, but more in a very personal way. We can thus infer that the legal and security dimension remained the main pillars of prison staff members' organizational culture, and the moral dimension is more valorized at personal level that at the professional community level.

Acknowledgement

This work was supported by a grant of the Romanian National Authority for Scientific Research and Innovation, CNCS-UEFISCDI, project number PN-II-RU-TE-2014-4-2967: Prisoners' Rights. Romania in the European context.

Notes

1 Aiud, Baia Mare, Bucureşti-Rahova, Colibaşi, Craiova, Drobeta Turnu Severin, Galaţi, Găeşti, Gherla, Iaşi, Miercurea Ciuc, Ploieşti, Tg. Jiu, Timişoara and Tulcea Prisons.

2 We need to remark here that human dignity in national legislation remains a fundamental principle, however, with an axiological central dimension and no legal operationalization in spite of the fact that it is often mentioned in the legal texts. In contrast, the prisoners' rights (in agreement with European recommendations regarding human rights and the rights of people deprived of their liberty) are addressed in a special section included in the national law, which details the obligations and the specific professional responsibilities of the prison staff.

3 For instance, 93.8% of the respondents strongly agreed with the following item: "The way in which the conjugal visits are organized respects the right of prisoners and their partners to intimacy and private life".

4 The results related to *The right to online communication* are not surprising considering that this right stipulated in the Law 254/2013 is a novelty in the penal field in Romania and that, according to the National Administration of Penitentiaries, the implementation of the necessary platforms that could facilitate the exercise of this right takes begins in 2015 and has to be finalized in 2016. Therefore, we can assume that the negative grades given by employees apply to those prisons with no such platforms at the time when the study was conducted. This argument is also supported by the high rate of non-responses (7.6%).

References

Cook, C. L., & Lane, J. (2014). Professional orientation and pluralistic ignorance among jail correctional officers. *International Journal of Offender Therapy and Comparative Criminology, 58*(6), 735–757.

Council of Europe, Committee of Ministers (1973). Resolution (73) 5 on the standard minimum rules for the treatment of prisoners, adopted on 19 January 1973. Retrieved from: https://rm.coe.int/CoERMPublicCommonSearchServices/DisplayDCTMContent?documentId=09000016804fac9a

Council of Europe, Committee of Ministers (1987). Recommendation R (87) 3 on the European prison rules, adopted on 12 February 1987. Retrieved from: https://rm.coe.int/16804f856c

Council of Europe, Committee of Ministers (2006). Recommendation Rec (2006)2 of the Committee of Ministers to member states on the *European Prison Rules adopted on 11 January 2006*. Retrieved from: https://rm.coe.int/european-prison-rules-978-92-871-5982-3/16806ab9ae

Crewe, B. (2009). *The Prison Society. Power, Adaptation, and Social Life in an English Prison.* Oxford: Oxford University Press.

Cullen, F. T., Latessa, E. J., Burton Jr., V., & Lombardo L. X. (1993). The correctional orientation of prison wardens: Is the rehabilitative ideal supported?. *Criminology, 31*(1), 69–92.

Cullen, F. T., Lutze, F. E., Link, B. G., & Wolfe, T. N. (1989). The correctional orientation of prison guards: Do officers support rehabilitation? *Federal Probation, 53*, 33–42.

Dâmboeanu, C., & Pricopie, V. (eds.) (2017). *Human Rights in Prison. A Sociological Approach.* Bucharest: Ars Docendi.

Dâmboeanu, C., Pricopie, V., Thiemann, A., Mihaiu, S., & Chirazi, G. (2017). *Raport de recomandări privind politicile penale naţionale în context european* [Report of recommendations on national penal policies in the European context]. ClujNapoca: CA Publishing.

Duffee, D. (1994). The correction officer subculture and organizational change. *Journal of Research in Crime and Delinquency, 11*(2), 155–172.

Farkas, M. A. (1999). Correctional officer attitudes toward inmates and working with inmates in a "Get Tough" era. *Journal of Criminal Justice, 27*(6), 495–506.

Farkas, M. A., & Manning, P. K.. (1997). The occupational culture of corrections and police officers. *Journal of Crime and Justice, 20*(2), 51–68.

Frezzo, M. (2015). *The Sociology of Human Rights*. New Jersey: John Wiley and Sons.

Garland, D. (1991). Sociological perspectives on punishment. *Crime and Justice, 14*, 115–165.

Hallsworth, S. (2002). The case for a postmodern penalty. *Theoretical Criminology, 6*(2), 145–163.

Jurik, N. (1985). Individual and organizational determinants of correctional officer attitude toward inmates. *Criminology, 23*(3), 523–539.

Kifer, M., Hemmens, C., & Stohr, M. K. (2003). The goals of corrections: Perspectives from the line. *Criminal Justice Review, 28*(1), 47–69.

Lambert, E. G., Hogan, N. L., & Barton Shannon M. (2002). Satisfied correctional staff: A review of the literature on the correlates of correctional staff job satisfaction. *Criminal Justice and Behavior, 29*(2), 115–143.

Lambert, E. G., Hogan, N. L., & Jiang, S. (2008). Exploring antecedents of five types of organizational commitment among correctional staff. It matters what you measure. *Criminal Justice Policy Review, 19*(4), 466–490.

Lambert, E. G., & Paoline III, E. A. (2008). The influence of individual, job, and organizational characteristics on correctional staff job stress, job satisfaction, and organizational commitment. *Criminal Justice Review, 33*(4), 541–564.

Law 275/2006 on *the execution of custodial sentences and measures imposed by judicial bodies in criminal proceedings*. Abrogated and replaced by Law 254/2013. Law into force from 18 October 2016 to 31 January 2014.

Law 286/2009, *Criminal Code*, published in the Official Gazette of Romania Part I, no. 510/24.07.2009. Entered into force on 1st February 2014.

Liebling, A. (2004). *Prisons and Their Moral Performance. A Study of Values, Quality, and Prison Life*. Oxford: Oxford University Press, Clarendon Studies in Criminology.

Ministerul Justiţiei, Administraţia Naţională a Penitenciarelor (2007). *Sondaj de opinie la nivelul personalului din unităţile sistemului penitenciar*. Raport de cercetare [Survey among staff members of the units within the prison system. Research report]. Bucharest: National Administration of Penitentiaries.

Nylander, P. -A., Lindberg, O., & Bruhn, A. (2011) Emotional labour and emotional strain among Swedish prison officers. *European Journal of Criminology*, 8(6), 469–483.

Resolution no. 157/2016 *to approve the Regulation implementing Law 254/2013 on the execution of custodial sentences and measures imposed by judicial bodies in criminal proceedings*, in force as of 11 April 2016, as amended and supplemented by Resolution no. 593/24.08.2016, published in the Official Gazette of Romania, Part I, no. 664 of 30.08.2016.

Shamir, B., & Drory, A. (1982). Some correlates of prison guards' beliefs. *Criminal Justice and Behavior, 8*(2), 233–249.

Shannon, S. K. S., & Page J. (2014). Bureaucrats on the cell block: prison officers' perception of work environment and attitudes toward prisoners. *Social Service Review, 88*(4), 630–657.

Tew, J., Vince, R., & Luther, J. (2015). Prison culture and prison violence. *Prison Service Journal, 221*, Special Edition *Reducing Prison Violence*, 15–19.

Tewksbury, R., & Mustaine, E. E. (2008). Correctional orientations of prison staff. *The Prison Journal, 88*(2), 207–233.

Whitehead, J. T., & Lindquist, C. A. (1989). Determinants of correctional officers' professional orientation. *Justice Quarterly, 6*(1), 69–87.

11

THE ASSESSMENT OF REMEDIAL MEASURES IN ENGLAND AND WALES TO THE PROOF OF THE WITHDRAWAL

A two-fold test

Rosaria Pirosa

Introduction

This chapter aims at focusing on the "stabilisation" of the English and Welsh approach in matter of the assessment of remedial measures, especially with regard to disenfranchisement and whole-life imprisonment. The relationship between the United Kingdom and the European Court of Human Rights (ECtHR) needs to be placed in the context of the "Brexit affair" which leads to the consideration of, on the one hand, the permanence of the standards in the protection of prisoners' rights established by the Court – and therefore on the connection between the Human Rights Act 1998 and the European Convention – and, on the other hand, the challenges that the Strasbourg judge has to face. The chapter intends to consider the recent perspectives on the European case law and on the interpretations of the ECtHR in the United Kingdom as a diagnostic tool to deal with the role of the ECtHR and the possible future of the Court itself in the European system of protection of rights.

Beyond the boundaries of the relationship between the United Kingdom and the European Court

The relationship between the United Kingdom and the ECtHR[1] has to be interpreted in the light of the "Brexit affair" which leads to evaluation of, on the one hand, the persistence of the standards in the protection of prisoners' rights established by the Court (Padfield, 2007:1–20 especially 2)[2] – and therefore the constant debate on the Human Rights Act 1998[3] as the domestic law that gives effect to the European Convention on Human Rights (ECHR) within the United Kingdom[4] – and on the other hand, the challenges that the Strasbourg judge has to face.

DOI: 10.4324/9780429317033-15

What has been defined as a "peculiar relationship" between the ECtHR and the English Courts in matter of disenfranchisement and life imprisonment has brought to light the "British exceptionalism" outside the boundaries of this territory.

As Lord Neuberger argued, "the idea of Courts overruling decisions of the UK Parliament, as is substantially the effect of what the Strasbourg and the Luxembourg Courts can do, is little short offensive to our notions of constitutional propriety" (Lord Neuberger, 2014). This point of view represented the paradigm of the tension that has taken shape between some Member States and the ECtHR and of the general criticism addressed to this body, whose legitimacy to act as a subsidiary legislator is contested (see Spano, 2018: 473–494). Under this perspective, the inherent political nature of the judicial power extends to compress sovereignty of the States. But the United Kingdom was also the main actor in advancing what Paulo Pinto de Albuquerque (2017) called a deeper criticism, of a legal nature,[5] which questioned the evolutionary interpretation of the Court. In this debate, it is interesting to note that prior to the Human Rights Act 1998, the UK courts thought that British common law should have been capable of this type of evolutionary change.[6]

In *Tyrer v United Kingdom,* for the first time the Court used the expression "convention as a living instrument"[7] affirming the principle according to which the Convention must be interpreted in the light of current conditions.

In *Demir v Turkey,*[8] the Court reiterated that the convention is a living instrument that must be interpreted in the light of current conditions, and according to the developments in international law, to reflect the progressively growing standard in the field of human rights protection. And perhaps it is no coincidence that the founding principle of evolutionary interpretation was recently questioned in *Hassan v. United Kingdom,*[9] where the Grand Chamber has stated that international human rights law (IHRL) applies to international armed conflict in conjunction with international humanitarian law (IHL) but has come to admit, as requested by the Government, that the IHL, i.e. the Third and Fourth Geneva Conventions relating to internment, can be used to qualify and, in practical terms, to weaken IHRL standards.

The principle of evolutionary interpretation of the Convention has been upset to include a new reason for detention under Article 5, that is internment under IHL; the rule has been interpreted as broadening the conditions for detention and decreasing those for the re-examination under the Geneva Conventions. As a matter of fact, Lord Hoffman argued that the proposition that the Convention is a "living instrument" is the banner behind which the Strasbourg Court has assumed the power to translate into norms what is believed is required by "European public order".[10]

Therefore, the failure to enforce the pilot-judgement Greens and M. T.[11] and the chequered jurisprudence of the Strasbourg Court with regard to the whole-tariff order can be conceived in the light of a relationship, which can be conceived not only as a specific affair, but with Brexit after the withdrawal, it could also be a diagnostic tool to focus the role of the ECtHR and the possible future of the Court itself in the European system of protection of rights. In this context, as a matter of fact, Paulo Pinto de Albuquerque (2017) questions the "existential crisis of the Court".[12]

Looking at the choices of the Court in matter of life imprisonment: "the development of differential treatment may have temporarily secured the remit of the Court by appeasing Britain but, if it continues to advance and embed itself, then the long-term future of the court cannot be so easily guaranteed" (Pettigrew, 2018:16–26, especially at 26). Assuming that the political standing of nations influences the court's judgements, this issue calls into question the doctrine of the margin of appreciation and, consequently, the very principles on which the court was founded in order to not risk that the "margin should be wider for those States which are supposed 'to set an example for others' and narrower for those States which are supposed to learn from the example".[13]

Disenfranchisement: the symbolic origin of English and Welsh "exceptionalism"

The origin of the tension between the English and Welsh system and the European institutions (in this regard, see Creighton, Padfield, and Pirosa, 2018) can be identified in the failure to implement the *Hirst* judgement. In *Hirst v. United Kingdom*,[14] the Grand Chamber had held, by a majority, that the generalized deprivation of the right to vote for all persons detained following a criminal conviction and for the duration of their detention "irrespective of the nature of gravity of their offence and their individual circumstances" was a general, automatic and indiscriminate restriction, incompatible with the right to vote under Article 3 of Protocol 1 of the European Convention. Given the nature of the Court's decision, the finding of a violation entailed the duty for the Member State to change its internal rules relating to the right to vote,[15] confirmed following a wide public debate on the occasion of the approval of the *Representation of the People Act* in 2000. The *Hirst* case was a moment from which the request of national sovereignty and the principle of subsidiarity of the international guarantee mechanism, on one side, and the supporters for a more effective and incisive judicial review by the Court, on the other side, faced each other. However, the Strasbourg Court's interpretation, in the *Hirst* judgement, was a prelude to a systemic approach and, therefore, not focused on the individual case. Unlikely *Scoppola v. Italy*,[16] the European Court, since the normative provisions related to the disenfranchisement directly and immediately affected the applicant's position, had held that the examination of their compatibility with the Convention was justified "without regard to the question whether, had the measure been drafted differently and in a way which was compatible with the Convention, the applicant might still have been deprived of the vote".[17] In other words, the Court had expressly refused to consider the case from a perspective of individual justice, not asking whether, in the specific case, the deprivation of vote for the period of detention against the applicant (sentenced to a term of discretionary life imprisonment) respected the requirements of proportionality, taking into account the crime for which he was convicted (manslaughter on diminished ground of responsibility), but focusing rather on the different question whether the applicable legal framework allowed and assessment of the proportionality of the measure.

This is the beginning of the deep tension between the United Kingdom, one of the founding Members of the Council of Europe, and the Strasbourg Court, which led the latter, given the inertia of the English and Welsh system in executing the sentence – in a subsequent and very similar case – to the procedure of the pilot judgement,[18] with the indication of general measures pursuant to Article 46 ECHR. The Court found a violation of Article 3 of Protocol 1 of the Convention yet, even after years of the United Kingdom failing to implement the judgement, it was not sanctioned in anyway. The apparent indifference to this behaviour has had a lasting negative effect on the European system of human rights protection, extending to other Contracting States that have noted an approach of favour and discrepancy. In July 2015, after the European Court found that the Russian ban on prisoner voting right violated the Convention in *Anchugov and Gladkov v Russia*,[19] considering the British refusal to capitulate to the ECtHR after the decision in *Hirst* and in *Greens and M. T.*, Russia introduced a Parliamentary Act in order to provide the supremacy of the Russian Constitution in the enforcement of the ECtHR decisions, allowing the judgements of Strasbourg to be overruled. These events have helped highlight how the issue of the conflict between the United Kingdom and the European Union has affected other States, and with Brexit, these conflicts will have to find a place in the Council of Europe. In this sense, the Council of Europe should not ignore the criticism addressed to the Court.

The case of the United Kingdom leads us to take into account that a relevant aspect of the consideration of administrative and management policy of the Court should concern the procedures of pilot judgement, given that Member States, evaluating the ECHR, should take into account "if it enters into the domain of proactive penal policy rather than being strictly confined to the domain of the law of the Convention".[20] Even without criticism, it is difficult for the Court to strategically advance its more ambitious aims because of a suboptimal machinery of execution of its judgements (Dzehtsiarou, and Tzevelekos, 2020: 1–6, especially 5–6; in this regard, see Pettigrew, 2015). As we will see in detail, with regard to life imprisonment, however, the Court's retreat from its own interpretative principles has been crucial in this matter.

Life imprisonment in the English and Welsh system: an overview in the light of the *Hutchinson* case

The ECHR had an impact on life imprisonment in Europe in ways that go beyond the debate about whether whole-life imprisonment infringes fundamental human rights. It is not just necessary to consider the so-called judicial ping-pong between the Courts in Strasbourg and London about whether English procedural law provides individuals with life sentences for which no minimum period has been set with a realistic prospect of release, but also taking into account whether other developments in English and Welsh life imprisonment law have shaped.

Thanks to a series of decisions of the ECtHR, life prisoners now have their release on parole determined by a Parole Board,[21] which is required to act like a court with a range of procedural safeguards, rather than by politicians deciding in private. Catherine Appleton and Dirk van Zyl Smit note, however, that the reform of the parole process may not have a transformative impact on the number of life sentence prisoners in custody or the lengths of time served prior to release. The interventions of the ECtHR have provided that those individuals who are sentenced to life imprisonment have a public hearing at which their minimum terms are determined. The vast majority of them (excluding only the small number who have whole-life orders) also know that after they have served this term their release will be decided by a body required to meet key due process standards. Appleton and van Zyl Smit argue that the human rights weakness in the system in England and Wales lies not in the procedure but "the growing frequency with which life sentences are imposed and the increasing time that life prisoners have to serve before they are released" (Appleton, and van Zyl Smit, 2016: pos. 4745–5266 of 12484).

In this sense, we can focus on the opportunity to reform the rule that requires the mandatory imposition of life sentences for a broadly defined crime of murder,[22] which amounts to a very comprehensive category, resulting in a key factor in explaining the life imprisonment rate.[23] As a matter of fact, the English and Wales jurisdiction provides for a mandatory sentence of life imprisonment for all persons convicted of murder, but it requires an increase in the minimum periods that persons convicted of murder have to serve before they can be considered for the release. Legislation establishes starting points for the minimum terms that judges should consider for murders of different kinds.[24] Connecting the criminal norms to their enforcement, a more flexible and coherent sentencing regime for murder would be a significant tool to review the current system as whole, in particular the determinants of the high indeterminate sentencing prisoners (Mitchell, and Roberts, 2012). As the scientific literature underlines, the increasing number of prisoners is strictly connected with policy choices and penal cultures. Policy choices in matter of life imprisonment show the reference to retention and public protection and penal culture shows the reference to public opinion. No exception for the United Kingdom.

Within Europe, the United Kingdom has the highest rate of life imprisonment per hundred thousand of national population (13 per 100,000 of national population, with 12.7 for England and Wales, 19.2 for Scotland and 8.3 for Northern Ireland[25]). Looking at the worldwide American exceptionalism (50.3 per 100,000 national population), we can identify a sort of British exceptionalism in the European context in this sense as well.[26]

Under current legislation, the judge establishes what is called "minimum term", namely what was known as the tariff period of life imprisonment that must be served in custody, considering instance of retribution and deterrence. In particular cases, exceptionally serious murders, the judge may even impose a "whole life order", which involves that no minimum term is set for release. Once the minimum term has been served, life prisoners are eligible for the consideration of release on licence by the Parole Board and they are under the jurisdiction of the probation service, with the potential for recall to prison.

Therefore, the English and Welsh approach in matter of whole-tariff order can be also considered in the light of the wider phenomenon of post-conviction indefinite detention, primarily linked to the imprisonment for public protection that was provided by Sections 224–236 of the *Criminal Justice Act 2003* (on the fixed-term sentences, see Creighton, and Arnott, 2009: especially 534–548). According to this discipline, an IPP sentence was imposed to any person convicted of serious offence, if the Court was "of the opinion that there is a significant risk to members of the public of serious harm occasioned by the commission of further specified offences".[27] This sentence was struck down under Section 123 of the *Legal Aid, Sentencing and Punishment of Offenders Act* (LASPO) 2012, which came into force on 3 December 2012,[28] but since 2003, it implied that the convicted person could be kept in prison indefinitely. As van Zyl Smit and Appleton note, the change was not made retrospective and thousands of individuals sentenced to IPP remain in prison (Appleton, and van Zyl Smit, 2016: pos. 4841, 12848). After the abolition of the IPP sentence, the number of persons serving indeterminate sentences in England and Wales has started to diminish, but thousands of inmates remain have gone beyond their formal minimum term.[29] As a matter of fact, they are subject to administrative recall and so even though the numbers of unreleased IPPs reduced, many then found themselves back in prison. "It is paradoxical that a system can improve its procedures significantly and yet end up incarcerating more indeterminate sentence prisoners for longer periods".[30]

The *Criminal Justice Act 2003* gives judges the power to set minimum terms without the interference of the Secretary of State but requires them, when setting the minimum term to serve by a convicted murderer, to have regard to principles set out in Schedule 21 to the Act. This provision remains the main critical aspect of the English and Welsh legislation. With regard to whole life order, English Courts and the European Courts intervened many times in recent years.

In the pivotal decision *Vinter and Others v United Kingdom*,[31] the Grand Chamber held that the administration of whole-life orders in England and Wales violates Article 3 of the ECHR because it excludes a real prospect and a practical possibility of release. The Strasbourg judge established that a sentence of life imprisonment compliant with Article 3 must be reducible *de jure* and *de facto*.[32] The ECtHR found the lack of an appropriate review procedure in the domestic law. In the previous case of *R. v Bieber*[33] and in the subsequent cases of *R. v Newell* and *McLoughlin*[34] – the judicial response to *Vinter*[35] – the view of the English Court of Appeal was radically different. This judicial body affirmed that an appropriate mechanism of release is already in place and the prospect of review is anchored in the power of the Secretary of State to release any prisoner on compassionate grounds in "exceptional circumstance"[36] under Section 30 of the *Crime Sentences Act* in a manner compatible with Article 3 of the Convention. According to *McLoughlin*, the statutory power of compassionate release, describing it as having a "wide meaning"[37] beyond its literal wording, allows and requires the evaluation of penological ground for incarceration. This conclusion can attract criticism because it requires that the Secretary of State to limit his discretionary power not taking into account the narrow parameters of the "Lifer Manual",[38] although this set of provisions is established by the very Secretary of State. The Fourth Section of the ECtHR[39] and then the Grand Chamber in *Hutchinson*[40] overruled the interpretation of the English and Welsh law adopted in *Vinter*, accepting the Court of Appeal's argument and the claim that the administrative discretion would be carried out in a way which allowed the assessment of penological grounds without any real evidence to support this and ended up holding that the whole-life sentence regime was at that point Convention compliant.

> In England and Wales, the unfortunate effect of *Hutchinson* is likely to be that whole-life orders will continue to make the life sentences to which they attach irreducible in practice.
>
> *van Zyl Smit, and Appleton, 2019: 47*

This case can be considered a crucial phase in the relationship between the United Kingdom and the Court of Strasbourg but first of all a way to focus on the role of the ECtHR in the protection of prisoners' rights. There were a number of decisions like *Murray v The Netherlands*,[41] *Matiošaitis v Lithuania*[42]and *Petukhov v Ukraine*[43] that confirmed that formal provision to assure release may be not exhaustive with the regard to the criteria set out in *Vinter.*[44] As a matter of fact, the conventional obligation to reduce whole-life imprisonment is declined according to specific procedural rules. This requires a concrete prospect of release for the person sentenced; the communication of the conditions and of the mechanisms which make *de facto* the sentence reducible at its outset; it implies that the prisoner has to know the term in which the review of his sentence will take place and can be requested; it involves the duty determining the progress in rehabilitation and, consequently, assessing the ongoing justification of the custody.[45] It must be clear "what a prisoner must do to be considered for release and under what conditions"[46] and these conditions must be made known to the prisoners, to the extent they can gain a "precise cognizance" of such requirements.[47] Given that penological justifications for imprisonment are not immutable, the Court in *Vinter* established that a periodic review, suggested at the point of 25-year imprisonment, should take place to evaluate if it is penologically justified to keep an offender imprisoned. Although Section 30 of the *1997*

Act did (and does) not fulfil these procedural criteria, the United Kingdom did not amend it. Albeit the UK Government did not provide examples of judicial review of a refusal by the Secretary of State to release a life prisoner, the ECtHR is "satisfied" that a "significant judicial safeguard is now in place".[48] There is no case law that explains any meaning given to "exceptional circumstances" and the "Lifer Manual" – the only current possible avenue to release – has not been revised for clarity. It is noteworthy, in that regard, that no whole tariff prisoner has ever been released in the United Kingdom.

In *Lendore*,[49] the UK Privy Council conceives *Hutchinson* as confirming a fair Article 3 standard and strengthening the United Kingdom's position.[50] That Court defined cases like *Trabelsi* that providing "objective, pre-established criteria" as an example of misapplication of Article 3 fortunately reframed by *Hutchinson*. This decision is linked with *McLoughlin* and, especially with the argument articulated by Lord Thomas, according to whom it is "difficult to specify *in advance* what such circumstances might be, given that the heinous nature of the original crime justly required punishment by imprisonment for life".[51]

In *Hafeez v Secretary of State for the Home Department*,[52] the application leads the High Court to take into account the domestic leading decision *R (Wellington) v Secretary of State for the Home Department*[53] in matter of extradition in the light of *Trabelsi v Belgium* where the Strasbourg judge found a violation of the ECHR Article 3 for the State to extradite an individual sentenced to life imprisonment to the United States of America, exposing him or her to a treatment without any prospect of release. But the High Court, not strictly bound to comply with ECtHR judgement, dismissed Mr Hafeez's application, holding, unlike the European Court established with regard to Belgium,[54] that the US system in sentencing life imprisonment is compatible with the ECHR Article 3. In this regard, the English judge criticizes Strasbourg's view in *Trabelsi*.[55] On 24 March 2020, responding to the application of Mr Muhammed Asif Hafeez, the European Court handed down a decision[56] where it stated that it relied on the argument of the incompatibility of the extradition to the US with the European Convention, considering the risk of life imprisonment without parole but primarily the real risk that conditions in the federal detention centres were inhuman due to Covid-19 pandemic.

It needs to take into account these English decisions, in the wider context of the indeterminate sentences and of the United Kingdom's prison system as whole, not in the limited one of the whole-tariff order. As a matter of fact, in 2013, in *Osborn and Booth v The Parole Board*,[57] the UK Supreme Court held that prisoners serving indeterminate sentences should usually be permitted an oral hearing before the Parole Board when release can be considered and when the Parole Board is requested to assess licence conditions (on this issue, see Arnott, and Creighton, 2014).

As van Zyl Smit and Appleton note: "while the procedural protections for the release processes relating to most prisoners serving indeterminate sentences are being strengthened, English courts are not scrutinizing those procedures for prisoners subject to whole-life orders with equal care" (Appleton, and van Zyl

Smit, 2016: pos. 4984 di 12484). This can be framed as the result of a historical trend by the UK Government to circumscribe the judicial discretion in this matter, conceiving the judicial power as potentially insufficient to protect "public protection". In this regard, we can find a progressive element of the English and Welsh life sentence system. On this basis, most life prisoners serve the first part of their sentence under a high-security regime together with other sentenced prisoners, and from there, they proceed to prisons with a medium level of security and, subsequently, to a low-security regime or to open prison conditions where they have the opportunity to leave prison. Accredited programmes are designed to address deficits in thinking skills, violent and sexual offending and substance abuse. But, in practice, persons don't attend and complete these programmes. The Secretary of State has the power to recall a life-sentenced prisoner to prison without prior consultation with the parole board, referring to the parole board only thereafter (Padfield, 2012: 34–45).

The contrast is less evident if we consider that the access to rehabilitation was not adequate for prisoners in indeterminate sentences and it can thwart the real possibility of demonstrating successful rehabilitation before the Parole Board.[58] The Committee of Ministers and the Committee for the Prevention of Torture have worked to adopt penal policies that are aimed at resocializing prisoners (Cp. van Zyl Smit, and Snacken, 2009: 375–376). The Recommendation on Conditional Release (Parole), adopted by the Committee of Ministers of the Council of Europe, defines the relevance of conditional release: "Conditional release should aim at assisting prisoners to make a transition from life in prison to a law abiding life in the community through post-release conditions and supervision that promote this end and contribute to public safety and the reduction of crime in the community". As van Zyl Smit and Appleton underlined "one weakness of the English system is that, while the Parole Board has an absolute power to order release, it has no power to compel the prison authorities to take specific steps that are necessary to prepare the prisoner for potential release" (van Zyl Smit, and Appleton, 2019: 250).

This systemic lack is increased with the lockdown conditions. According to the data of the Prison Reform Trust, the anti-pandemic measures have reduced opportunities to take part in rehabilitation activities for the 11,000 prisoners serving indeterminate sentences (9,000 unreleased; 2000 recalled). This means that they cannot demonstrate to the Parole Board their progress and that the risk they pose has been reduced.[59]

Therefore, in general, the ECtHR case law calls into question English and Welsh sentencing and release policies and practices and the length of the minimum terms that all prisoners sentenced to mandatory life imprisonment must serve before they can even be considered for release. In particular, there is no mechanism able to protect the right to hope of the whole-tariff prisoner – which is fundamental to the human dignity of all persons[60] – to prohibit *de facto* whole life sentence, which is a sentence where the prospect of review is denied and the punishment part of life sentences is undetermined.[61]

> Being sentenced to life imprisonment, or to an indeterminate period of imprisonment, brings a unique pain to the experience of incarceration, since it removes the certainty of release on a given date in the future. Furthermore, the painfulness of indeterminacy may be more pronounced for individuals sentenced to life imprisonment without parole (LWOP), who have little or no prospect of release.
>
> *(van Zyl Smit, and Appleton, 2019: 179)*

For, however, leniently the ECtHR might have treated the UK government in *Hutchinson*, it has made it clear in a series of recent judgements that it will hold other contracting parties to reasonably exacting standards (Dyer, 2020: 484–590). In particular, the *Murray* judgement relied on the individualization and progression principles to be applied in evaluating whether a life-sentenced prisoner had a *de facto* possibility of release[62] and these criteria are also supported by international non-European instruments.[63] The legal effect of the *Hutchinson* decision is circumscribed to England and Wales that remain one of the jurisdictions in the global scenario in which the narrow provisions ensure that life imprisonment without parole is practically irreducible.[64]

The compliance of the English and Welsh legislation on compensation with the European Court of Human Rights case law: an indicator

After Brexit and during the post-transitional phase that will end on January 2021, the question is how the protection of prisoners' rights in England and Wales can be framed in the European context. Recently this issue has been emerged with regard to the violation of Article 6 (2) ECHR.

In this regard, we will focus on the case *R (Hallam and Nealon) v Secretary of State for Justice*,[65] which can be considered an indicator of the English Courts' approach, and especially of the Supreme Court of the United Kingdom, with regard to the ECtHR case law. The appeals concerned the entitlement to compensation of persons whose criminal convictions were subsequently quashed for being unsafe. The Secretary of State for Justice refused the applications for compensation under Section 133 of the *Criminal Justice Act 1988*[66] on the ground that the new evidence did not show beyond reasonable doubt that they had not committed the offences. The appellants argued that the requirement contained in Section 133 that a new or newly discovered fact must show beyond reasonable doubt that the person did not commit the offence, in the absence of which they are unable to claim compensation, is incompatible with the presumption of innocence contained in the ECHR Article 6 (2).

The appeal obliged the Supreme Court to take into account whether it should have departed from its previous decision in *R (Adams) v Secretary of State for Justice*[67] in the light of the decision in *Allen v United Kingdom*,[68] where the ECtHR held that an applicant's Article 6 (2) right was not violated "where the conviction rendered the conviction unsafe, because, had it been available at the time of trial, a reasonable jury might or might not have convicted".

Lord Mance who delivered the leading judgement refuses to depart from *Adams* or follows the case law of the ECtHR if and insofar the ECtHR may have, in the past, gone further than this.[69] Lady Hale also considered the ECtHR's jurisprudence in this area to be evolving and it was not appropriate for the Court to make a declaration of incompatibility in proceedings brought by an individual in respect of whom the ECtHR would be unlikely to find a violation.[70] In this regard, the opinion of Lord Wilson is very significant because he argues that he "cannot subscribe to the ECtHR analysis in this area, despite the high professional regard in which he holds its judges, the desirability of a uniform interpretation of article 6 (2) throughout the states of the Council of Europe",[71] because "his belief that there is no room left for constructive dialogue between this court and the ECtHR, and his recognition that the appellants are likely to prevail before the ECtHR in establishing a violation of their Convention rights".[72] Having regard to the "unsettled state of the ECtHR's case law", Lord Lloyd-Jones did not affirm that Section 133 is incompatible with the Convention.

In his dissenting opinion, Lord Reed, the President of the Supreme Court, expressed a different idea:

> Whilst it may be appropriate for this Court to decline to follow the ECtHR in certain circumstances, no circumstances of that kind exist here: the Grand Chamber's judgement in Allen was carefully considered, is based on a detailed analysis of the relevant case law, is consistent with a line of authority going back decades, and has been followed by the ECtHR subsequently.[73]

The judge did not accept that the Supreme Court should deliberately adopt a construction of the Convention which it knows to be out of the step with the ECtHR's approach, established by numerous judgements and confirmed at the level of the Grand Chamber. Agreeing with Lord Reed, Lord Kerr notes that there exists the requisite link between the concluded criminal proceedings and the compensation proceedings, which is the test articulated in a clear and constant line of Strasbourg jurisprudence. Therefore, this decision is a demonstration of different perspectives on the European case law and on the interpretations of the ECtHR in the United Kingdom.

The British set-up should not only be conceived as exceptional and Eurosceptic, because the United Kingdom is probably emblematic of challenges that the whole European human rights system is currently facing with regard to Russia, Poland and Hungary. At the same time, criticism towards the European Court must consider that the Court's judgement might not give impetus to proper reforms but the "Court's output, seen as an *acquis*, acquire a certain meta-function" (Dzehtsiarou, and Tzevelekos, 2020: 5), as a matter of fact "by means of its judgement the Court impact on the fabric of legal order in the respondent state".[74] Notwithstanding the ancient and deep national traditional and political opposition to European institutions, this also happened in England and Wales.

Notes

1 Under Article 50 of the Treaty on the European Union, on 29 March 2017, the British Government communicates to the Council of Europe its intention to withdraw from the European Union. On that date, the British Parliament, after the question posed by the UK Supreme Court on the consultative nature of the referendum held on 26 June 2016 ended with the result of 48.17% for "remain" against 51.9% for "leave", approved it. For further information, see https://www.gov.uk.

2 "Following the 'Brexit' vote of June 2016, the pressure for change coming from European institutions is increasingly likely to be resisted. And standards in prison have generally been declining in recent years, not improving".

3 In this regard, we can consider especially Article 3 of the Act which states that "So far as it is possible to do so, primary legislation and subordinate legislation must be read and given effect in a way which is compatible with the convention rights" (Human Rights Act 1998, s. 3) and the Article 6 concerning the acts of public authorities that provides: "It is unlawful for a public authority to act in a way which is incompatible with a Convention right" (*Human Rights Act 1998*, s. 6). In the United Kingdom, the executive is legally obliged to discharge his duties in accordance with the European Convention of Human Rights.

4 Intentions to repeal the *Human Right Act*, which binds the United Kingdom to act in accordance with the European Convention, have been expressed, by the current Prime Minister as well, and vigorously after *Vinter*. As Andrew Dyer notes with regard to irreducible life sentence: "One of the reasons for the lower level of protection in UK is the 'weak form' model of judicial review for which the Human Rights Act provides" (Dyer, 2020: 484–590, especially 489). Cp. *Human Rights Act 1998*, UK, sec. 4.

5 Paulo Pinto de Albuquerque underlined two forms of criticism with regard to the ECtHR, the political one and the legal one. Cp. P. Pinto de Albuquerque (2017).

6 In 1991, the House of Lords recognized that marital rape is a crime for the first time and the ECtHR upheld their approach. Cp. *R v R* [1991] UKHL 12.

7 *Tyrer v United Kingdom*, 1978, 2, EHRR at 31.

8 *Demir v Turkey*, 2009, 48 EHRR 54 at 146–154, check.

9 *Hassan v. United Kingdom*, GC, App. n. 29750/09, September 16, 2014.

10 Lord Hoffmann, "The Universality of Human Rights", available at: www.judiciary.gov.uk/media/speeches/2009/speech-lord-Hoffmann-19032009.

11 *Greens and M.T. v United Kingdom*, (2011) 53 EHRR 21.

12 Cp. P. Pinto de Albuquerque, "Is the ECHR facing an existential crisis?", Speech delivered at the Mansfield College, Oxford, April 28, 2017.

13 *Hutchinson v United Kingdom* 2015, dissenting opinion of Judge Paulo Pinto de Albuquerque at 40.

14 *Hirst v. United Kingdom* (No. 2) GC, (2006) 42 EHRR 41.

15 Cp. Council of Europe, Committee of Ministers, Hirst against the United Kingdom, no. 2, Interim Resolution CM/Res DH (2009) 160, December 3, 2009.

16 *Scoppola v Italy* (No. 3), GC (2013) 56 EHHR 19.

17 *Hirst v. United Kingdom*, at 72.

18 *Greens and M.T. v United Kingdom*, cit.

19 *Anchugov v Russia*, App.nos 11157/04 and 15162/05, July 4, 2013.

20 This is the paraphrase of the point of view expressed by Judge Kūris in *Matiošaitis v Lithuania* mentioned in the following pages of this chapter: "The Lithuanian authorities clearly had to be aware of the prevailing – and very strong – trend in the post-Vinter development of the Court's case law pertaining to the alleged irreducibility of life imprisonment. They were obliged not to dismiss this trend, but to take into account if this enters into the domain of proactive penal policy rather than being strictly confined to the domain of the law of the Convention, as interpreted in the pre-Vinter case law" (Kūris in *Matiošaitis v Lithuania*, Judge Kūris at 8).

21 The Council of Europe emphasizes that in the context of structuring the release process, "the most important decision to be made is which criteria will be used whether a prisoner can or cannot be granted release", Council Recommendation (2003) *on Conditional Release (parole), Explanatory Memorandum* at 18.

22 In England and Wales, the definition of murder includes intentional homicide as well as instances where the offender, while intending only grievous bodily harm, causes death, see Mitchell, and Roberts (2012: 16).

23 In England, Wales, Scotland and Northern Ireland, life imprisonment may be imposed for a wide range of offences, including adult rape and burglary even where no homicide occurs in the commission of the offence. Only in the United Kingdom (0.1%) and in Georgia (11.7%) are any prisoners serving life imprisonment for drug offences. See van Zyl Smit, and Appleton (2019: 141).

24 The *Criminal Justice Act of 2003* sets out in a schedule various starting points for trial judges that they have to adopt in relation to various degrees of seriousness from 15 years to a whole life order, where there would be no minimum period.

25 *Council of Europe Annual Penal Statistics: Prison Populations, Surveys 2016* (Strasbourg: Council of Europe, 2018, check new data). Institute for Criminal Policy Research, World Prison Brief, point out 13.4.

26 van Zyl Smit and Morrison wrote on the "Scottish exceptionalism" in "The Paradox of Scottish Life Imprisonment", *European Journal of Crime, Criminal Law and Criminal Justice*, 28 (2020), pp. 76–101. On the contiguity between death penalty and life imprisonment without parole in England and Wales, see Pettigrew (2016: 1–15).

27 *Criminal Justice Act 2003*, s. 226, 1 b.

28 The LASPO 2012 replaced IPP sentences with new Extended Determinate Sentences (EDS). While technically not indeterminate, they both extend the period of custody that offenders serve and revoke automatic release at a fixed point in their sentence. In this regard, see the current set-up: Report of Prison Reform Trust "Prison: the facts. Bromley Briefings Summer 2019", despite its abolition in 2012, over nine in ten people (91%) serving an IPP sentence are still in prison having passed their tariff expiry date – the minimum period they must spend in custody and considered necessary to serve as punishment for the offence (p. 8), available at: http://www.prisonreformtrust.org.uk/Portals/0/Documents/Bromley%20Briefings/Prison%20the%20facts%20Summer%202019.pdf

29 According to the Report of Prison Reform Trust "Prison: the facts. Bromley Briefings Summer 2019", despite its abolition in 2012, over nine in ten people (91%) serving an IPP sentence are still in prison having passed their tariff expiry date – the minimum period they must spend in custody and considered necessary to serve as punishment for the offence (p. 8), available at: http://www.prisonreformtrust.org.uk/Portals/0/Documents/Bromley%20Briefings/Prison%20the%20facts%20Summer%202019.pdf. Data sources: Table 1.9, Ministry of Justice (2019) Offender management statistics quarterly: October to December 2018, London: Ministry of Justice.

30 *Ibidem*.

31 *Vinter* [2016] 63 EHRR 1.

32 In this sense the previous *Kafkaris v Cyprus* GC (2009) 49 EHRR 35, at 98.

33 *R. v Bieber* [2008] EWCA Crim 1601, [2009] 1 All ER 295.

34 *R. v McLoughlin* [2014] EWCA Crim 118; [2014] 1 WLR 3964.

35 In the general election, the Conservative Party promoted the paper "Protecting Human Rights in the UK", which expresses the will to break with the Strasbourg Court.

36 According to the judicial reasoning of the Court of Appeal, since the meaning of exceptional circumstances would evolve under common law, it is not necessary a further explanation of release procedures for whole life prisoners. *McLoughlin* [2014], at 36, check.

37 *McLoughlin* [2014], at 33.

38 The criteria that must be met by a prisoner to be considered for release are provided for the Chapter of the Indeterminate Sentence Manual ("the lifer manual") issued by the Secretary of State as *Prison Service Order 4700* and is restricted, in its wording, to compassionate release when a prisoner is terminally ill.
39 *Hutchinson v United Kingdom* (2015) 61 EHRR 13.
40 *Hutchinson v United Kingdom* GC, App. no. 5792/08, January 17 2017.
41 *Murray v The Netherlands* (2017) 64 EHHR 3. The Grand Chamber focused on the individualization and progression principle to ascertain whether a life-sentenced prisoner has a *de facto* possibility of release.
42 *Matiošaitis v Lithuania*, Applications nos. 22662/13, 51059/13, 58823/13, 59692/13, 59700/13, 60115/13, 69425/13 and 72824/13, May 23, 2017.
43 *Petukhov v Ukraine (No 2)*, Applications no. 41216/13, March 12, 2019. The Court held that the Ukrainian rules lack clarity regarding the applicable tariff period so that "prisoners who receive a whole life sentence do not know from the outset what they must do in order to be considered for release and under what conditions" (para 174). According to *Murray v The Netherlands*, the Strasbourg judge also established that the State haș "a positive obligation to secure prison regimes to life prisoners which are compatible with the aim of rehabilitation and enable such prisoners to make progress towards their rehabilitation" (para 181).
44 To compare the ECtHR approach in *Matiošaitis* and in *Hutchinson* in the application of the *Vinter* criteria, see Graham (2018: 258). The author notes that "the Court in Matiošatis (...) emphasized to a much greater extent the reducibility of the sentence de facto and the clarity of associated criteria for this; asserted a higher standard of proof; applied greater scrutiny to the State's claims, and, crucially, seemed to reassert the strand of jurisprudence that Article 3 requirements must be present from the start of the sentence, a facet so gravely overlooked in Hutchinson". To focus on this issue, M. Pettigrew mentions, "Politics, Power and Parole in Strasbourg: Dissociative Judgement and Differential Treatment at the European Court of Human Rights". Referring to *Matiošaitis v Lithuania* and the judgement rendered earlier in the year by the Grand Chamber in Hutchinson v United Kingdom, Mark Pettigrew underlines that "the real difference between the two, it is submitted, is of the political power of the respective nations at the level of the threat that they pose to the court by virtue of remaining or withdrawing from its remit" (p. 16).
45 These criteria integrate the so-called *Vinter* review. On this issue, see van Zyl Smit, Weatherby and Creighton (2014: 59–84).
46 *Vinter v United Kingdom* (2013) 63 EHRR 1 at 122.
47 *Trabelsi v. Belgium* (2015) 60 EHRR 21 at 137.
48 *Hutchinson v United Kingdom*, at 53.
49 *Lendore* v *Attorney General of Trinidad and Tobago* [2017] UKPC 25 WLR 3369.
50 *Lendore* at 70.
51 *R. v McLoughlin* [2014] cit., Lord Thomas at 36.
52 *Hafeez v Secretary of State for the Home Department* [2020] EWHC 155 (Admin).
53 *R (Wellington) v Secretary of State for the Home Department* [2018] UKHL 72.
54 In the pre-Vinter era, in *Harkins v United Kingdom* and *Ahmad v United Kingdom*, the European Court held the United Kingdom would not violate the ECHR Article 3 if the applicants were extradited to the United States. Cp. *Harkins v United Kingdom* (2012) 55 EHRR 19; *Ahmad v United Kingdom* (2013) 56 EHRR 1.
55 "The Court considered that, even if some detailed consideration of the review scheme in the United States were appropriate, on this issue the judgement in Trabelsi was wholly unreasoned", *Hafeez v Secretary of State*, para 56.
56 *Hafeez v United Kingdom*, App. no 14189/20, March 24 2020.
57 *Osborn and Booth v Parole Board* [2013] UKSC 61 [2013] 3 WLR 102. See also *R (Haney, Kaiyam, and Massey) v the Secretary of State for Justice* [2014] UKSC 66, [2015] A.C. 1344.

58 *James, Well and Lee v United Kingdom*, 2012.
59 Representing the Howard League for Penal Reform and the Prison Reform Trust, Simon Creighton, founding partner of Bhatt Murphy Solicitor in London, issues the government with a letter before action over what they alleged was the government's failure to respond effectively to the coronavirus pandemic in prisons, cp. https://www.lawgazette.co.uk/lawyer-in-the-news/lawyer-in-the-news-simon-creighton-bhatt-murphy/5104116.article.
60 *Vinter v United Kingdom*, Concurring opinion of Judge Power-Forde.
61 The English law provides for a distinction between the punishment part of the life sentence and the part designed to incapacitate the life prisoner in order to reduce risk to society.
62 "The Contracting Parties to the Convention have a positive obligation to promote resocialization of prisoners namely by providing and implementing an individualized sentence plan. This is the very first time that the Court has acknowledged the crucial importance of an individualized sentence plan for the promotion of resocialization of prisoners, that importance being reinforced by a statement of principle of the Grand Chamber", *Murray v The Netherlands*, Concurring opinion of Paulo Pinto de Albuquerque at 2, check.
63 UN General Assembly, *United Nations Standard Minimum Rules for the Treatment of Prisoners*, December 17, 2015, especially Rules 4, 87 and 90.
64 Haiti, Honduras, Israel, Mexico, Turkey and the United States.
65 *R (Hallam and Nealon) v Secretary of State for Justice*, [2019], UKSC 2.
66 This provision has been amended by section 175 of the Anti-social Behaviour, Crime and Policing Act 2014.
67 *R (Adams) v Secretary of State for Justice* [2011], UKSC 18.
68 *Allen v United Kingdom*,
69 *R (Hallam and Nealon) v Secretary of State for Justice*, [2019], UKSC 2, para 48.
70 *Ibidem*, paras 78–82.
71 *Ibidem*, para 94.
72 *Ibidem*.
73 *Ibidem*, para 174.
74 *Ibidem*. We can affirm that the ECtHR judgements have an impact even if they are not properly enforced.

References

Books and Articles

Appleton, C., van Zyl Smit, D., "The paradox of reform: Life imprisonment in England and Wales", in D. van Zyl Smit, C. Appleton (eds.), *Life Imprisonment and Human Rights*, Oxford: Hart Publishing, 2016, kindle, pos. 4745-5266 of 12484.

Arnott, A., Creighton, S., *Parole Board Hearings. Law and Practice*, Legal Action Group, London, 2014.

Creighton, S., Arnott, H., *Prisoners. Law and Practice*, Legal Action Groups, London, 2009.

Creighton, S., Padfield, N., Pirosa, R., "England and Wales: An uncertain relationship with European institutions", in G. Cliquennois, H. de Suremain (eds.), *Monitoring Penal Policy in Europe*, Routledge, London-New York, 2018.

Dyer, A. "Irreducible Life Sentences, Craig Minogue and the Capacity of Human Rights Charters to make a Difference", *UNSW Law Journal*, 43 (2020), 2, pp. 484–590.

Dzehtsiarou, K., Tzevelekos, V. P., "The Conscience of Europe that Landed in Strasbourg: A Circle of Life of the European Court of Human Rights", *The European Convention on Human Rights Law Review*, 1 (2020), 2, pp. 1–6.

Graham, L., "From Vinter to Hutchinson and Back Again? The Story of Life Imprisonment Cases in the European Court of Human Rights", *European Human Rights Law Review*, 2018 (2018). Available at SSRN: https://ssrn.com/abstract=4087763 or http://dx.doi.org/10.2139/ssrn.4087763

Lord Neuberger, Cambridge Freshfields Annual Law Lecture 2014, "The British and Europe", February 12, 2014.

Mitchell, B., Roberts, J., *Exploring the Mandatory Life Sentence for Murder*, Hart Publishing, Oxford, 2012.

Padfield, N., "Monitoring Prisons in England and Wales: Who Ensures the Fair Treatment of Prisoners?", *Crime Law and Social Change*, 70 (2007), 1, pp. 1–20, especially p. 2.

Padfield, N., "Recalling Conditionally Released Prisoners in England and Wales", *European Journal of Probation*, 4 (2012), pp. 34–45.

Pettigrew, M., "A Tale of Two Cities: Whole of Life Prison Sentences in Strasbourg and Westminster", *European Journal of Crime, Criminal Law and Criminal Justice*, 23 (2015), pp. 281–299.

Pettigrew, M., "American Policy British Politics: Whole of Life Imprisonment and Transatlantic Influence", *International Journal of Comparative and Applied Criminal Justice*, 40 (2016), 3, pp. 1–15.

Pettigrew, M., "Politics, Power and Parole in Strasbourg: Dissociative Judgement and Differential Treatment at the European Court of Human Rights", *International Comparative Jurisprudence*, 4 (2018), 1, pp. 16–26.

Spano, R., "The Future of the European Court of Human Rights – Subsidiarity, Process-Based Review and the Rule of Law", *Human Rights Law Review*, 18 (2018), 3, pp. 473–494.

van Zyl Smit, D., Appleton, C., *Life Imprisonment. A Global Human Rights Analysis*, Harvard University Press, Cambridge, 2019.

van Zyl Smit, D., Morrison, K., "The Paradox of Scottish Life Imprisonment", *European Journal of Crime, Criminal Law and Criminal Justice*, 28 (2020), pp. 76–101.

van Zyl Smit, D., Snacken, S., *Principles of European Prison Law and Policy: Penology and Human Rights*, Oxford University Press, Oxford, 2009.

van Zyl Smit, D., Weatherby, P., Creighton, S., "Whole life Sentences and the Tide of European Human Rights Jurisprudence: What is to Be Done?", *Human Rights Law Review*, 14 (2014), 1, pp. 59–84.

Legislation and Documents

Council of Europe Annual Penal Statistics: Prison Populations, Surveys 2016.

Council of Europe, Committee of Ministers, Hirst against United Kingdom, no. 2, Interim Resolution CM/Res DH, 2009, 160, December 3 2009.

Council Recommendation, 2003, on Conditional Release (parole), Explanatory Memorandum.

Criminal Justice Act 2003.

Human Rights Act 1998.

Prison Service Order 4700, 2010.

UN General Assembly, United Nations Standard Minimum Rules for the Treatment of Prisoners, December 17, 2015.

Cases European Court of Human Rights

Ahmad v United Kingdom, 2013, 56 EHRR.

Anchugov v Russia, App.nos 11157/04 and 15162/05, July 4 2013.

Demir v Turkey, 2009, 48 EHRR 54.

Greens and M.T. v United Kingdom, 2011, 53 EHRR 21.

Hafeez v United Kingdom, App. no 14189/20, March 24 2020.
Harkins v United Kingdom, 2012, 55 EHRR 19.
Hassan v United Kingdom, GC, App. n. 29750/09, September 16 2014.
Hirst v United Kingdom (No. 2) GC, 2006, 42 EHRR 41.
Hutchinson v United Kingdom, 2015, 61 EHRR 13.
Hutchinson v United Kingdom GC, App. no. 5792/08, January 17 2017.
Kafkaris v Cyprus GC, 2009, 49 EHRR 35.
Matiošaitis v Lithuania, Applications nos. 22662/13, 51059/13, 58823/13, 59692/13, 59700/13, 60115/13, 69425/13 and 72824/13, May 23 2017.
Murray v The Netherlands, 2017, 64 EHRR 3.
Petukhov v Ukraine (No 2), App. no. 41216/13, March 12 2019.
Scoppola v Italy (No. 3), GC, 2013, 56 EHRR 19.
Trabelsi v Belgium, 2015, 60 EHRR 21.
Tyrer v United Kingdom 1978) 2, EHRR.
Vinter v United Kingdom (2013) 63 EHRR 1.

The United Kingdom

Hafeez v Secretary of State for the Home Department, 2020, EWHC 155 (Admin).
Lendore v Attorney General of Trinidad and Tobago, 2017, UKPC 25 WLR 3369.
Osborn and Booth v Parole Board, 2013, UKSC 61 [2013] 3 WLR 102.
R (Adams) v Secretary of State for Justice, 2011, UKSC 18.
R. *v Bieber* [2008] EWCA Crim 1601, 2009, 1 All ER 295.
R (Hallam and Nealon) v Secretary of State for Justice, 2019, UKSC 2.
R. *v McLoughlin*, 2014 EWCA Crim 118; 2014, 1 WLR 3964.
R (Haney, Kaiyam, and Massey) v the Secretary of State for Justice, 2014, UKSC 66, [2015] A.C. 1344.
R v R, 1991, UKHL 12.
R (Wellington) v Secretary of State for the Home Department, 2018, UKHL 72.

News and Websites

On the Brexit: https://www.gov.uk.
On the initiative of Simon Creighton with regard to the government' failure to respond effectively to the coronavirus pandemic in prisons: https://www.lawgazette.co.uk/lawyer-in-the-news/lawyer-in-the-news-simon-creighton-bhatt-murphy/5104116.article.
On the Lord Hoffmann's speech on the Universality of Human Rights: www.judiciary.gov.uk/media/speeches/2009/speech-lord-Hoffmann-19032009.
On the percentage of inmates who serving an IPP sentence are still in prison having passed their tariff expiry date and on the LASPO Act 2012: http://www.prisonreformtrust.org.uk/Portals/0/Documents/Bromley%20Briefings/Prison%20the%20facts%20Summer%202019.pdf.

12

SYSTEMIC EFFECTS AND DASHED EXPECTATIONS

The two tales of prison litigation in Germany

Christine Morgenstern and Mary Rogan

Introduction

The control of prisons and the protection of those in prison rest on two pillars: Institutional oversight and prison monitoring by national and international bodies as the first pillar and individual complaints procedures, including the possibility to challenge prison decisions before a court as the second pillar. In this chapter, we will concentrate on two aspects of this combined protection system in the German context. First, we will look at prison litigation in Germany and highlight its overall impact on the prison system by introducing the legislative framework and analysing leading cases and recent case law. Second, we will explore in how far its practice keeps the legislation's promise by looking at the individual prisoner's possibility to access the courts and find redress when their rights have been infringed.

Prison litigation in the German context

The Constitutional basis: Fundamental rights and the citizen's right to complain

The German *Grundgesetz* (Basic Law, BL) of 1949 forms the constitutional basis for legislation, execution of state decisions and jurisprudence. It was drafted in 1948/1949 under the impression of the dictatorship and gross human rights violations during the Third Reich. Being aware of the weaknesses of its predecessor, the Weimar Constitution of 1919, the protection of human dignity was put to the forefront (Article 1 BL) and strong mechanisms were established to ensure that the executive respects fundamental rights and dignity. One of these safeguards concludes the Basic Law's Fundamental Rights Section and guarantees legal protection in Article 19 BL: 'Should anyone's rights be violated by public authority, he has recourse to the courts'.

DOI: 10.4324/9780429317033-16

Federal and state actions in Germany are usually based on detailed statutory legislation and a sophisticated regulation of administrative procedures. They are, following Article 19 BL, subject to judicial review by the various judicial branches, including a strong administrative jurisdiction. Despite this approach, effective and independent judicial oversight over prisons was not effectuated until the 1970s. Two decisions of the Federal Constitutional Court (FCC) (further outlined below) compelled the German legislator to introduce formal complaints procedures as part of primary prison legislation.

The Prison Acts: Prison oversight and the prisoner's right to complain

As a result, in 1977, the Prison Act (PA 1977) came into force. It regulated rights and duties of prisoners, prisons and the prison administration. It retained the established oversight system by the Ministries of Justice of the Federal States (*Länder*) and added a court procedure.

Departments of the Ministries as 'Higher prison authorities' are responsible for the overall organisation, including staff, material and financial resources and supervise and inspect prisons. As part of the Ministries, however, they are also directly involved in prison policy and often penal politics more generally. Other institutions can additionally be viewed as monitoring bodies, in that they can hold all public institutions to account, including prisons, at least by requesting information. These are parliamentary bodies, in particular the petition committees that exist in all, or ombudspersons who exist in some Federal States. North Rhine Westphalia is the only Federal State that has assigned a special ombudsperson for prisons (*Justizvollzugsbeauftragter*). On the prison level, prison committees (*Anstaltsbeirat*, literally translated as 'advisers to the prison') can be seen as a monitoring bodies. They consist of independent individuals (often nominated by political parties or other local or regional players and therefore perhaps less independent that envisaged) who have free access to prisoners. They can, inter alia, forward complaints to the prison governor and try to mediate conflicts. When these boards were established in 1977, the legislator had hoped to create a mechanism to link the inside to the outside and contribute to involve civil society in prison matters. Whether this endeavour was successful is dubious – in the literature, the prison committees hardly play a role. Prisoners will address representatives of all these bodies usually in writing, but in the case of ministerial officials and the prison committees they should also be able to contact them when they visit the prison.

As an innovation, the PA 1977 introduced a comprehensive system of complaints procedures and judicial review in a dedicated chapter on 'legal remedies'. It is not a two-tier system because the two forms can be applied by a prisoner independently from each other. The first option is an internal complaints mechanism, according to which every prisoner can directly 'apply to the head of the institution with requests, suggestions and complaints on matters concerning himself'. The second option is a judicial complaint. A designated chamber of the Regional Court was created (*Strafvollstreckungskammer,* here referred to as Special Prison Chamber) to deal with them and other decision relating to the prisoner, namely the decision on early release. The idea behind creating a specialised chamber was to establish the jurisprudence of specialised judges who are particularly knowledgeable about and acquainted with the prisons located near the court. The decision can be appealed to the Higher Regional Court, and the possibility of appeal exists for both the prisoner and the prison. Following the approach of Art. 19 BL, each and any decision taken in prison and even simple actions of prison guards such as not knocking at the prisoner's cell door can be the subject of such a judicial complaint.

In addition, prisoners have the possibility of a constitutional complaint to the FCC once all other judicial remedies are exhausted. It was established with the creation of the FCC in the 1950s and is (and was from the beginning) accessible for all citizens, including prisoners – two constitutional complaints led to the landmark decision mentioned above and should be taken as a first proof for the importance of judicial decisions on prisons in Germany.

In September 2006, a major Constitutional Law Reform was enacted that redistributed the legislative competences for prison legislation to the Federal States (*Länder*). Regional differences are a notorious feature of both sentencing styles and prison policy, even when both were based on the same legislation. The changes did not affect the judicial complaints procedures for prisoners (sec. 109–121 PA), as this specific part of the PA 1977 remained in force. Nevertheless, it was feared that different regional developments in prison legislation could change the quality of prison sentences as such and would tear apart what should be a uniform approach to punishment. A detailed analysis of the impact of the reform is beyond the scope of this chapter. The general assessment is that it could have been worse and that many of the 16 new Prison Acts even introduced useful new regulations.

No dedicated statistics exist that would measure for example how many or how often prisoners complain before the courts, and no data on the outcome, length of procedure is collected. Statistics exist, however, on the volume of cases dealt with by the courts, including the caseload of judicial complaints before the Special Prison Chamber.[1] When comparing the number of judicial complaints to the number of prisoners in a longitudinal perspective, no clear picture emerges. At least the significantly decreasing number of prisoners has not led to a significantly lower number of complaint cases; if at all, rather the opposite is the case: In 1997, the courts dealt with 8,051 prisoner complaints; the highest number can be found for 2005 (12,481). In recent years, it has been between 10,000 and 11,000 per year (10,261 in 2019).

Falling short of expectations: The judicial complaint of prisoners reflected by research, practice and prison reform initiatives

In the years after the new Prison Act came in force, empirical prison research flourished, but the complaints system remains an under-researched area. The most important study was published in 1981 by Diepenbruck. He analysed prisoner files and interviewed prison staff, judges and prisoners in three Federal States. The aim of his study was an evaluation of the reformed complaints system and particularly the newly introduced judicial complaint; he wanted to know if they were effective and in practice can strengthen prisoner's rights. Aware of the interplay between informal and formal ways of complaining, the practical impediments for complaints and the bureaucracy involved, he developed a typology of complainants. Among these are the querulous prisoners who need to be distinguished from the prisoner who often complains because he has been provoked. Another type is the prisoner who complains once but then is silenced by disappointment and yet another the prisoner who is fearful from the start. In his interviews, the prisoners were sceptical about their chances of success, they feared repressions by staff, sometimes by other prisoners, and saw prison staff, Ministry and court as one 'front'. Diepenbruck (1981) also looked at the success rate of different forms of complaints: One third of all complaints before the prison director were solved in a way that the prisoner reached either what he wanted or another form of solution he could accept. When this was not the case, prisoners usually did not go further (only in 12% of these cases, they sought a judicial remedy). Complaints to the court were only successful in 3–6% of all cases. Hardly ever an appeal was launched after a case lost before the court.

In the 1980s, two more studies contributed to our understanding of judicial complaints. One found that the system was not applied in a way that was beneficial to the aim of resocialisation because both prison administrations and courts gave away the chance to show prisoners that they were taken seriously as complainants before court (Laubenstein 1984). Another study showed that most prisoners involved in judicial complaint cases did not have a legal representative; mostly, because they did now know how to get one, and because this field was not attractive for defence lawyers (Litwinski and Bublies 1989).

In the 1990s, two studies disagreed on how the system of judicial complaints could be made more effective for prisoners: Analysing statistical data from over 1600 complaints procedures in the largest German State, North Rhine Westphalia (NRW), Kamman (1991) confirmed a quite low success rate – less than 10% – and analysed the different reasons for failure. He reported a difficult relationship between judges and prison authorities. Critical of the usually written procedure, he suggested to hold preliminary mediatory hearings with all parties involved. This idea of a quasi-problem-solving court, however, did not find many followers because a risk for the impartiality of judges was feared (Feest and Lesting 2009). A decidedly critical approach was taken in a study by Feest, Lesting and Selling (1997: 202, Feest and Lesting 2009: 675) who coined the phrase of 'refractory prison authorities': They showed that defiance of prison administration to implement court decisions where prisoners had won their cases went beyond some peculiar, isolated cases. They also found that the courts themselves were very reluctant to intervene and must be, in particular because of the wide discretion for prison authorities, regarded as 'impotent' (Feest, Lesting and Selling 1997: 202).

While for these authors more and/or better judicial protection of prisoners was indispensable, two later studies critically framed the system of judicial complaints as 'juridification' or 'judicialisation' of the prison. Wingenfeld (1998) described the courts' task to control decisions by prison staff as nearly unmanageable because of the many vague rules in the Prison Act that leave (too) much room for discretion. The second study (Bergmann 2003) deals with the implications of court complaints for daily prison practice. Particularly interesting are findings that describe (drawing on Christie 1985) how judicial complaints contribute to the 'expropriation of conflicts'. In her study, prisoners generally were reluctant to go to court because they are afraid of drawbacks inside prison. They did, however, think that conflicts were solvable within the prison and that staff often finds a constructive way of dealing with conflicts. Interestingly, some prisoners thought that prison staff is happy to be challenged about difficult decisions because in that way it is the Ministry or the court that takes the ultimate responsibility for an unpopular decision (Bergmann 2003). Generally, the author finds 'ambivalent' or even 'negative effects' (Bergmann 2003: 217, 266) of a formalised complaints system that opens the way to the courts; she claims that by the judicial clarification of certain rules and practices the prisons lose the necessary room for manoeuvre and tend to make decisions 'court proof' instead of effectively addressing the situation.

A recent study focused on remand prisoners and their special legal and practical possibilities to complain before a court about detention matters (Graebsch, Descarpes and Lederer 2018). It painted a particular bleak picture, finding that conditions of pretrial detention are rarely addressed by defence lawyers because they focus either on pretrial orders and try to get their clients released, or on the trial proceedings.

To conclude, the studies mentioned indicate that internal, often informal, complaints mechanisms seem to be accepted as conflict solving options and means of in-prison communication. They mostly agree in their findings that judicial complaints, in contrast, have not fulfilled the expectations the legislator and prison policy experts had in the 1970s; they are assessed as disappointing regarding both procedure and outcome.

European and international prison monitoring and litigation: An additional safety net?

In addition to domestic legislation, European standards and norms have been and remain important for German prisons. The European Convention on Human Rights (ECHR) is regularly applied by German courts in prison cases. Even if most of these are concluded within the German system, the traditional assumption that domestic standards are higher than the European standards has been shattered at least to a certain extent as German prisoners have won cases even cases relating to inhuman treatment according to Art. 3 ECHR (see below for more details).

Another important European player in this field is the European Convention for the Prevention of Torture and Inhuman or Degrading Treatment or Punishment, adopted in 1989, was ratified by Germany in 1990. Its monitoring body, the European Committee for the Prevention of Torture (CPT), visited Germany ten times.[2] Its influence in Germany can be described as discreet but noticeable in some areas (Cernko 2014, Morgenstern 2018). The reports by the CPT repeatedly describe typical problems found in other Member States as well. One example is the lack of suitable out of cell activities being (e.g. CPT 2012: 28). In the last regular visit report, the CPT concentrated on special institutions for mentally ill offenders. For prisons, progress regarding accommodation, sanitation and treatment programs was acknowledged, but the CPT is critical about the striking contrasts between establishments visited in the different Federal States (CPT 2017: 6).

Germany also has ratified the Optional Protocol to the United Nations Convention against Torture (OPCAT) on 4 December 2008 and set up a National Preventive Mechanism (NPM). This NPM consists of one body responsible for Federal authorities, and a second one that is responsible for the monitoring of all institutions for the deprivations of liberty on the State level, namely prisons. Their annual reports present a compilation of all activities and are published online in German and English.[3] Additionally, visit reports are published online shortly after the visits. The range of concerns raised is broad. Criticism by UN Bodies and the CPT referred to understaffing and underfunding of the German NPM (CPT 2022). Nevertheless, the body (with recently increased staffing) performs many visits to various forms of institutions; for example, during the Covid-19 pandemic, it has been a valuable source of information on how prisons dealt with this difficult situation (generally reporting positive outcomes).

Case law and consequences

Leading cases by the FCC: Paving the way for prison reform

As indicated above, the FCC played an important role for prison reform in Germany. In the reformatory climate of the 1970s that sought to address social problems and influenced for example labour and education law, prison reform progressed. Retributive punishment was discredited, and the aim of social reintegration (*Resozialisierung*) gained more and more popularity. Notwithstanding an ongoing critical discourse, it became and remained the leading principle for sentence enforcement (Morgenstern 2015). One important facilitator was the Federal Constitutional Court (FCC) that shaped prison policy for years to come.

Up to the 1970s, the prevailing concept of a special – lesser – legal status of prisoners had created a so-called special power relationship between this kind of citizen and the state (*besonderes Gewaltverhältnis*). Under this concept, restrictions of fundamental rights were justified by the objectives of punishment and the 'nature of the institutionalised relationship'.[4] No precise statutory basis was deemed necessary and all interventions could be based on administrative regulations. In 1972, the Federal Constitutional Court (FCC) outlawed this concept.[5] The FCC argued that a prisoner, as any other citizen, has and retains all rights unless they are restricted by statutory law. Therefore, it is a prisoner's right to challenge decisions of the prison administration. This decision was a landmark in German prison history as it ultimately forced the legislator to pass a statutory Prison Law and to introduce an effective system of judicial protection for prisoners. The substantive counterpart of this decision followed one year later: The FCC argued that every offender has a right to resocialisation that accrues from his or her constitutional rights to personal liberty and respect for human dignity as well as the state's duty to care for all citizens.[6]

The FCC must be credited for its ongoing commitment to spell out the meaning of fundamental rights in the prison context. It must not be forgotten, however, that its decisions were and are based on judicial complaints by prisoners willing to go the long way, because cases can only be brought before the FCC after all other legal remedies are exhausted. In the 1970s, this was a relatively complicated procedure, involving courts not familiar with prison matters. Since 1977, prisoners can bring the case before the above-mentioned Special Prison Chamber of the Regional Court and appeal to the Higher Regional Court before the so-called constitutional complaint to the FCC is available to them.

Until today, constitutional complaints and the decision by the FCC have direct influence on prison life and impact for many prisoners: While decisions only refer to the individual prisoner and sometimes do not go beyond this special case due to its nature, others must be implemented for all prisoners under the right to equal treatment. Three relatively recent examples illustrate the wide range of issues that have been brought to the FCC by way of constitutional complaint. The first important issue is prison leave or other pre-release relaxation measures (*Vollzugslockerungen*). Here, the FCC, drawing on the principle of resocialisation, has underlined several times that a prognosis on future behaviour is only possible when the prisoner gets a chance to show that he or she is not abusing leave or other opening measures. It is thus essential that these relaxation measures are granted, or that there is at least a fair chance to get them. While this topic often is connected to resettlement, it has direct impact on prison life: The court explained that it follows from Art. 1 BL (respect for human dignity) that prison authorities must counter the risk of 'prison deprivation' by allowing contact to the outside world by – if needed accompanied – prison leave.[7] The second example relates to restricted possibilities and high costs of telephone calls in prisons. When a prisoner finally brought this issue before the FCC, the court argued that the prison authorities' duty to care obliged them to protect the financial situation of prisoners and thus, that it infringes the principle of resocialisation to provide only very expensive telephone systems.[8] Other seemingly small problems find their way to the courts as the third example shows: The decision dealt with writing materials, mainly used for writing complaints, that were not provided by the prison authorities. The FCC found that the rejection of this request was never explained properly to the prisoner. It found that the rejecting decisions as such were dubious, as they were not well founded (not reasoned at all), and thus against the law. The prisoner had to be compensated for his expenses.[9]

The contribution by other courts, including the European Court of Human Rights

Going backwards in the court hierarchy described above, the prisoner must appeal to the Higher Regional Court of the Federal State (*Oberlandesgericht, OLG*)[10] if a complaint to the Regional Court was not successful (see § 116 PA 1977, so-called further complaint). It will only review questions of law, not questions of fact. As mentioned, one reason for low success rates before the courts is that the PA often gives room for discretion, which limits the possibilities for a judicial review. To avoid further splintering of the judicial practice in Germany, however, decisions by the Higher Regional Courts are important. While successful further complaints always have been described as very rare in the research mentioned above, the creation of the 16 new Prison Acts seems to have slightly increased the number of further complaints.[11] To give just one example of the courts' efforts to provide for the uniform use of the law: According to older jurisprudence, prisoners can be punished with disciplinary measure when they deny the prison authorities to take a urine sample, but this is inadequate when it happens for the first time. The new Prison Act of Thuringia could have been understood, however, in a way that even the first incident can justify a disciplinary measure. The Special Prison Chamber of the relevant (lower) Regional Court had decided accordingly, as did the respective Chamber in the neighbouring State, Hesse. In 2014, the Higher Regional Court of Frankfurt in Hesse decided that this would be against the law; the Higher Regional Court of Thuringia in Jena followed.[12] Prisoners in both cases thus had succeeded with their further complaint; jurisprudence insisted on a uniform approach and outlawed the sweeping practice of taking disciplinary action against anyone who refuses to provide urine samples. Comparable blanket or random measures, such as random strip searches, have been outlawed by the FCC (see below).

Leaving the domestic courts aside for a moment, it must be noted that a complaint to the European Court on Human Rights (ECtHR) is possible for prisoners as a very last resort (see also Morgenstern and Dünkel 2018). This has been important in cases where the FCC denied access on formal grounds – something that often happens in prison cases and can, at least partly, be attributed to the overload of cases the FCC is confronted with. The ECtHR may then step in. In three of these cases (so far), it even found violations of Art. 3 ECHR by German prison authorities. Two of the cases referred to unjustified strip searches, one to a lack of adequate medical treatment. In the first case, the appellant had been complaining about his prison conditions and fought with prison staff. He was taken to a security cell, where he was strip-searched and apparently left naked for seven days. Even if placement might have been justified initially because of the danger to himself or others, depriving him of his clothes during his entire stay there constituted inhuman and degrading treatment.[13] In the second case, the Court stated that Art. 3 ECHR includes an obligation on prison authorities to seek independent medical advice on the appropriate treatment for a drug-addicted prisoner – the German authorities had failed to do so.[14]

The most recent case again dealt with the complaint of a prisoner who had been strip-searched.[15] The court argued that the repeated searches included embarrassing positions and were intrusive; they had no legitimate purpose, as they had been ordered before or after visits against one in five prisoners at the relevant time regardless of security concerns relating to the individual prisoner. On all occasions on which the applicant had been searched, he had visits from public officials. Owing to the absence of a legitimate purpose for these repeated random searches, the feeling of arbitrariness and the feelings of inferiority and anxiety associated with them, they had gone beyond the inevitable element of suffering or humiliation connected to imprisonment. They had therefore diminished the applicant's human dignity and had amounted to degrading treatment. It must be noted, however, that this practice had been declared unconstitutional in Germany as well and prisons in Germany are not allowed these random strip searches any longer.[16] The problem in the case brought before the ECtHR was that the domestic courts refused legal aid for a procedure to seek compensation for the non-pecuniary damage the appellant had suffered because of these searches. Interestingly, the decision was almost not discussed in German expert circles and if it was, only under a procedural aspect, the flawed compensation procedures German legislation provides (Neumann 2020).

Judicialisation revisited: On the recent impact of court decisions

As demonstrated, a wide variety of issues and problems are brought before different courts successfully by prisoners. The court decisions may change problematic practices and therefore have beneficial impact on all prisoners and prison climate more generally. Other cases, however, may simply impact on the procedure or even have detrimental effects. Practitioners are increasingly critical of decision coming from the ECtHR and the FCC and sometimes bluntly attack them as being detached from prison realities (Arloth 2019). Defiance and indeed 'refractoriness' as mentioned above may be the result.

In addition, prisons are not only held accountable before the Special Prison Chamber upon initiative of prisoners as described above. Other forms of litigation may include civil proceedings to receive monetary compensation for ill-treatment.[17] There are also a few cases of criminal litigation, with a recent example that impacted heavily on many people working in prison: Two senior prison staff were found guilty of causing death by negligence. They had transferred a prisoner with multiple convictions for traffic offences to an open institution. During day release, this prisoner was seen driving a car by police officers although he was obliged not to do so. In a wild car chase over the motorway, he caused an accident that left a woman dead. He was later convicted of murder. In the proceedings against the two prison officers, the public prosecution and the court of first instance argued that prison staff had not sufficiently assessed the risk the man had posed and therefore their positive prognosis that he would not commit new crimes, abscond or otherwise abuse his day release was 'obviously wrong'. Understandably, the decision was perceived as a threat by many. Since then, prisons may be more reluctant to grant leave or other relaxations and ministries are keen to avoid negative headlines, resulting at least in one Federal State in an initiative to curtail these possibilities and change the law accordingly (Kubink and Henningsmeier 2019). It was met with great relief when the German Supreme Court quashed the decision in November 2019 and acquitted the two officers. Emphasising the aim of resocialisation, the judges argued that risks of relaxations such as temporary prison leave must be considered carefully but cannot be completely excluded in all cases: The law accepts a residual risk and the prisons' prerogative to assess it.[18]

Access to justice for prisoners

Turning to those whose rights are at stake, research from the beginnings found problems of access to justice for prisoners (Diepenbruck 1981, Graebsch, Descarpes and Lederer 2018, Litwinski and Bublies 1989). These problems can be found on various levels: Prisoners must be informed about their possibilities and rights and they must understand them – this is particularly difficult for prisoners who do not speak German and may be relevant for a huge share of the many foreigners detained in German prisons (depending on the region, up to 76% in remand detention; Morgenstern 2018). Even when they understand their options, they must trust the system in so far as they see a chance to win a case before the court. They must also have a chance of support in prisons (for example by social workers, or, in case of non-natives, by interpreters) and in court proceedings by lawyers. The Prison Act provides for legal aid in certain cases, but it seems to be hardly granted in practice. Research on pretrial detention (Morgenstern 2018) has shown that in Germany, despite a traditionally strong belief in the independence, quality and integrity of judges, a growing need exists to provide for equality of arms, to professionalise the proceedings and thus to involve more lawyers. Only few of them, however, can claim expertise in prison matters. Prison cases are seen as complicated and certainly not financially rewarding (see also Graebsch et al. 2018). An ongoing research project will shed more light on this issue.[19] First findings confirm earlier research in as far as a significant proportion of prisoners remain passive and do not want to formally complain (within prisons or before a court) even if they do have grievances. The reasons given are complex, but the feeling that they will not be heard or even that there will be reprisals play an important role. The most important reason, however, seems to be that 'it's useless anyway' (Morgenstern et al. 2020).

Conclusion: Litigation for prisoners or for the prison system?

It is certain that German prisons are subject to an intricate set of legislation and standards that have been developed to ensure the protection of prisoners' rights and proper functioning of the prison system. Prison inspection visits must be expected regularly from five different bodies with additional bodies having the right to visit.[20] Potentially, monitoring activities in the widest sense can be performed by up to 14 different domestic or international bodies and institutions.[21] For prisons, this means that they must be able to prepare, usually on short notice, for visits. Far more often, however, their accountability work means to present written statements to courts and other bodies. This complex net of different accountability measures could well be experienced as 'audit explosion' described in public management and for prisons (Bennett 2014: 449). However, a closer look reveals that in a large country such as Germany with about 180 prisons, the burden on each prison remains small: While all prisons must deal with issues, their prison committees will raise and cases their prisoners bring against them before the courts, even the oversight performed by the Ministry of Justice may not be felt heavily, depending on the number of prisons and the ministerial commitment to prison problems in the respective state. Moreover, the bodies mentioned here have different tasks: Some are concerned with individual cases, some with issues concerning the prison as such (for example infrastructure, security concerns or staff resources) or general prison policy while for example the CPT's mandate is restricted to the prevention of torture and ill-treatment. In the best of worlds, they could represent a complimentary system of accountability mechanisms. Whether they do in practice, depends, on the quality of monitoring and a consistent approach to the way the monitoring tasks are performed.

As for litigation, we have tried to show that systemic effects of court decision in prison matters have been visible since the 1970s. Often they influenced prison practice in a positive way and forced the legislator and prison administrations to change their approaches. Without restraints imposed by courts, their insistence on the implementation of the principle of resocialisation, penal policy and politics could have led to a more punitive climate in Germany. Nevertheless, many experts have been very critical on the judicialisation, and 'on the ground', in prisons, prisoners do not seem to trust the system of judicial complaints. Can we still speak of a successful system (as, for example, in Morgenstern and Dünkel 2018)?

The fact that each and every decision or action taken by the prison authorities can be made subject to a judicial review in itself has a moderating, preventive effect because staff and prison authorities must always be aware that they may held accountable to what they have done. The cases mentioned above and the rich jurisprudence show that this is not only a remote possibility but also can always happen. Together with the dense net of monitoring and oversight activities, comprehensive institutional and legislative prerequisites for some sort of 'quality control' are in place to secure a generally decent and humane prison system. We have to conclude, however, that the system has significant flaws: It does not do justice to the individual case, the individual prisoner. While more research is needed to clarify the extent of these problems, it is clear that vulnerable prisoners are impeded in their to access justice. Some cases only lead to further proceduralisation – prisoners get better reasoned decisions, but not what they actually wanted in substance. Even when the need for reform is visible and acknowledged within the prison system (as, for example, in the above-mentioned telephone case), it is delayed until a court decision finally makes it unavoidable. In that way, the weakest in the system, the prisoner, carries the burden to effectuate reform (that often only arrives when she or he is long gone). Much more needs to be done to make prison litigation a tool that benefits the individual prisoner more than the prison system.

Notes

1 Statistisches Bundesamt 2020 (and earlier), Statistik "Strafgerichte", Table 3.1. Geschäftsentwicklung Landgerichte, Sonstiger Geschäftsanfall, 'Verfahren nach §§ 109, 110, 138 StVollzG'.
2 All visits are documented on the website of the CPT (http://www.cpt.coe.int/en/states/deu.htm). The last visit took place in December 2020 with targeted visits to remand prisons or prison sections. Nothing on this visit has been published yet.
3 www.nationale-stelle.de/index.php?id=74&L=1.
4 For example, Kammergericht Berlin, Neue Juristische Wochenschrift 1969: 672.
5 In the official collection of the FCC decisions BVerfGE 33, 1.
6 So-called Lebach decision, BVerfGE 35, 202.
7 BVerfG, 23 May 2013, 2 BvR 2129/11; BVerfG, 19 January 2016, 2 BvR 3030/14; BVerfG, 19 September 2019 – 2 BvR 1165/19.
8 BVerfG, 8 November 2017, 2 BvR 2221/16.
9 BVerfG, 4 October 2017, 2 BvR 821/16.
10 Some *Länder* have two or more Higher Regional Courts, NRW has three.
11 At least more decisions are published in the relevant database (www.beck-online.de).
12 OLG Frankfurt a.M., 2 December 2014, 3 Ws 937/14 (StVollz); OLG Jena, 6 April 2018, 1 Ws 411/16.
13 Hellig v. Germany, 20999/05, 7 July 2011.
14 Wenner v. Germany, 62303/13; Judgement of 1 September 2016. The domestic authorities had not examined the necessity of drug substitution treatment regarding the criteria set by the relevant domestic legislation and medical guidelines, nor accessed the help of expert medical advice. Despite the applicant's previous medical treatment with drug substitution therapy for 17 years, no follow-up had been given to the opinions expressed by external doctors on providing the applicant with that treatment again.
15 Roth v. Germany, 6780/18 and 30776/18, 22 October 2020.
16 BVerfG, 5 November 2016, 2 BvR 6/16 and further decision by Higher Regional Courts.
17 This is rarely successful, exceptions are a few cases where prisoners had been placed in overcrowded cells, e.g. Kammergericht Berlin, 27 January 2015, 9 U 232/12.
18 Bundesgerichtshof, 26 November 2019 - 2 StR 557/18.
19 www.tcd.ie/law/research/PRILA/.
20 These are the respective Ministry of Justice, the National Preventive Mechanism, the Prison Committee, in North Rhine Westphalia the Prison Ombudsman and in some other Federal States the Citizen's Ombudsman, and the CPT. Extraordinary visits

could be paid by the Petition Committee of the Federal States, bodies of the United Nations such as the Working Group on Arbitrary Detention or the Sub-Committee for the Prevention of Torture (Human Rights Council 2015) as well as the European Commissioner for Human Rights (Article 6, Resolution [99] 50 on the Council of Europe Commission for Human Rights).

21 These are those mentioned above, and in addition the domestic courts in ordinary and prison cases, the FCC, bodies of the State or the Federal Parliament and, on the international level, the European Court of Human Rights and potentially the European Court of Justice. All of them have the right to request information from public administration bodies, including prisons.

References

Arloth, F. (2019). Editorial. Forum Strafvollzug 68, 323–324.

Bennett, J. (2014). Resisting the Audit Explosion: The Art of Prison Inspection. Howard Journal of Criminal Justice 53, 449–467.

Bergmann, M. (2003). Die Verrechtlichung des Strafvollzugs. Herbolzheim: Centaurus.

Cernko, D. (2014). Die Umsetzung der CPT-Empfehlungen im deutschen Strafvollzug. Berlin: Duncker & Humblot.

Committee for the Prevention of Torture (2012). Report to the German Government on the visit to Germany from 25 November to 7 December 2010, CPT/Inf (2012) 6, Strasbourg, 22 February 2012.

Committee for the Prevention of Torture (2017). Report to the German Government on the visit to Germany from 25 November 2015 to 7 December 2015, CPT/Inf (2017) 13, Strasbourg, 1 June 2017.

Committee for the Prevention of Torture (2022). Report to the German Government on the periodic visit to Germany from 1 to 14 December 2020, CPT/Inf (2022) 18, Strasbourg, 14 September 2022.

Diepenbruck, K. -H. (1981). Rechtsmittel im Strafvollzug. Göttingen: Universitätsverlag.

Feest, J. and Lesting, W. (2009). Contempt of Court: zur Wiederkehr des Themas der renitenten Strafvollzugsbehörden. In: Müller, H. E., Sander, Günther M. and Válková, H. (eds.): Festschrift für Ulrich Eisenberg zum 70. Geburtstag, München: Beck, 675–691.

Feest, J., Lesting, W. and Selling, P. (1997). Totale Institution und Rechtsschutz: Eine Untersuchung zum Rechtsschutz im Strafvollzug. Opladen: Westdeutscher Verlag.

Graebsch, C., Descarpes, P. and Lederer, C. (2018). Improving the protection of fundamental rights and access to legal aid for remand prisoners in the European Union, WP3, Empirical Study: The actors of legal protection, their professional practices and the use of law in detention, 21 November 2018, www.prisonlitigation.org/eupretrialrights/ (accessed 11 February 2020).

Human Rights Council (2015). Report of the Working Group on Arbitrary Detention. Follow-up mission to Germany. A/HRC/30/36/Add.1 http://ap.ohchr.org/documents/dpage_e.aspx?si=A/HRC/30/36/Add.1. (accessed 11 February 2020).

Kamman, U. (1991). Gerichtlicher Rechtsschutz im Strafvollzug. Centaurus: Pfaffenweiler.

Kubink, M. and Henningsmeier, I. (2019). Verantwortung im Behandlungsvollzug. Forum Strafvollzug 68, 331–337.

Laubenstein, K. (1984). Verteidigung im Strafvollzug. Zugleich ein Beitrag zu dem Rechtsschutzverfahren nach den §§ 109 ff. StVollzG. Dissertation: Frankfurt a. M.

Litwinski, H. and Bublies, W. (1989): Strafverteidigung im Strafvollzug. München: Beck.

Morgenstern C. and Dünkel F. (2018). Monitoring prisons in Germany: the role of the European Court of Human Rights. In: Cliquennois, G. and de Suremain, H. (eds.): Monitoring Penal Policy in Europe. London: Routledge, 21–36.

Morgenstern, C. (2015). 'Der Resozialisierungsgrundsatz' – Social Reintegration as the dominant narrative for community punishment in Germany? In Robinson, G. and McNeill, F. (eds.): Community Punishment. A European Perspective. London: Routledge, 72–94.

Morgenstern, C. (2018). Die Untersuchungshaft. Eine Untersuchung unter rechtsdogmatischen, kriminologischen, rechtsvergleichenden und europarechtlichen Aspekten. Baden-Baden: Nomos.

Morgenstern, C., Van der Valk, S., Aizpurua, A. and Rogan, M. (2020). The silent majority – who is (not) complaining in German prisons? Presentation for the Annual Meeting of the Law and Society Association (online-event), 29. Mai 2020 (unpublished)

Neumann, E. (2020). Würdeverletzungen haben ihren Preis. https://verfassungsblog.de/wurdeverletzungen-haben-ihren-preis/ (accessed 11 February 2021).

Wingenfeld, A. (1998). Die Verrechtlichung des Strafvollzugs und ihre Auswirkungen auf die judikative Entscheidungspraxis. Aachen: Shaker.

INDEX

For Product Safety Concerns and Information please contact our
EU representative GPSR@taylorandfrancis.com Taylor & Francis
Verlag GmbH, Kaufingerstraße 24, 80331 München, Germany